The Slave Power

SOUTHERN CLASSICS SERIES

John G. Sproat and Mark M. Smith, Series Editors

The Slave Power

Its Character, Career, and Probable Designs

Being an Attempt to Explain the Real Issues
Involved in the American Contest

John E. Cairnes

New Introduction by Mark M. Smith

University of South Carolina Press

Published in cooperation with the
Institute for Southern Studies and the South Caroliniana Society
of the University of South Carolina

Introduction © 2003 University of South Carolina

First cloth edition published by Parker, Son and Bourn, 1862; enlarged edition published by Macmillan, 1873

This paperback edition published in Columbia, South Carolina, by the University of South Carolina Press, 2003

Published in Columbia, South Carolina, by the
University of South Carolina Press

Manufactured in the United States of America

07 06 05 04 03 5 4 3 2 1

Library of Congress Cataloging-in-Publication Data

Cairnes, John Elliott, 1823–1875.
    The slave power : its character, career, and probable designs : being an attempt to explain the real issues involved in the American contest / John E. Cairnes ; new introduction by Mark M. Smith.
        p. cm. — (Southern classics series)
    Originally published: 2nd ed. London : Macmillan, 1863. with a new introduction.
    "Published in cooperation with the Institute for Southern Studies and the South Caroliniana Society of the University of South Carolina."
    Includes bibliographical references.
    ISBN: 1-57003-522-9 (pbk. : alk. paper)
    1. Slavery—Political aspects—United States—History—19th century. 2. Slavery—Economic aspects—United States—History—19th century. 3. United States—History—Civil War, 1861–1865—Causes. 4. United States—Politics and government—1783–1865. 5. United States—Economic conditions—To 1865. 6. Slavery—Political aspects—Southern States—History—19th century. 7. Slavery—Economic aspects—Southern States—History—19th century. 8. Southern States—Politics and government—1775–1865. 9. Southern States—Economic conditions—19th century. I. Title. II. Series.

E458.2.C334 2003
973.7'11—dc22   2003062171

CONTENTS

Chapter I.
Introductory.—The Case Stated.

Chapter II.
The Economic Basis of Slavery.

Chapter III.
Internal Organization of Slave Societies.

Chapter IV.
Tendencies of Slave Societies.

Chapter V.
Internal Development of Slave Societies.

Chapter VI.
External Policy of Slave Societies.

Chapter VII.
The Career of the Slave Power.

Chapter VIII.
The Designs of the Slave Power.

Chapter IX.
General Conclusions.

SERIES EDITOR'S PREFACE

As Mark Smith attests in his balanced and discerning introduction to this southern classic, John Elliott Cairnes's early attempt to identify the cause of the Civil War sparked a war of words that has continued from the time it appeared in 1862 to the present day. Given the arguments Cairnes set forth, especially his emphasis on slavery as the "first cause," doubtless the controversy was inevitable. In the event, it ultimately involved, directly or indirectly, many notable historians and economists on both sides of the Atlantic— John Stuart Mill, Thomas Carlyle, Richard Cobden, and Karl Marx, for example, in the early years; Eugene Genovese, Kenneth Stampp, William Miller, Abraham Hirsch, and Harold Woodman, more recently. The book continues to have relevance because it was successful, as Smith notes, in interweaving so many threads in the complex fabric of the American Civil War.

Southern Classics returns to general circulation books of importance dealing with the history and culture of the American South. Sponsored by the Institute for Southern Studies and the South Caroliniana Society of the University of South Carolina, the series is advised by a board of distinguished scholars who suggest titles and editors of individual volumes to the series editors and help establish priorities in publication.

Chronological age alone does not determine a title's designation as a Southern Classic. The criteria also include significance in contributing to a broad understanding of the region, timeliness in relation to events and moments of peculiar interest to the American South, usefulness in the classroom, and suitability for inclusion in personal and institutional collections on the region.

John G. Sproat
Series Editor

INTRODUCTION

Today's specialists in antebellum U.S. history and general readers alike will find familiar the following argument from the early 1860s:

> The Southerners had for many years governed the Union. They had done so with a view to their own peculiar institution of slavery; the object of their policy being to increase as far as possible the number of Slave States, and so keep up their power in the Senate, and maintain and extend that state of things which, for economical reasons, are essential to the existence of slavery. No doubt it is true that slave labour is wasteful, superficial, inefficient, and applicable to only the rudest processes. Hence, as the slave population increases, an enormous area is required for its

I remain grateful to Barbara Bellows, Eugene Genovese, Alex Moore, John David Smith, and Jack Sproat for their helpful suggestions on the content and nature of this introduction. My thanks also to Kathy Hilliard for her timely help.

employment, and hence no doubt the slaveowners were anxious to make every other consideration bend to that of introducing new Slave States
into the Union.*

The argument summarizes the main findings of J. E.
Cairnes's *The Slave Power: Its Character, Career, and
Probable Designs: Being an Attempt to Explain the Real
Issues Involved in the American Contest,* a book first
published in 1862 and reissued, in a revised and
enlarged format, a year later. While Cairnes's interpretation was not entirely original, the very familiarity of
the argument testifies to the book's influence at the time
of its publication and its impact on the writing of antebellum Southern history and Civil War causation.†

  John Elliott Cairnes was born at Castlebelling-
ham, Ireland, in 1823 and died in England in 1875.

---

* "England and America," *Fraser's Magazine* 68 (October 1863): 422.
  † In 1969 Harper Torchbooks reissued what was then the most recent
edition, to my knowledge, of Cairnes's book. Harold D. Woodman introduced that edition with erudition and sophistication. Since Woodman's
introduction a good deal of scholarship has been written. See, for example, the only biographical treatment of Cairnes—Adelaide Weinberg's
1973 study, *John Elliot Cairnes and the American Civil War: A Study in
Anglo-American Relations* (London: Kingswood, 1973). Part 2 of Weinberg's study consists of letters of great interest, written between Cairnes
and Sarah Blake Shaw (1862–68). It should be noted that "Mrs. Weinberg's untimely death unfortunately prevented revision of the whole
work and addition of further notes before publication." See Joseph M.
Hernon Jr., rev. of Weinberg, *Civil War History* 21 (September 1975):
283–84. There is some inconsistency between the spellings of "Elliott,"

Although his father considered him academically unexceptional, he had sufficient wherewithal to graduate from Trinity College, Dublin, with his B.A. in 1848 and his M.A. two years later. In 1856 he won the Whately professorship of political economy at Trinity College, which he held for the five-year duration of the chair. A year later he published *The Character and Logical Method of Political Economy,* which "marked him as a disciple of John Stuart Mill," a man with whom Cairnes shared a close relationship for the rest of his life. In 1859 he was appointed professor of political economy and jurisprudence at Queen's College, Galway, where he wrote *The Slave Power.* Cairnes married in 1860 and in the same year injured his knee in a hunting accident, "the consequences of which were ultimately fatal to his health." He moved to London in 1865, and there he was soon appointed professor of political economy at University College. Despite his deteriorating physical condition, especially his bouts with rheumatic gout, he remained intellectually vital until his death.*

with some sources opting for the single "t," others for "tt." Both Weinberg and Cairnes's entry for the *Dictionary of National Biography* (London: Oxford University Press, 1949–50), III: 668–69, use the single "t." In his review of Weinberg's book, Hernon calls it a mistake, although it might simply be a difference between American and English spellings (294). "Elliott" is the spelling used in this introduction.

Dictionary of National Biography, III: 668–69. See also the entry in *Encyclopedia of the Social Sciences* (New York: Macmillan, 1948), III: 140; Weinberg, *John Elliot Cairnes,* 11–16.

While it is true that Cairnes's methodology—one influenced by John Stuart Mills's orthodox school of political economy—was coming under attack by European economists such as W. Stanley Jevons, Alfred Marshall, and Leon Walras who employed "mathematics to illustrate and explain economic doctrines to give precision to classical doctrines," Cairnes was nevertheless recognized as one of England's eminent nineteenth-century economists. His attention to the interaction between politics and economics—itself a product of his commitment to the tenets of classical political economy—gave his work analytical strength, lasting influence, and broad appeal. He also published several essays in 1873, including one on the value of gold, a work later verified and acknowledged by Jevons. "Cairnes at the time of his death," reads the entry in the *Dictionary of National Biography*, "was undoubtedly at the head of living economists."*

---

* Harold D. Woodman, Introduction, in J. E. Cairnes, *The Slave Power* (New York: Harper Torchbooks, 1969), xxvi, xxiv, xxv, xxxi. On Mill and Cairnes and classical economic thought, see Evelyn L. Forget, "J. S. Mill and J. E. Cairnes on Natural Value: The Role of Expectations in Late-Classical Thought," *History of Political Economy* 21 (Spring 1989): 103–21; on Jevons and Cairnes, see R. D. Collinson Black, "Jevons and Cairnes," *Economica* 27 (August 1960): 214–32; and on correspondence between Mill and Cairnes, see George O'Brien, "J. S. Mill and J. E. Cairnes," *Economica* 10 (November 1943): 273–85. *The Slave Power* was a product of a year's worth of lectures on the Confederacy that Cairnes prepared and delivered while at Queen's College. Parker, Son, and Bourn

Even though his view of political economy harkened back to the classical school of Adam Smith, Cairnes was on the radical side of intellectual thought in the nineteenth-century Anglo-American world. At one end of the philosophical spectrum stood those who tended to look backward in order to safeguard the future from social revolution. These conservatives included Southern slaveholders, proslavery ideologues, and some notable British intellectuals, such as Scottish historian and critic Thomas Carlyle. While Carlyle and Southern proslavery ideologues differed in many respects, as did the proslavery thinkers themselves, and while the dialogue between British conservatives and Southern planters was more muted than the more frequent and acerbic exchanges between Southern slaveholders and British antislavery activists, some British intellectuals and proslavery

in London published the original version of the book in 1862; Carleton's of New York published the first American edition later that year. Although that version was probably an unauthorized reprint, Carleton nevertheless advertised it as a second edition, the only change being a preface added by an "American editor" and the addition of the Emancipation Proclamation (issued in September 1862) at the book's end. In 1863 Macmillan issued a proper second edition. The changes were more substantive, with expansions in the text and the addition of several appendices, and it is this second edition (the English second edition) that is reprinted here. See A. N. J. Den Hollander, "Countries Far Away— Countries at a Distance," *Comparative Studies in Society and History* 9, no. 4 (1967): 363–64.

thinkers nonetheless shared "pre-industrial and religious values" and fretted over the prospect of "secularism, capitalist greed, and 'mob rule.'" Carlyle warmed to the Confederate cause, defended slavery, and highlighted the hypocrisy of British antislavery supporters who denounced bondage but ignored the perils of free wage labor and its deleterious effects on industrial workers. Although he later tempered his views, Carlyle's 1849 defense of slavery did not go unnoticed in the South, and *De Bow's Review* reprinted his thoughts on the matter in 1850.*

At the opposite end of the spectrum stood so-called radical liberals, led most prominently in Britain by John Stuart Mill, utilitarian economist and philosopher. Using rational criticism, Mill unapologetically

---

*T. Peter Park, "John Stuart Mill, Thomas Carlyle, and the U.S. Civil War," *Historian* 54 (Fall 1991): 93. In general consult Eugene D. Genovese, *The Slaveholders' Dilemma: Freedom and Progress in Southern Conservative Thought, 1820–1860* (Columbia: University of South Carolina Press, 1992). It should be noted that many English liberals expressed sympathy for the Confederacy because the Southern cause was reminiscent of several European nationalist movements and because Southern politicians defended free trade, something that tariff-happy Republicans did not endorse. See the remarks on this matter in Woodman, Introduction, xvi–xvii. For exchanges between some proslavery thinkers and English abolitionists and on the proslavery critique of Smithian political economy, see Drew Gilpin Faust, ed., *The Ideology of Slavery: Proslavery Thought in the Antebellum South, 1830–1860* (Baton Rouge: Louisiana State University Press, 1981), 168–205 (James Henry Hammond), 290–91 (George Fitzhugh).

denounced traditional institutions, championing
instead the benefits of individual liberty and a con-
cern for the common good. Thus Mill was firmly in the
radical liberal camp of his day and applauded the
benefits of free labor society and political democracy,
the very things Carlyle and his followers saw as the
beginning of the end of secure, workable, and orderly
civil society. Liberal radicals, including free-trade
activist Richard Cobden, socialist Thomas Hughes,
and fellow political economist John Elliott Cairnes,
numbered among Mill's supporters. In many ways the
American Civil War focused the British debate concerning slavery and freedom, and it was a debate that
found clear, powerful expression in Cairnes's *The Slave
Power.* *

Cairnes's book, then, must be understood within the
context of mid-nineteenth-century Britain, itself
deeply divided on the questions of the U.S. Civil War
and the impact of capitalist revolution on its own society. As R. J. M. Blackett's recent study shows, British
views on the meaning of the war and what role, if any,
Britain was to play were bewildering in their complexity and changed over time. Although there was a
good deal of sympathy with the Union, events some-
time strengthened the hand of pro-Confederate
sympathizers in Britain. For example, the Union's

* Park, "John Stuart Mill, Thomas Carlyle, and the U.S. Civil War," 96.

adoption of the Morrill tariff in February 1861 and
the serious spat over the *Trent* affair in November of
that year spurred British nationalism and generated
serious tensions between the Union and Britain. The
Trent incident, in which Union naval officer Charles
Wilkes removed Confederate envoys James Mason and
John Slidell from a British mail packet, the *Trent*—an
event Britain deemed insulting, tantamount to piracy,
and a violation of international law—could well have
led to war had not the Union issued an apology for
Wilkes's behavior. Moreover, British intellectuals were
themselves divided over the desirability of wage labor,
the appropriateness of democracy, and, from a less
theoretical perspective, the extent to which a Union
victory would threaten British imperial and economic
power.*

Despite strong British support for the Union, it is
fair to say that Cairnes did not win the war for public
opinion with his book. James Spence's *The American
Union,* one of the most influential, pro-Confederate
tracts, proved even more popular. It was not published
until late in 1861 and had gone through four editions
by the spring of 1862. While Spence's book "was to be
only the first of many such contributions to the

*R. J. M. Blackett, *Divided Hearts: Britain and the American Civil
War* (Baton Rouge: Louisiana State University Press, 2001), 21–22,
89–121.

Southern Cause in Britain," it was certainly the most admired not least because it reassured his audience that, though relevant to the conflict, slavery was not at the root of the Civil War. Instead, Spence argued, the conflict was a product of sectional and geographic differences between two disparate regions, a consequence of wrangles over tariffs between an agricultural South and industrializing North. Furthermore, Spence claimed, for the Confederacy to earn its place among nations, it would have to accept the gradual abolition of slavery. Spence saw the South's decision to secede as essentially reasonable, and he worked hard to counter the argument that the war was about the moral dimensions of human bondage.*

Cairnes's *The Slave Power* was the main counter to Spence's study. Although Cairnes's book did not approach the popularity of Spence's *The American Union, The Slave Power* nevertheless resonated in Britain. Most obviously (and predictably), the book earned lavish praise from Cairnes's mentor, John Stuart Mill, who had encouraged Cairnes to write the study. Mill also agitated to get the book favorable reviews and publicity, which, in fact, it did, with Harriet Martineau profiling it in the *Daily News*. While

---

*Brian Jenkins, *Britain and the War for the Union* (Montreal: McGill-Queen's University Press, 1980), II: 35–36. Note, too, Ephraim Douglass Adams, *Great Britain and the American Civil War* (New York: Russell & Russell, 1958), II: 112; Blackett, *Divided Hearts,* 24, 139–40.

several British reviewers wondered whether a Northern victory was really in England's economic and political interest, *The Slave Power* nevertheless earned positive reviews in the *National Review,* the *Economist,* and the *Anti-Slavery Reporter,* among others, principally because Cairnes had done such a good job of exposing slavery's "ruinous effects on agriculture, on industry generally, and on social well-being and development." Cairnes's book drew favorable responses from significant figures, including, for example, Charles Darwin, and the copies purchased by Mudie's, at the time one of the world's greatest libraries, were in great demand.*

Cairnes disagreed sharply with interpretations that stressed tariffs as a cause of the Civil War, noting that the relatively liberal tariff of 1857 had done nothing to forestall the South's secession. No, Carnes maintained, slavery was the principal cause of the war, and that end did not justify the South's claim to political sovereignty and independence. But while Cairnes was "appalled by the thought of a Southern victory," he was "by no means convinced of the desirability of the Union's complete restoration." The North's expressed desire to reunify the nation, Cairnes worried, might

---

* Jenkins, *Britain and the War for the Union,* II: 37–39. The favorable review quoted is from W. R. Greg in the *North British Review,* cited in Woodman, Introduction, xxxix. On fears that a Union victory would hurt Britain, see *ibid.,* xxxix–xl.

lead the Union to offer concessions to the South. Cairnes instead preferred confining slavery where it currently existed but with a new border at the Mississippi River, thus placing the South "in a territorial straightjacket" that in turn "would eventually lead to the painless extinction of the hated institution."*

In a way Cairnes's book—and his argument that slavery was the cause of the war—was always going to be of limited appeal, at least until the Union actually made slavery an issue in the war. "The undeniable fact that the leaders of the Union had earlier refused to declare war on slavery, and in words if not in deeds had persistently denied that this was their purpose," notes Brian Jenkins, "discouraged many British abolitionists and led them to conclude that the struggle could not be justified." Ultimately, though, Abraham Lincoln's Emancipation Proclamation seemed to prove that Cairnes had been right—that the war was at least in part about slavery, even if the Union had been shy to recognize the fact initially.†

---

* Jenkins, *Britain and the War for the Union*, II: 37. Cairnes's interest in Southern slavery did not evaporate when the war ended. In 1865 he published an essay in which he argued that the South's freedpeople had to be custodians of their own rights lest former planters use their economic and political authority to reassert their influence. See "The Negro Suffrage," *Macmillan's* 16 (August 1865): 334–43. Note, too, Weinberg, *John Elliot Cairnes*, 114–20.

† Jenkins, *Britain and the War for the Union*, II: 39, 40, 269.

If Cairnes lost the sales battle for his book, he won
in other ways. Both classical economists and the most
revolutionary thinkers of the nineteenth century, for
example, applauded Cairnes's analysis. Karl Marx in
the first volume of *Capital* (a work Marx planned
before, during, and immediately after the American
Civil War), cited Cairnes's *The Slave Power* several
times, all favorably. In his examination of "The Labour
Process and the Valorization Process," Marx con-
trasted the efficiency of capitalism with slavery's
tendency to use "only the rudest and heaviest implements," citing the 1862 edition of Cairnes's study to
that effect. More significant, Marx quoted Cairnes at
length in his discussion of the working day and the
callousness of markets for labor under both slavery
and freedom. Marx applauded Cairnes's argument
that slave deaths through overwork in the rice fields of
Georgia and "the swamps of the Mississippi" were
"repaired from the teeming reserves of Virginia and
Kentucky." This trade in turn led to further exploita-
tion since slaves could be worked hard and replaced
with relative ease and frequency, courtesy of Virginia
especially. Although Marx's point was to suggest that
"For slave trade, read labour-market, for Kentucky
and Virginia, Ireland and the agricultural districts
of England, Scotland and Wales, for Africa, Germany,"
he considered Cairnes's depiction of the workings

and effect of the Southern slave trade accurate on the essentials.*

Trying to measure the influence of Cairnes's antislavery work in Britain is also complicated because historians disagree on how best to characterize the British position on the Civil War. Philip S. Foner in *British Labor and the American Civil War* (1981) takes a hard Marxist line, making the argument that the majority of the British working class sympathized with Southern slaves and supported the Union. Conversely Mary Ellison's local study *Support for Secession: Lancashire and the American Civil War* (1972) argues that Lancashire workers endorsed the Confederacy. Whatever the competing views, however, it is

---

* Karl Marx, *Capital: A Critique of Political Economy. Volume One,* trans. Ben Fowkes (New York: Vintage, 1977), 304n.18, 377–78. The "initial plan of *Capital,*"explains Ernest Mandel,"was drawn up in 1857; the final plan dates from 1865–6."*Ibid.,* 27. On Marx's view of the American Civil War, see *Marx and Engels on the United States* (Moscow: Progress Publishers, 1979), 79–224. As Peter J. Parish astutely (and wryly) remarked:"European readings of the significance of the Civil War were often confused and unpredictable. The differing interpretations of its liberal message, and the competing claims for sympathy of American and Southern nationhood, no doubt go a long way to explain the broken pattern of European reaction. Certainly the Civil War created some very strange bedfellows. It is hard to see what else but pro-Northern sympathies could ever have rallied behind one standard such a motley group as Karl Marx, Czar Alexander II, John Bright, Bismarck, Victor Hugo, Robert Browning and John Stuart Mill."Peter J. Parish, *The American Civil War* (New York: Holmes and Meier, 1975), 648.

probably fair to say that just as abolitionists in the northern United States embraced Cairnes's book, lauding the authority a respected economist had given to their cause, so British public opinion generally was "strongly influenced" by the work. Not all British reviews were wholly in agreement with Cairnes, of course. "We do not dispute Mr. Cairnes's forcible statement of the evils of slavery, both moral and economical," offered the *Edinburgh Review* in October 1862, "although we think that he has somewhat exaggerated the latter, and has somewhat overstated the inherent necessity, which slavery imposes, of seeking fresh soils." Nevertheless Mill's review of the book did much to help its sales both sides of the Atlantic. As Dutch historian A. N. J. Den Hollander has remarked, "The book was generally well-received in Great Britain notwithstanding Britain's widespread sympathy for the Confederacy." On the whole contemporary British reviews tended to applaud the book, and most criticisms were of specific points, not a wholesale rejection of the work. All in all, it is fair to say that, as Joseph M. Hernon Jr. puts it, "[p]robably no book of its time exercised greater influence in shaping British public opinion on the American Civil War than John Elliott Cairnes's *The Slave Power*."*

*Philip S. Foner, *British Labor and the American Civil War* (New York: Holmes and Meier, 1981); Mary Ellison, *Support for Secession: Lancashire and the American Civil War* (Chicago: University of Chicago

Unsurprisingly Cairnes came in for vigorous attack—some of it warranted—by Southern loyalists and Confederates. Almost as soon as the 1862 edition appeared in print, Southern newspaper correspondents derided its tone and blasted its argument. South Carolina's *Charleston Mercury,* for example, noted the book's publication on September 18, 1862. "The Yankees are rejoicing over an antislavery book recently published by a Mr. Cairnes," reported the *Mercury,* explaining, "Cairnes is caustic on us," describing "our cause" as "wholly evil." A University of Virginia mathematics professor and Southern nationalist, Albert Taylor Bledsoe challenged Cairnes on several fronts in his book *Is Davis a Traitor; or, Was Secession a Constitutional Right Previous to the War of 1861?* (1866). Bledsoe pointed to Cairnes's painful misreading of the so-called three-fifths clause or vote, arguing, "No such thing as a 'three-fifths vote' is known to the Constitution of the United States; and the name is the coinage of ignorance." Yet even Bledsoe recognized the accuracy of Cairnes's argument concerning the South's

Press, 1972). For a study that finds a broad range of sympathies, see Joseph M. Hernon Jr., *Celts, Catholics and Copperheads: Ireland Views the American Civil War* (Columbus: Ohio State University Press, 1968). See also Weinberg, *John Elliot Cairnes,* 68–70. Quotations from Park, "John Stuart Mill, Thomas Carlyle, and the U.S. Civil War," 98; *Edinburgh Review,* 236 (October 1862): 558; Den Hollander, "Countries Far Away— Countries at a Distance," 364; Hernon, rev. of Weinberg, 283.

need to expand and acquire political power in order to preserve slavery and protect property rights. The difference between Cairnes and Bledsoe on this matter was simple. Both thought expansion essential to Southern survival, but the former thought the tendency pernicious while the latter considered it desirable.*

Northern reaction to *The Slave Power* was usually and understandably more favorable. Cairnes's critique of Southern slavery and political manipulations earned favorable comment in a wide variety of Northern sources, and the book was cited to support points of history concerning American economic development. Mary L. Booth's *History of the City of New York* (1867) cited Cairnes's study to note the trajectory of Northern history, and Henry Darling invoked the book to drive home a point about the increase in

---

*"The News from Richmond," *Charleston Mercury,* September 18, 1862; Albert Taylor Bledsoe, *Is Davis a Traitor; or, Was Secession a Constitutional Right Previous to the War of 1861?* (Baltimore: Innes & Company, 1866), 220, 240. On the three-fifths clause, Bledsoe noted, "It was in counting the number, not those who should vote, but only of those who should make up the basis of representation that five slaves were reckoned equal to three white persons, or to three free negroes" (220). Cairnes's explanation of the clause is in *The Slave Power,* 195–96. Harold Woodman errs uncharacteristically when he notes that Cairnes's book was "Ignored in the South." See Woodman, Introduction, xli.

cotton demand and the role of the cotton gin in his study *Slavery and the War* (1863).*

The Northern press was also favorable toward *The Slave Power.* The *Living Age* of Boston reprinted John Stuart Mill's lengthy *Westminster Review* article in its November 15, 1862, issue. The review was nothing less than sympathetic and congratulatory. Cairnes, contended Mill, brought to bear a keen intellect on the question, as should be expected from a "first-rate political economist," a "moral and political philosopher," and a scholar who appreciated the close relationship between economics and politics. Although Mill was quick to endorse almost all of Cairnes's points concerning the inefficiency of slave labor and the attendant rise of the southern Slave Power, he hesitated to second Cairnes's suggestion that a workable compromise would be to limit slavery's expansion at the Mississippi River. Mill was most impressed with the author's prose and analysis ("artistic as well as scientific") and the timeliness of the book's publication. "A work more needed," said Mill, "could scarcely have been produced at the present time," and it was

*Mary L. Booth, *History of the City of New York* (New York: W. R. C. Clark, 1867), 838; Henry Darling, *Slavery and the War: A Historical Essay* (Philadelphia: J. B. Lippincott, 1863), 182–83, 189.

likely to sway English constituencies who still favored the South.*

Not all Northerners accepted all of Cairnes's claims. Reviewers for the *Chicago Tribune*, the *North American Review*, the *New York Tribune*, the *New York Times*, and *Harper's Weekly*, while sympathetic to Cairnes's overall analysis, roundly rejected his claim that the best strategy for ending slavery was containment. More pointedly, James R. Gilmore—a Bostonian who excelled in accurately depicting the evils of Southern bondage and who shared Cairnes's abolitionist sympathies—considered Cairnes's study first-rate but prone to distortion on some important points. In his 1864 book, *Down in Tennessee*, he bashed Cairnes less for his argument that slavery created a class of "mean whites" but more for his exaggeration of the number of poor, landless whites in the South. Gilmore called *The Slave Power* a "very valuable and generally accurate account," but he disagreed with Cairnes's argument that "In the Southern States, no less than five millions of human beings are now said to exist in a condition little removed from savage life." Cairnes's five million "mean whites," or "white trash," Gilmore thought "a very great error." "The very idea is

* "The Slave Power," *Living Age*, no. 963 (November 15, 1862): 303, 315; Park, "John Stuart Mill," 97. See also John Stuart Mill, *Dissertations and Discussion: Political, Philosophical, and Historical* (New York: Henry Holt, 1882), III: 264–99; Weinberg, *John Elliot Cairnes*, 40–42.

preposterous," he explained, "for if it were so, one-half of the Southern people would be paupers, and no community could exist which had to support that proportion of non-producers." Gilmore did not deny the existence of a class of "mean trash" in the South, but, he insisted, "they are a comparatively small class," as the "census shows that they cannot number above half a million." Gilmore thought Cairnes entirely wrong to lump the South's yeomen and small-farm owners—men with "a sturdy independence, and an honest regard for each other's rights"—into one undifferentiated mass of poor Southern whites.*

If contemporary British and American reaction to *The Slave Power* was mixed, the same may be said of the book's reception among modern historians. Cairnes's influence lingered and informed a good deal of twentieth-century historical work on slavery. For example, in his groundbreaking study *The Political Economy of Slavery,* Eugene D. Genovese begins his discussion on the productivity of Southern slave labor: "Although the debate on slave productivity is an old one, few arguments have appeared during the last hundred years to supplement those of contemporaries like John Elliott Cairnes." Cairnes, explains Genovese,

---

*On these and other reviews, see Woodman, Introduction, xli; Weinberg, *John Elliot Cairnes,* 40–67. James R. Gilmore, *Down in Tennessee, and Back by Way of Richmond* (New York: Carleton, 1864), 182–83. Gilmore wrote this book under the pseudonym Edmund Kirke.

Genovese, cont'd

"made the much-assailed assertion that the slave was so defective in versatility that his labor could be exploited profitably only if he were taught one task and kept at it. If we allow for exaggeration, Cairnes's thesis is sound."* Although Genovese believed that Cairnes's argument that slavery exhausted Southern soils was "simplistic and mechanistic," Genovese did not consider him wrong on the matter; in fact, he thought his basic, "traditional" argument superior to the revisions offered by Avery O. Craven and Charles Ramsdell. Much of Genovese's analysis endorsed Cairnes's assessment of both Southern economic development and his understanding of the cultural mind-set of the Southern planters. Like Cairnes, Genovese located the planter's expansionist tendency in the "economics, politics, social life, ideology, and psychology" of the slaveholders.†

Other social historians also engaged Cairnes. Although he disagreed with a good deal of *The Slave Power*, Kenneth M. Stampp took seriously Cairnes's

---

* Eugene D. Genovese, *The Political Economy of Slavery: Studies in the Economy and Society of the Slave South* (Middletown, Conn.: Wesleyan University Press, 1989; orig., 1965), 43.

† Genovese, *The Political Economy of Slavery*, 243. Avery O. Craven, *Soil Exhaustion as a Factor in the Agricultural History of Virginia and Maryland, 1606–1860* (Urbana: University of Illinois Press, 1926); Charles Ramsdell, "The Natural Limits of Slavery Expansion," *American Historical Review* 16 (September 1929): 151–71.

argument, using it as a foil in his landmark 1956 study, *The Peculiar Institution: Slavery in the Ante-Bellum South.* While Stampp doubted Cairnes's contention that slaves were incapable of working efficiently in either field or factory, he read Cairnes closely enough to note rightly that the economist understood that planters kept slaves for cultural as well as economic reasons, that a program of compensated emancipation would fail precisely because slaveholders owned slaves for prestige, and that Cairnes acknowledged that slavery was sufficiently profitable to still remain in existence by 1860. For Stampp, though, Cairnes was a man hostage to his own classical liberal doctrines, doctrines about the moral and economic desirability of free wage labor that led him to discount and downplay the efficiency of antebellum bondage. As Stampp explained, while proslavery ideologues and liberal economists agreed that slavery was unprofitable, they parted company when it came to the appropriateness of human slavery. Cairnes's training and worldview, argued Stampp, left him little room to entertain the idea that slavery could be economically efficient.*

Given that social historians such as Eugene Genovese have found much of value in Cairnes's argument

---

* Kenneth M. Stampp, *The Peculiar Institution: Slavery in the Ante-Bellum South* (first published, New York: Knopf, 1956; reissued, New York: Vintage, 1989), 393, 397, 399, 386, 388, 383–384. Stampp mistakenly identifies Cairnes as "the English economist" (384).

and given Cairnes's reputation as a first-rate economist, it is ironic that most modern economic historians
have been critical of *The Slave Power.* Roger L. Ransom, for example, while noting the popular appeal and
plausibility of Cairnes's thesis, nevertheless disagrees
with virtually everything that Cairnes's claimed, especially concerning the South's perceived need for slavery's expansion. Economic historian Claudia Dale
Goldin likewise challenges Cairnes. While she notes
that Cairnes was among the first to consider the problems slaveholders faced in trying to maintain slavery
in an urban setting, Goldin disproves Cairnes's claim
that urban slavery was unsustainable.*

Other economic historians were even more critical.
Writing in 1978, Gavin Wright challenged Cairnes's

---

* Roger L. Ransom, *Conflict and Compromise: The Political Economy
of Slavery, Emancipation, and the American Civil War* (New York: Cam-
bridge University Press, 1990 ed.), 6, 9, 53–55; Claudia Dale Goldin, "A
Model to Explain the Relative Decline of Urban Slavery: Empirical
Results," in Stanley L. Engerman and Eugene D. Genovese, eds., *Race
and Slavery in the Western Hemisphere: Quantitative Studies* (Princeton:
Princeton University Press, 1975), 430–31, 428. Several eminent historians—U. B. Phillips and Lewis Cecil Gray as well as Richard C. Wade—
agreed with Cairnes's point that slavery and urbanism and industrialism
were incompatible because of the threat posed by insurrections and runaways in such environments. U. B. Phillips, "The Economic Cost of Slaveholding in the Cotton Belt," *Political Science Quarterly* 20 (June 1905):
257–75; Lewis Cecil Gray, *History of Agriculture in the Southern U.S.
to 1860* (Gloucester, Mass.: Peter Smith, 1958), I: 470; Richard C. Wade,
Slavery in the Cities: The South, 1820–1860 (New York: Oxford University Press, 1964), 3. See also Robert William Fogel and Stanley L.

claim that "the slave economy depended upon continued acquisition of fresh land, and that this expansionism was on an inevitable collision course with the
desires of free white Northern settlers." Argues
Wright, "there is no evidence to indicate that they
[Southern planters] were 'feeling the pinch' of land
shortage in the 1850s." Moreover, there remained a
large amount of prime, uncultivated cotton land
"within the 1860 boundaries of the slave states," a
point that Cairnes noted but tended to gloss over.
Wright also points out that "improved acreage was
growing more rapidly than population in every cotton
state; the rise in land values reflected these ongoing
improvements." Given such evidence, Wright asks, "can
we reasonably believe that Southerners were politically agitated over soil exhaustion in the midst of the
spectacular cotton yields of the late 1850s?" All in all,
Wright concludes, "the land-expansion hypothesis as
argued by Cairnes and his followers is an economic
Hamlet without the prince."*

Engerman, *Time on the Cross: The Economics of American Negro Slavery*
(Boston: Little, Brown, 1974), 1:63.

  * Gavin Wright, *The Political Economy of the Cotton South: Households, Markets, and Wealth in the Nineteenth Century* (New York: Norton,
1978), 131–33. On these matters, see also Gray, *History of Agriculture in
the Southern United States to 1860,* I:640–42. Note, too, Michael Tadman,
"The Demographic Cost of Sugar: Debates on Slave Societies and Natural Increase in the Americas," *American Historical Review* 105 (December 2000): 1541n. 20.

Despite such criticisms it is clear that Cairnes influenced modern economic historians partly because of his association with classical political economy. Historians sympathetic to the classical school found it shaping their working assumptions. "I was startled to discover," writes Robert William Fogel, reflecting on the findings he and Stanley Engerman presented in *Time on the Cross,* "the numerous ways in which masters relied on rewards to elicit labor—a device I had assumed was almost entirely absent since David Hume, Adam Smith, John E. Cairnes, and most of the other classical writers had identified this lack as the fatal flaw in slavery as an economic system."* Fogel and Engerman indeed spent some time tackling Cairnes's arguments in *Time on the Cross.* On one level Fogel and Engerman indicted Cairnes for the "polemical nature of the work," arguing that Cairnes, "alarmed at the widespread sympathy among Englishmen for the southern struggle for 'self-determination,' sought in this volume to demonstrate that both morality and economic self-interest dictated that Great Britain should refrain from intervening in the Civil War on behalf of the Confederacy." They also chastised the Irish economist for his heavy reliance on the observations of antebellum Southern society by Northern

---

*Robert William Fogel, *Without Consent or Contract: The Rise and Fall of American Slavery* (New York: Norton, 1989), 393–94.

F.L.Olmsted

architect and traveler Frederick Law Olmsted. They acknowledged, however, that Cairnes differed from the Northern traveler in some important respects. While Olmsted tended to explain the supposed inferiority of slaves with reference to race, Cairnes opted to stress the condition of slavery as the cause of inefficient slave labor. Moreover, "whereas Olmsted cited the tendency of slave agriculture to reduce the fertility of land as one of the many shortcomings of the peculiar institution, Cairnes elevated this feature to central importance, making the degradation of land an inescapable consequence of the employment of slave labor." In fact, Cairnes went even further and essentially reformulated Olmsted's clumsy claim that slavery was generally unprofitable. Cairnes realized that such an assertion raised more questions than it answered. As Fogel and Engerman put it, Olmsted's "argument led to unanswerable conundrums. Why did the system take root in the first place and why did it persist in the South for more than two hundred years? And, if the system was generally unprofitable, why shouldn't opponents of slavery merely wait for the operation of the market to force the system out of existence?"*

* Fogel and Engerman, *Time on the Cross*, I: 181–87.

Here Cairnes revised Olmsted's assertion by arguing not that slavery was inherently unprofitable but
only that it tended toward inefficiency and that, moreover, there were several conditions under which slavery could prove profitable. If demand existed for a
crop that could be grown more efficiently on a large
scale, if labor could be concentrated to keep the cost of
supervising the slaves low, if soils were of a sufficiently
high fertility "and practically unlimited in extent,"
and if there was a mechanism for transferring slave
labor (an interregional slave trade), then, according to
Cairnes, slavery could be profitable. Thus Cairnes
could argue that because the South possessed these
qualities, Southern slavery was profitable even though
the system in the abstract was inefficient and certainly inferior to free wage labor. In this way Cairnes
explained why slavery had taken root in the South
and not in the North, and the analysis enabled him to
argue that slavery's future was contingent on its
expansion. Anticipating a distinction made by economic historian Harold D. Woodman, Cairnes maintained that, while slavery was profitable for individual
planters, it in fact damaged the Southern economy
generally because it hindered the development of
commerce and manufacturing, the true keys to
macroeconomic success.*

*Ibid., 181–87; Harold D. Woodman,"The Profitability of Slavery: A
Historical Perennial," *Journal of Southern History* 29 (August 1963):
303–25.

While Fogel and Engerman presented Cairnes's argument in its correct light with the appropriate subtlety and qualifications, they were also right to argue that, such caveats notwithstanding, Cairnes "did little to test the evidential basis of these arguments. He accepted as proven Olmsted's contentions that southern slave labor and white labor were less efficient than northern labor. He also accepted as proven the rapid and steadily declining fertility of lands worked by slaves." In other words it was Cairnes's "failure to consider seriously the validity of this set of alleged facts that constitutes the basic flaw in his analysis of the economics of slavery." Cairnes, they concluded, "simply never came to grips with the basic empirical issues on which that indictment must stand or fall."*

Cairnes's *The Slave Power* has also come in for some detailed commentary and criticism by modern historians, not all of which is based on his failings as an economist. In a searching evaluation of Cairnes's book, A. N. J. Den Hollander argues that Cairnes's depiction of Southern slaveholding society was misleading, suggesting that the South's planter class was too small to constitute a "Slave Power." Whether or not this is the case, as classes do not have to be large in order to wield political influence, Den Hollander's points concerning Cairnes's methodology are worth noting. Per Den Hollander, Cairnes started "from a few

* Fogel and Engerman, *Time on the Cross,* I: 188–89.

general premises," buttressed them with "comment on
the part of eye-witnesses," and thereby established
conclusions that "then became the basis for further
argumentation." Den Hollander agrees that Cairnes
relied too much on travel accounts, adding that
Cairnes "preferred to use their convictions, generalizations, and interpretations rather than their immediate
observations. To these he resorted only when they fitted his own presentation and argumentation. In other
words: he ignored that which conflicted with his own
mode of thought."*

Den Hollander does not deny Cairnes's erudition
and, in fact, argues that it was his learning and eloquence that proved so persuasive to the "uninformed
layman." But he does question the reality of Cairnes's
description. What *The Slave Power* offered, states Den
Hollander, "was really nothing but a grotesquely inaccurate picture of that faraway country with which
Europe was so heavily preoccupied in those days."
Moreover, it "presented to the reader a social world
which not only did not exist but which could not have
existed." Echoing some contemporary reviews, Den
Hollander questions both Cairnes's characterization
of the South's poor whites and his estimate of their
numbers, noting that criticisms from reviewers led
Cairnes to reduce his estimate of the numbers of poor

*Den Hollander, "Countries Far Away—Countries at a Distance,"
365–66.

whites from five million in the first edition of *The Slave Power* to four million in the 1863 edition. But if there were four million incurably indolent poor whites, wonders Den Hollander, how did the slave South function? He suggests that it could not have and so doubts the accuracy of Cairnes's description of poor whites, which historians of the Southern yeomen have also questioned in recent years. As several modern historians have argued, it is unhelpful to talk about a large class of lazy poor whites; rather, it is more reasonable to examine various types of yeomen and nonslaveholders, to gauge the extent of their involvement in the antebellum South's burgeoning market economy, and to consider their tenacious commitment to republicanism.*

* *Ibid.,* 366,367,362–76; Frank L. Owsley, *Plain Folk of the Old South* (Baton Rouge: Louisiana State University Press, 1949); J. Mills Thornton III, *Politics and Power in a Slave Society: Alabama, 1800–1860* (Baton Rouge: Louisiana State University Press, 1978); Lacy K. Ford, Jr., *Origins of Southern Radicalism: The South Carolina Upcountry, 1800–1860* (New York: Oxford University Press, 1988); Steven Hahn, *The Roots of Southern Populism: Yeoman Farmers and the Transformation of the Georgia Upcountry, 1850–1890* (New York: Oxford University Press, 1983); Charles C. Bolton, *Poor Whites of the Antebellum South: Tenants and Laborers in Central North Carolina and Northeast Mississippi* (Durham: Duke University Press, 1994); Bradley G. Bond, *Political Culture in the Nineteenth-Century South: Mississippi, 1830–1900* (Baton Rouge: Louisiana State University Press, 1995); Harry L. Watson, "Conflict and Collaboration: Yeomen, Slaveholders, and Politics in the Antebellum South," *Social History* 10 (October 1985): 273–98; Donald L. Winters, "'Plain Folk' of the Old South Reexamined: Economic Democracy in Tennessee," *Journal of Southern History* 53 (November 1987):

How then to account for Cairnes's wildly inaccurate claims? "That he only exaggerated the mistakes already made by others is not a satisfactory answer. Many untruths had been written before," maintains Den Hollander. Rather, Cairnes's main faults reside in his unwitting immersion in a journalistic tradition that simply encouraged the reiteration of some commonly accepted points about the South—especially its putative three-class structure (planters, slaves, poor whites)—and in his heavy reliance on travel accounts. This became most apparent, according to Den Hollander, in Cairnes's central argument that slavery necessarily led to soil erosion and thereby mandated the Slave Power's manipulation of federal policy. Den Hollander also criticizes Cairnes's methodology. While Cairnes "did not try to conceal exceptions to his generalizations," he nevertheless argued "that those exceptions did not carry much weight" and so was guilty of "selective handling of his sources" and unwilling to explore the implications of evidence that contradicted his working assumptions. Then there was the matter of Cairnes's own moral values and the way they shaped his study. Den Hollander points out that while

565–86; Stephanie McCurry, *Masters of Small Worlds: Yeoman Households, Gender Relations, and the Political Culture of the Antebellum South Carolina Lowcountry* (New York: Oxford University Press, 1995). Cairnes responded to criticisms of his estimates on the number and significance of "poor whites" in appendix D in the second edition of *The Slave Power.*

"Cairnes did not have a high opinion of America as a nation," he especially disliked the South and its peculiar institution and that his "antipathy led him to concentrate upon slavery and to seek in it the key to the understanding of Southern society, a fatal bias that, nevertheless, one can understand." Such a predilection combined with his methodological inclination to see the world in binary moral terms of good or bad led him to write a book whose logic became self-fulfilling. "Cairnes did not really investigate the South," argues Den Hollander, "he investigated slavery in the South," projected his dislike of slavery onto the South as a whole, and refused "to paint a picture accurately reflecting the complexity of Southern society."*

Historian William L. Miller was even more caustic, dismissing the belief that *The Slave Power* was a book grounded in solid, broad evidence. "Though Cairnes cites formally or informally over 100 different items," notes Miller, "by far his chief source of information on matters economic was the work of the American journalist and landscape architect F. L. Olmsted." Olmsted's works—principally his two most influential travel accounts of the South—were, according to Miller, cited thirty-four times, "three times the number of citations accorded the work of any other author."

* Den Hollander, "Countries Far Away—Countries at a Distance," 367–68, 370, 373, 374–75.

More damning still, in Miller's opinion, Cairnes did not make fullest use of helpful—and challenging— economic material from *De Bow's Review*. While he cited work by agricultural reformers Edmund Ruffin and James Henry Hammond, for example, he neglected to explore the implications of some of their positions. While Cairnes cited Ruffin, he failed to explain that Ruffin believed that slavery did not destroy land. In fact Miller suggests a scholarly sleight of hand by Cairnes: "On the whole, Cairnes assembled a good bibliography and made such use of it as to convince many who lacked time or disposition to examine his sources with some care."*

---

*William L. Miller, "J. E. Cairnes on the Economics of American Negro Slavery," *Southern Economic Journal* 30 (April 1964): 333, 335, 336. For Phillips's criticism of Cairnes see his *American Negro Slavery* (New York: D. Appleton, 1918), 356. Like all works, Miller's itself is a reflection of its time and, as such, has weaknesses. Note especially his claim that "the disciplinary institutions and practices of American Negro slavery prevented formation of strong family ties," a point now considered inaccurate, in large part as a result of Herbert G. Gutman, *The Black Family in Slavery and Freedom, 1750–1925* (New York: Pantheon, 1976). See also Fogel and Engerman, *Time on the Cross,* I: 170. Earlier historians tended to be more forgiving of Cairnes's method and also applauded the moral commitment he brought to his work. In their 1931 study Donaldson Jordan and Edwin J. Pratt remark that Cairnes's book, "a lucid review of American history and a formidable indictment of the South," was "effective because the author, though not without an underlying passion for righteousness, was scientific rather than sentimental." Moreover, Cairnes, unlike Mill, remained "an active worker in the

Miller objected to Cairnes's findings on additional grounds. Like others, he considered Cairnes's initial estimates of the number of poor whites in the South in 1860 grossly exaggerated. He also believed that Cairnes "overestimated the contribution of slave-breeding to the income of planters in Virginia, Maryland, and Kentucky." It is true that Cairnes undoubtedly exaggerated the extent to which slaveholders moved westward in their hungry pursuit of land. While it remains clear that the wealthiest planters in parts of Georgia and Alabama moved often, it is also the case that between 1850 and 1860 nonslaveowners were marginally more likely than slaveowners to move westward even though, when slaveholders did move, they tended to go greater distances.*

Given all of these criticisms—some of them quite damning—it is worth asking what remains of value in *The Slave Power.* Most obviously, Cairnes's book captured something of the essence or spirit of the coming

Northern cause" during the course of the war. Donaldson Jordan and Edwin J. Pratt, *Europe and the American Civil War* (Boston and New York: Houghton Mifflin, 1931), 74–75.

  * Miller, "J. E. Cairnes on the Economics of American Negro Slavery," 338, 339–40; James Oakes, *The Ruling Race: A History of American Slaveholders* (New York: Knopf, 1982), 77; Donald F. Schaefer, "A Statistical Profile of Frontier and New South Migration, 1850–1860," *Agricultural History* 59 (October 1985): 563–78.

cf. note for references

of the American Civil War. At the broadest level, many historians "do largely agree with Cairnes and Mill that a conflict between slave and liberal-capitalist economic systems was an underlying cause of the Civil War." And while much work has been done on a variety of other possible underlying causes of the war, the notion that slavery, far more than tariffs and party formation, caused the war still enjoys considerable currency.*

Cairnes's ability to link economics and politics also made his study of lasting value. Cairnes was hardly the first to use the term *The Slave Power,* and he was as vague in its precise definition as others who employed it. Cairnes described the Slave Power as "that system of interests, industrial, social, and political, which has for the greater part of half a century directed the career of the American Union." As David Brion Davis rightly remarked, such "definitions were fairly

---

* Park, "John Stuart Mill, Thomas Carlyle, and the U.S. Civil War," 98. Echoes of Cairnes can be found in Eric Foner, *Free Soil, Free Labor, Free Men: The Ideology of the Republican Party before the Civil War* (New York: Oxford University Press, 1970); Kenneth M. Stampp, "Race, Slavery, and the Republican Party in the 1850s," in his *The Imperiled Union: Essays on the Background of the Civil War* (New York: Oxford University Press, 1980), 105–35; and Mark M. Smith, *Listening to Nineteenth-Century America* (Chapel Hill: University of North Carolina Press, 2001). For an interpretation that stresses the party politics behind the coming of the war, see, most obviously, Michael Holt, *The Political Crisis of the 1850s* (New York: Wiley, 1978).

cf. ref. below

commonplace," and "they seldom indicated whether the Slave Power was confined to the wealthier planters, or whether it embraced all slave owners, including women, the executors of estates, and residents of border states; whether it was a purely political interest, . . . or represented a total culture or civilization; and whether it included Northern business and political interests that supported Southern demands, as well as Southern politicians who had no personal ties with slavery."* That much said, Cairnes and other contemporaries used the term "Slave Power" as shorthand to describe an actual Southern ascendancy in the federal government. After all, between 1788 and 1850 slaveholders occupied the presidency for fifty years and eighteen out of the thirty-one Supreme Court justices in those years were slaveholders. As Leonard L. Richards, a recent student of the Slave Power, argues: "Slaveholders were generally in control."†

In other words, while Cairnes's book is limited in some important respects, he did manage to fashion a persuasive argument linking what was in fact an impressive Southern and slaveholding power in the

*David Brion Davis, *The Slave Power Conspiracy and the Paranoid Style* (Baton Rouge: Louisiana State University Press, 1969), 19–20.

† Leonard L. Richards, *The Slave Power: The Free North and Southern Domination, 1780–1860* (Baton Rouge: Louisiana University State Press, 2000), 9–10.

federal government with some very loud and agitated calls on the part of planters for the need for slavery's expansion westward.

Some planters undoubtedly believed that slavery's economic future was anchored in the drive into new territories. Although it remains clear that slavery could have flourished economically while not expanding westward, slaveholders—for a raft of psychological, social, cultural, and political as well as economic reasons—firmly believed that they had to expand and reserved the constitutional right to do so. As slaveholders heard increasingly shrill claims from Northern supporters of free soil and free labor to expand westward, they became sensitive about their own desire and need to counter the Northern vision of the future with their own claim to expand bondage to the west and so preserve their peculiar institution in time. Cairnes captured the spirit and tenor of this mind-set, one effectively summed up by Eugene Genovese. "It is difficult but unnecessary," writes Genovese, his ear turned toward Cairnes, "to assess the relative strength of the roots of slavery expansionism." Fear of economic stagnation, loss of political independence, the growing ascendancy of a worldview based on wage labor all "supported and fed the taproot—the exigencies of slaveholder hegemony in a South that fought against comparative disadvantages in the world market and that found itself increasingly isolated morally and politically." In short, "The existence of a threatening economic process," such as the rise of wage labor in the west, "would have been enough to generate fear and suspicion, even without the undeniable hostility arising in the North on political and moral grounds."Cairnes himself said as much, pointing to the"roots"of slavery and Southern identity. Without emancipation, Cairnes argued, "The lust of power will still be generated by the associations and habits of domestic tyranny, and the ambition of slaveholders will still connect itself with that which is the foundation of their social life, and offers to them their only means of emerging from obscurity. In a word, all those fundamental influences springing from the deepest roots of slave society"combined to"mould the character and determine the career" of the Slave Power. Cairnes's argument retains currency less because he got the economics right but more because he captured the spirit of the Southern mind-set. In this regard the political economist was a better observer of Southern culture and the mind of the master class than he was an economist.*

* Genovese, *The Political Economy of Slavery,* 251; Cairnes, *The Slave Power,* 263–64. On Cairnes's weaknesses as an economist, see Woodman, Introduction, xxix–xxxi esp.

Another strength of Cairnes's work resides in his methodology, something usually criticized by scholars. Cairnes's very methodology led him to attend less to the minutiae of evidence and more to the importance of overarching tendencies, a methodological proposition shared in part by others of his ilk and time. As Abraham Hirsch explains, "Cairnes, more strongly than any other of the major methodologists, felt that the validity of economic theory is established by the truth of the assumptions on which it rests." Cairnes argued that a theoretical conclusion "can neither be established nor refuted by an appeal to the records ... that is to say, by statistical or documentary evidence bearing on the course of industrial or commercial affairs." Rather, Cairnes suggested that an attention to premises, those "expressing a tendency deduced from certain principles of human nature," would facilitate understanding of the essential, core habits of a given society operating under particular conditions.* Even by William L. Miller's estimation, such an approach gave the book a powerful appeal. At the time, "Cairnes' thesis seemed to explain much, and it enlisted economic arguments to support those primarily ethical or political" issues that were of

---

*Abraham Hirsch, "J. E. Cairnes's Methodology in Theory and Practice," *History of Political Economy* 10 (Summer 1978): 322–23, 326.

paramount importance to contemporaries. As such, Cairnes's argument "became embedded in widely used textbooks on the economic history of the United States" so that even though he was incorrect on some essentials, the moral and ethical thrust of his argument still carries enormous currency in popular conceptions of the coming of the American Civil War principally because he willingly braided questions of history, economic development, and morality.*

Whatever Cairnes got wrong about the economics of Southern slavery, he was right about slaveholders' mind-set and their culture mainly because he remained true to the methodology and writing of classical political economy. As historian Harold D. Woodman explained with considerable insight: "The greatness of classical political economy before 1860 came from the breadth, the sense of history and morality, and the humanism of Smith, Ricardo, Mill, and others." By contrast neoclassical economics tends toward statistical abstractions and so loses a sense of

---

* Miller, "J. E. Cairnes on the Economics of American Negro Slavery," 341; Woodman, Introduction, xxxii–xxxiii. Cairnes's approach was influenced in part by the "holistic" system of Auguste Comte, the great French positivist. It argued for the kind of interwoven analysis Cairnes offered in *The Slave Power.* See Weinberg, *John Elliot Cairnes,* 17; J. E. Cairnes, "M. Comte and Political Economy," *Fortnightly Review,* 7 n.s. (May 1870): 579–602.

history and context. Ironically, Cairnes's methodological conservatism, his tendency to draw on an increasingly outdated way of understanding the world, helps make his study relevant a hundred and forty or so years after its initial publication.*

Mark M. Smith

* Woodman, Introduction, xlviii–xlix; Den Hollander, "Countries Far Away—Countries at a Distance," 367. Upon Cairnes's death in 1875, *The Slave Power* again earned warm applause, even from the *London Times,* which had been staunchly pro-Confederate. See Woodman, Introduction, xliii.

TO JOHN STUART MILL, ESQ.

Dear Sir,

I have great satisfaction in prefixing your name to the present work. Its appearance on my page will show that I have not engaged in speculation on an important subject without some qualification for the task. The sanction it gives to the views which I advocate will furnish an apology for the confidence with which they are urged—a confidence which, divided as opinion is on the subject of which I treat, might otherwise appear unbecoming. Lastly, the opportunity of connecting my name in public with that of one from whose works I have profited more largely than from those of any other living writer, was one which I could not easily forego.

Believe me, dear Sir,

With sincere respect,

Very truly yours,

J. E. CAIRNES.

1st May, 1862.

"I could easily prove that almost all the differences which are observed between the characters of the Americans in the Southern and Northern States have had their origin in slavery."—*Tocqueville.*

"If America ever undergoes great revolutions, they will be brought about by the presence of the blacks on the soil of the United States; that is to say, it will not be equality of conditions, but, on the contrary, inequality, which will produce them."—*Ibid.*

"African slavery as it exists among us—the proper status of the negro in our form of civilization—this was the immediate cause of the late rupture and present revolution. Jefferson, in his forecast, had anticipated this as the 'rock upon which the old Union would split.' He was right. What was conjecture with him is now a realized fact."—*A. H. Stephens, Vice-president of the Southern Confederacy.*

PREFACE

TO

THE SECOND EDITION.

THE remarkable change in the position of affairs in
North America, alike military and political, since
the first appearance of this work, now six months
ago, suggests the expediency of some remarks on
offering to the public a second edition. At that time
the Federal armies were triumphant at nearly all
points; the early surrender of the Confederate
capital was generally looked for; and even those
who were most anxious to believe in the hopeless-
ness of the task which the North had undertaken
placed their trust, rather in the heats of a Southern
summer, in the extent of the country to be
conquered, and in the resources of guerilla warfare
when the Northern forces should have penetrated
the Cotton states, than in the ability of the South
to defeat its opponent by regular military operations. No one in England at that time expected
what has since occurred—the evacuation of the
Southern territory by the principal Northern army

as the consequence of defeats sustained in a series of
pitched engagements. The writer of the present
work was certainly little disposed to make light of
the military qualifications of the new Confederacy ;
so far from this, his main object had been to depict
its formidable character—a task which he so performed as to have drawn upon him from some of
his critics the charge of exaggeration ; yet it now
appears that his error was of an opposite kind. The
military capacity of the Slave Power has proved on
trial to be greater than even those imagined who
were most disposed to magnify its prowess. What
is the bearing of this fact upon the following speculations ? It is this :—so far as those speculations
have proceeded upon the assumption of an established military superiority in the Free States, so far
they have for the present ceased to be applicable ;
on the other hand, so far as their aim was to hold
up to the world the new confederacy as the most
formidable antagonist of civilized progress which
has appeared in modern times—so far, that is to say,
as the main purpose of the present work was
concerned—so far, I apprehend, my position has
been indefinitely strengthened by the tenor of
events.

But the change in the posture of affairs has
introduced a new consideration. Has the military
success of the South been such as to justify us in

regarding its cause as definitively triumphant, and therefore in deprecating the further prosecution of the war by the North as a wanton waste of human life? Let us look at the facts. Notwithstanding the succession of defeats sustained by its principal armies, almost every position of importance which the North has at any time held since the war commenced, is still in its hands. At the present moment it holds, with the exception of eastern Virginia, all the Border States, and, with the exception of Vicksburgh, and Port Hudson, the whole course of the Mississippi. It holds besides most of the principal strongholds along the eastern and southern coast. On the other hand, not a foot of free soil is in possession of any Southern army. Were peace now established on the basis of *uti possidetis*, the North would gain, and the South would lose, nearly all the substantial objects for which the war has been waged. So much of Southern society as is susceptible of assimilation into the political system of the Northern people would be recovered; the Mississippi would be theirs; the Territories would be open for free colonization. On the other hand, the Slave Power would be thrown back into the corner of a continent; the field for its expansion would be cut off; and the cherished dream of a slave empire, "extending from the home of Washington to the palaces of Montezuma," would, at least for the present, have vanished. It would seem, then, that, to secure the substantial objects of the struggle, little more is necessary than that the North should make good the position which it at present holds. But it will be said that the war is carried on by the North for the specific object of restoring the Union, and that towards this end at least no real progress has been made. I grant that the restoration of the Union is still in the programme of the North—how far it is in the minds of its most thoughtful men is a different question. But conceding that the North seeks to restore the Union, and conceding also that the task of restoration is beyond its power, does it follow that there is nothing to be gained by a further prosecution of the contest? I apprehend it is only those who have attended to the ostensible, to the neglect of the real, issues of the war who will think so. The rationale of the revolution—always plain enough to those who were acquainted with the antecedents of the struggle and not blinded by terror of democracy, but now obvious to all eyes—is, that, under the guise of a constitutional question, a great social problem is being worked out. " States' rights," says Mr. Russell, " means protection to slavery, extension of slavery, and free trade in slave products with the outer world;" and so, on the other hand, the restoration of the Union on Republican principles, means the limitation, and ultimate extinction of slavery. Whatever plausibility there might have been at one time in denying this, there is none now. The social realities have burst the shell of constitutional figments in which they were incased ; and the conflict between slave and free society has now been actually proclaimed. In view of this—the real issue at stake, will it be said that there is nothing to be gained by a prolongation of the contest ? Let those who say so tell us upon what conditions peace would now be accepted by the South. With the actual military success which has attended its arms, with the liberal recognition which that success has met with from the nations of Europe, sustained as its cause has been by some of the leading journals of France and England,—is it to be supposed that the South, in this condition of its fortunes, would accept any terms short of those which would satisfy the known and plainly avowed purpose for which it has taken up arms ? That purpose has been to establish a Slave empire, self-sustained and capable of free expansion ; and the practical question now before the world is this—have matters arrived at that point at which this catastrophe has been proved to be inevitable— at which free society is bound to confess defeat ?

Before accepting this conclusion, let us remember what has just been stated—that, effectually to baffle the designs of the Slave Power, it is only necessary that the North should permanently make good the position which it at present holds. Is there anything in what has occurred to afford the slightest grounds for supposing that the North is not fully competent to accomplish this ? In point of material resources its superiority to its opponent is undeniable ; so that, if the contest becomes one of endurance, it is plain that physical exhaustion must first overtake the South. The struggle may indeed be abandoned from moral exhaustion ; but the possibility of this only deepens the obligation of all who recognize in the Northern cause the cause of human freedom, to sustain by the clear expression of their sympathy and approval the spirit of the people to whom this great charge is committed. But the present aspect of affairs gives promise, I think, of a decision in favour of freedom, speedier, and therefore more humane, than that which would result from the absolute exhaustion of the weaker combatant. This will appear if we consider the peculiar character of the contest, and the conditions under which it has been waged up to the present time.

The contest is one between two forms of society, which though embodied in political systems technically identical, are in reality antithetical in all their essential qualities. In the North we find a government broadly democratic alike in form and spirit ; in the South one democratic in form, but in spirit and essence a close oligarchy. For the purpose of war each of these political systems has its peculiar excellences and defects, its characteristic virtues and infirmities. This being so, before the superiority of either to the other, as a military agency, can be pronounced to be established, the systems, as wholes, with all their attributes alike of strength and weakness, must be submitted to the test. Now the mode in which the war has been conducted in America up to a recent time has been such as to give all the benefit of its peculiar strength, apart from its weakness, to one of the combatants, while to the other no corresponding advantage has been permitted : the weak side of the North has been brought prominently forward; while to that of the South has been secured absolute immunity from attack. On the side of the North publicity, divided councils, popular dictation, jealousy felt by the civil towards the military power, and, what is the natural consequence of this, constant interference by the civil magistrate with the plans of the military chiefs, —the inevitable incidents of popular government— have all played their part. To these have been opposed on the side of the South, the secresy, the unity of plan, and the absolute submission to the guidance of a few capable men, which are the natural and well-known features of an oligarchical rule. The result has been what might have been anticipated. At Bull Run General Scott was forced to sanction an advance against his better judgment

in deference to the popular will.   The plans of
MacClellan for the peninsular campaign were known
to the enemy the day after they were first discussed
in a council of war; and the combinations on which
he had subsequently counted for the capture of
Richmond—and which, in spite of the disadvantages
under which he laboured from the premature disclosure of his plans, would, in the opinion of the best
judges, have been successful, had he been permitted
to carry them into effect—were all rendered nuga-
tory by the pertinacious perversity with which the
civil power interfered to defeat them.   The disaster
at Fredericksburgh was but a repetition of the old
lesson.   A movement, apparently well conceived,
but which could only have been successful as a
surprise, broke down through want of concert.   It is
neither to inferiority in the Northern soldier, nor to
want of capacity in the Northern generals, that the
miscarriages of the North up to the present time can
fairly be attributed—the highest authority has borne
testimony to the merits of both*—but to causes

---

* "Je sais bien qu'il fallait gagner cette bataille et qu'on ne l'a
pas fait; mais ici la responsabilité est loin d'appartenir tout entière
à l'armée et à son chef.   Quels étaient les hommes qui, les obligeant
à une entrée en campagne intempestive, avaient ainsi révélé à l'en-
nemi le secret des opérations préparées contre lui avant que l'on fût
prêt à les éxecuter ?   Le général Mac-Clellan avait-il à répondre du
manque d'unité dans le but et dans l'action qui avait entravé les
mouvemens des armées fédérales depuis qu'on lui avait enlevé le
commandement en chef et la direction supérieure de toutes ces

incidental to the social and political system of the
Northern States. Indeed, looking at the extraordinary disadvantages under which the North has
laboured in this respect in connexion with the actual

armées ? Mac-Clellan enfin était-il responsable de l'amoindrisse-
ment systématique qui, en face de l'agglomération des forces ennemies lui avait enlevé successivement, depuis l'ouverture de la campagne, la division Blenker, donnée à Frémont, et les deux tiers du
corps de Mac-Dowell, sans compensation aucune, sans l'envoi d'un
seul homme pour combler les vides causés par le canon et les mala-
dies ? En dépit de toutes ces contrariétés, il était parvenu à conduire son armée sous les murs de Richmond; mais il n'avait plus
les moyens de frapper le grand coup qui trés probablement eût
terminé la guerre." . . . "Evidemment on avait besoin d'être
renforcé. Pouvait-on l'être ?" . . . "Les avant-postes de Mac-
Dowell étaient auprès de Bowlinggreen, à quinze milles de ceux de
Porter. Il n'eût fallu que le vouloir, les deux armées se réunis-
saient alors, et la possession de Richmond était assurée. Helas! on
ne le voulut pas. Je ne puis penser à ces funestes momens sans un
véritable serrement de cœur." . . . "Non-seulement les deux
armées ne se réunirent pas et ne communiquèrent même pas ensemble, mais l'ordre arriva par le télégraphe de Washington de brûler
les ponts dont on venait de se saisir." And, summing up the results
of the five days' fighting before Richmond, the writer bears testimony to the conduct of the Federal troops :—" Sans doute il y avait
eu, pendant le cours de cette difficile retraite, des momens de trouble et de désordre; mais quelle est l'armée qui, en pareille circon-
stance, y pourrait échapper complétement ? Il restait toujours ce
fait, qu'assaillie, au milieu d'un pays qui ne lui offrait que des
obstacles, par des forces au moins doubles des siennes, l'armée du
Potomac avait réussi à gagner une position où elle était hors de
péril, et d'où elle aurait pu, si elle avait été suffisamment renforcée,
s'il avait été répondu à la concentration des forces ennemies par
une concentration semlable, ne pas tarder à reprendre l'offensive."
—*Revue des Deux Mondes,* 15 October, 1862, pp. 842, '43, '44, '63.

results of the war, one cannot but admire the pluck, the energy, the unflinching devotion and indomitable resolution, which have been sufficient to neutralize so many blunders, and which still maintain the Federal armies, in spite of constant reverses, in the very foreground of their most advanced conquests. The miscarriages of the·North, then, are to be attributed to the inevitable weakness for war of the most popular form of government which the world has seen ; and herein, I apprehend, lies solid ground for hope ; for of the attributes of popular government none is more striking than its capacity to profit by disaster. A year's experience in the Crimea was sufficient to revolutionize our own military system ; and it is strange if the campaign in the peninsula, followed by the catastrophe at Fredericksburgh, has not sufficed to teach the North the lesson, that no extent of resources can, in military affairs, supply the place of discipline, concentration of strength, and submission to a single mind—qualities of which its opponent has furnished such admirable examples, and from the want of which it has itself so lamentably suffered.* But there is a still surer ground of

---

* The following from the *New York Times* shows that the lesson is beginning to be learned. " The rebels, notwithstanding all their trials and disappointments, have been patient. They have submitted with hardly a murmer to the management of their leaders, have not clamoured for intelligence, nor dictated plans, nor mourned over mishaps. They have exhibited remarkable trust and constancy."

hope. As I have just remarked, while the weak side
of the North has been freely exposed, that of the
South has hitherto remained secure against attack.
The slaves, who would gladly have filled the ranks of
the Federal armies, have hitherto, with the assent of
those armies, been doing the work of their enemies.
Those who should have been their allies have, as the
war has been conducted, been driven into the ranks
of their foes. We now see with what result. For
a year the Slave Power has contended on equal terms
with a nation of freemen, its match in soldierly qualities, numbering more than double its population, and
commanding more than quadruple its wealth. But
slave powers—great as is their capacity for war—
have, fortunately for civilization and human freedom, also their vulnerable side. That side has
hitherto been spared by the North : it now remains
to see what will be the consequence of assailing it.
The reasons which at the outset of the war restrained
the Federal government from dealing this blow were
natural and perhaps irresistible. The programme of
the Republican party had never gone beyond the
" limitation of slavery"; the conservative instincts
of the Northern people were strong;* the attitude

* " J'entends dire qu'il est dans la nature et dans les habitudes
des démocraties de changer à tout moment de sentiments et de
pensées. Cela peut être vrai de petites nations démocratiques,
comme celles de l'antiquité, qu'on réunissait tout entières sur une
place publique et qu'on agitait ensuite au gré d'un orateur. Je n'ai

of the Border states suggested compromise; the strength and determination of the Slave Power had not yet been proved;—finally, the responsible leaders of the nation "shrunk, as human nature will shrink, even, when most sincere, from accepting in a plain form a tremendous issue."* But the time for temporizing has passed. To delay the blow longer would be to trifle with the dearest interests of human freedom.

That the emancipation of slaves, as a belligerent measure, is thoroughly justifiable, is to my mind as clear as any proposition in the ethics of war. It is a weapon, of which every belligerent, to whom the chance has occurred, has in turn freely availed itself —England prominently among the number. The Constitution of the United States prohibits the emancipation of slaves, as a war measure, just as much and just as little as does the Constitution of England. In each case martial law is incompatible with the

rien vu de semblable dans le sein du grand peuple démocratique qui occupe les rivages opposés de notre Océan. Ce qui m'a frappé aux Etats-Unis, c'est la peine qu'on éprouve à désabuser la majorité d'une idée qu'elle a conçue et de la détacher d'un homme qu'elle adopte. Les écrits ni les discours ne sauraient guère y réussir; l'expérience seule en vient à bout, quelquefois encore faut-il qu'elle se répète." . . . "j'entrevois aisément tel état politique qui, venant à se combiner avec l'égalité, rendrait la société plus stationnaire qu'elle ne l'a jamais été dans notre occident."—*Tocqueville's Democratie en Amérique*, vol. ii. p. 290.

* ANGLO-SAXON in the *Daily News.*

ordinary legal rights of the citizen, but in each case a temporary recurrence to martial law may nevertheless be the only effectual means of permanently preserving those legal rights.   There is indeed a difference between the authority of the Federal government under the Constitution of the United States, and the authority of a purely national government like that of England ; but the difference is not one which affects the present argument.   The authority of the Federal government covers but a portion of the national life of the American people : it is a government of " enumerated powers ;" but within the range of those powers it is supreme, and, in relation to the acts to which those powers apply, it stands in precisely the same position towards every individual within the thirty-four states of the Union, as does the government of Great Britain to the individuals who compose the British nation.   " A government entrusted with such ample powers," says Chief Justice Marshall, delivering the judgment of the Supreme Court, " on the due execution of which the happiness and prosperity of the people vitally depend, must also be entrusted with ample means for their execution. . . . If the end be legitimate and within the scope of the Constitution, all means which are appropriate and plainly adapted to this end, and which are not prohibited by the Constitution, are lawful." The emancipation of the slaves of rebellious citizens is not prohibited by the Constitution, but on the contrary by very plain implication permitted, since it is provided that Congress shall have power " to make all laws that may. be necessary and proper to carry into execution the foregoing powers."* As to the lurid pictures of servile risings which fill the visions of our pro-slavery seers, they have already been abundantly falsified by events. In many districts the white population, including the wives and children of the planters, have been absolutely at the mercy of the negroes, who, if they were the savages they are described, might have freely given the rein to their propensities ; yet up to the present time not a single outrage of the slightest moment has occurred.† Nor is there the least probability that, if treated with ordinary humanity, the negroes will depart from the line of cautious moderation which they have hitherto followed. " They know," says one of themelves, " that naked hands are no match for broadswords, and that grubbing hoes will be sure to go down before cannon balls. The South

---

* Art. I. sec. 8. On which the comment of Hamilton in the *Federalist* is as follows :—" These powers ought to exist *without limitation,* because it is impossible to foresee or define the extent and variety of national exigencies, and the correspondent extent and variety of the means necessary to satisfy them."

† " Even our contemporary the *Index,* with all its energy, can get together no evidence of any worse atrocity than that ' a Mrs. Mock, in Florida, was *threatened* by a negro with bayonetting.' "— *Spectator,* 27th Dec., 1862.

was never better prepared for insurrection than now
—and the slaves know it.   They have no need to
prove their ability to fight, by rushing into the
whirlwind of uncertain and irregular war.   They
are now taking their places in the ranks of regular
troops, and distinguishing themselves for all the
qualities which are valuable in the soldier."*   How
long this moderation may last is another question,
and one of not less than awful gravity.   As we read
the sanguinary recitals which now fill the telegrams
from the Southern States, it is impossible not to
recall the savage scenes which once followed similar
atrocities.   It is not inopportune to remark that the
massacres of St. Domingo were preceded by a cold-
blooded murder committed by the ruling caste on
an unoffending man.   A coloured officer, Colonel
Ogé, the bearer from the Convention of a decree,
not of emancipation to the slaves, but merely conferring citizenship on the free blacks, was for no
other offence than this seized by the planters, and
broken on the wheel.†   Provocation far exceeding
the murder of a single innocent man has already
been given to the negroes of the Southern States.
A recent telegram announces that twenty of these
men had been deliberately slaughtered in cold blood
by the commanders of the principal Confederate

* *Douglass's Monthly.*
† Alison's *History of Europe*, vol. viii., p. 170.

army in the West, and for what crime ?—simply
because they were found in charge of waggons belonging to the Union army—a service, which, from
the commencement of the war, the negroes have not
ceased to perform for the armies of the South.   We
have seen torrents of vituperative eloquence directed
against the author of the proclamation of emancipation because of the possible evils which may flow
from a measure of justice ; but against the perpetrators of this actual atrocity, and others no less
black, not a single syllable of reprobation has yet
been uttered by those indignant sticklers for the
claims of humanity.*   Might it not be well if they
were to remind their vigorous and brilliant friends
of the fate of the murderers of Ogé ?

The denial to a belligerent of the right to emancipate his enemies' slaves is a position so monstrous
that to expose its absurdity the facts need only to
be stated.   To illustrate the principle by the case

* The following are the terms in which the *Saturday Review*
comments on the proclamation of Jefferson Davis, authorizing the
wholesale murder of the negro population :—"That part of the
proclamation, which refers to the negro insurgents, is more excusable [than that which orders the execution of General Butler and
his officers], although it is *probably impolitic.*"   From another
article under the same date it would seem that the objection to
even the "least excusable portion" is rather of a technical than a
moral nature:—"The portion of the document which denounces
vengeance against officers serving under General Butler is *hardly
reconcileable with the laws of war.*"

before us, what is contended for is this:—it is claimed that the South shall be permitted to employ its slaves in forwarding in every conceivable way the business of the war—producing food and clothing for the army, raising earthworks and fortifications, transporting stores and munitions of war, doing generally the work of the camp—nay (for this has happened in some instances) actually taking part in hostile operations in the field ; while the North shall be precluded from adopting the only course which can effectually deprive its enemy of this formidable means of maintaining the contest. Services which are permitted to slave powers, when taken unjustly and by force, are to be denied to free nations when voluntarily rendered. It is not enough that " a barbarous and barbarizing" Confederacy should have extended to it the usages of civilized warfare; a claim of privileged exemption from the liabilities of ordinary belligerents is set up on its behalf ; and free nations are required to submit to the direst blows of their formidable antagonist without daring to wrest from its grasp the weapon which deals them.

But there is another aspect than any which has yet been adverted to, under which the new policy of the Northern government well deserves to be considered. The natural complement to the military emancipation of slaves is the formation of a negro army ; and this, I apprehend, is the crowning result towards which the growing complications of the struggle are now rapidly converging. In a recent article in the *Spectator*, the policy of a negro army has been discussed in a manner which may well arrest the attention of American statesmen. Fully appreciating the abounding difficulties of the actual situation, the writer, with true political instinct, seizes upon the sole guiding clue from the bewildering maze.

" In the first place, the negro would probably supply the North as good or even a better military *matériel* than the mean whites supply to the South. They are quite as strong and quite as hardy, apparently quite as courageous, nearly as intelligent, much more *faithful* if well treated, and much more deeply habituated to that obedient attitude of mind which is the essence of military discipline. The Northern army has always been a free and easy army ; fighting bravely it is said, but also determined to exercise the right of public opinion as to the moment when they have done their share. The notion seizes them in battle that they have accomplished all that *ought* to be expected of them, and then no officer can force them to do more.* This

* Describing the defeat at Gainshill (27 June, 1862), the writer in the *Revue des Deux Mondes* (18 Octobre, 1862, p. 859), already quoted, says :—" Il n'y a pas panique, on ne court pas avec l'éffare-

is not *business* in military affairs.   The Southern troops, accustomed to an aristocratic caste, do not judge for themselves in this way.   They *spend* themselves at the command of their officers.   And thus, too, it would, in all probability, be with a negro army. Their fidelity and their respect for the white race would alike keep tight the bonds of military authority, now so loose at the North.   The negroes would be Sepoys without any disposition to treachery, and with more than the Sepoy physique.   Moreover, they would be even less exposed to the malaria and exhaustion of the Southern climate than the Southerners themselves.   Again, the negro just released from slavery would thankfully accept low *wages* in the Northern army, instead of the enormous bounty and pay now claimed by every white volunteer ; and they would be as easy to satisfy with wholesome rations of any kind as the present army is hard. Every element of the soldier is to be found in the negro, unless it be natural military tastes, and this the *cause* now supplies.   There is physical strength and a body used to unlimited hardships.   There is deference of spirit, clanship as between man and man, and affectionate fidelity to superiors.   There is

ment de la peur ; mais, sourds à tout appel, les hommes s'en vont délibérément, le fusil sur l'épaule, comme des gens qui en ont assez et qui ne croient plus au succès."

the willing hand without the meddling head, and the greatest of all motives for desperate valour.

" But next, a large auxiliary negro army would help to solve a great political problem. Under the President's emancipation policy a great number of negroes must be attracted northwards, and the greatest jealousy is felt by the Northern labourer lest they should reduce his normal wages. By employing them freely in the army this danger would be partially averted, and a great boon conferred upon the Northern labourer, who dreads the drafting policy of the administration. In this way the half-reluctant States of the North would be *reconciled* to the first steps of the emancipation policy,—and if, as we hope, the regiments thus formed should prove the most effective and best-disciplined in the army, the military pride of the North would soon convert them to the President's policy,—for no susceptibilities of caste would be hurt by the glory of black regiments with white commissioned officers,—the unjust rule of war being that all display of public gratitude is lavished on the leader, however much is due to the followers.

" But not only would this policy enormously lower the cost of the army, spare the labour of the North, and reconcile the democrats to emancipation—but it might be made one of the most powerful elements in what we may call the foreign policy of the war ; for there would be no better means of avoiding all the dangers of servile insurrection than passing the fugitive slaves through the discipline of a military *régime*. The least indulgence of private licence or vindictiveness might then be punished by instant death without any undue austerity. In no way could a severer control be kept over the risks of emancipation on a large scale. And thus the natural European suspicion of all sudden emancipation would be best removed. Nor would this be all. One result of such a measure would be still more important. A negro army once established would probably become the nucleus of the permanent military system of the North,—and so a most important check upon the South. Of course, we are assuming what all Englishmen now assume, that absolute subjugation of the South is a dream, that the war is a question of boundaries,—a question, as mathematicians would say, of the maximum or minimum extent of the Slave Power. Now, assuming this, what could be more important, more decisive for the slavery policy of the South, than the existence of a negro army across the border,— capable of large increase, and ready and eager to act in all causes directly involving the extension or limitation of slavery ? The knowledge of such a fact would be by far the most effective check on slavery propagandism that could be exerted by the agency of human fear.

" In whatever light we contemplate the question, the principles involved in the creation of a negro army seem to us most pregnant of weighty result and gradual political transformations."*

With regard to the new matter in the present edition, I have a few words to say. It is, for the most part, introduced in expansion of topics which found a place in the former edition, but of which the course of events or of discussion, since its publication, has suggested the expediency of a fuller treatment. Besides additions of this nature, a considerable body of evidence will be found in the notes and appendices, chiefly, it will be observed, drawn from Southern sources. Much of this will doubtless be familiar to those who have already studied the social condition of the Southern States ; but, in the present state of opinion concerning Southern institutions, it has been thought advisable to supply the reader, as far as possible, with the means of verifying the accuracy of statements of fact. To one document, which will be found in the Appendix, I wish particularly to call attention —The *Philosophy of Secession*, by the Hon. L. W.

---

* *Spectator*, December 13, 1862.

Spratt. Mr. Spratt is the editor of the *Charleston Mercury*, one of the most influential papers in the South.   He represented Charleston in that South Carolina Convention which led the way in the secession movement ; and the confidence reposed in him by the people of South Carolina may be inferred from the fact, that he was one of the commissioners appointed by that—the leading secession state—in the most critical juncture of its history to expound its views before the other insurgent conventions.   We learn from the Hon. Andrew J. Hamilton, of Texas, that Mr. Spratt's essay has been " reproduced in the leading prints of the South, and spoken of in terms of commendation, and that up to this hour no man has lifted up his voice in criticism against any of the positions there assumed."   " I have heard," adds Mr. Hamilton, " the echoes of these sentiments in the streets, in the hotels, and at the festive board."   A statement of the central idea involved in secession proceeding from a writer occupying the position of Mr. Spratt, and which has received the sanction of the Southern press and of Southern society, cannot but deserve the attention of those who would understand the real meaning of the American revolution.   I desire no better justification for all that I have said respecting the character and aims of the Slave Power than is furnished by Mr. Spratt's essay.

One further remark I wish to make. Since the publication of the first edition of the present work, the aspect of affairs in America has undergone a vast change : in no instance have I attempted to meet this change by any modification of the positions originally assumed in this essay. If the course of events has tended in any degree to weaken the general force of my argument, I am prepared to accept the loss of credit which may on this account fairly attach to my speculations. It is my conviction, however, that experience has greatly strengthened all its principal positions. One fact will perhaps appear inconsistent with this statement —the triumph of the democratic party at the recent elections ;—an òccurrence which may be thought to militate against the expectation which I have expressed of a rapid growth of anti-slavery sentiment in the North. But in truth it warrants no inference of the kind. The significance of the democratic triumphs, as interpreted by the whole Northern press, is simply this—distrust of the competency of the administration, and dissatisfaction with the management of the war. The occurrence is one of the same kind as a change of government from the Whigs to the Tories would have been in this country during the agony of the Crimean conflict. Had this occurred, no one acquainted with political parties here would have regarded it as an indication that liberal principles had retrograded in England. It would have signified simply a demand for a more energetic prosecution of the war ; and this is also the explanation of the Republican defeats. There is moreover another consideration which should be taken account of in attempting to estimate the significance of these party gains and losses. Under the influence of the logic of events, opinion in America is rapidly moving away from the old political landmarks. In a pamphlet just issued from the New York press, which I have now before me, the emancipation proclamation is vigorously defended by a writer, " called by some a pro-slavery man," and who, as he tells us, " at the last state senatorial election voted for the democratic candidate." On the other hand, as we learn from the correspondent of the *Daily News*, there are " Republicans pure, who are heart and soul in the war, and ready to sacrifice their last son and last cent in order to bring it to an honourable conclusion, who have voted for Seymour in sheer weariness of disgust."*

* " With reference to the slavery question," said General Butler, in a recent speech at New York, "his views had undergone a radical change during his residence at New Orleans. . . . He thought he might say that the principal members of his staff, and the prominent officers of his regiments, without any exception, went out to New Orleans hunker [Americanese for extreme pro-slavery] Democrats of the hunkerest sort, for it was but natural that he

But it is idle to dwell upon such incidents as these with the broad facts of the past year before us. Let me here briefly enumerate them. Slavery has been abolished in the District of Columbia. It has been excluded from the Territories. An effective anti-slave-trade treaty has been negotiated with Great Britain. The President, for the first time in the history of the United States, has propounded a scheme for universal emancipation. Two slave states have returned members to Congress pledged to an emancipation policy. The legislature of one slave state has voted emancipation by immense majorities. Lastly, the President, in his capacity of commander-in-chief has proclaimed immediate emancipation in all the insurgent states, and has authorized the raising of a negro army. These are the grand achievements of the Northern States in the past year—the monuments of a revolution—fearful as is the cost at which its results have been obtained—as hopeful and as rapid as any which the history of mankind records.

should draw around him those whose views were similar to his own, and every individual of the number had come to precisely the same belief on the question of slavery as he had put forth in his farewell address to the people of New Orleans. This change came about from seeing what all of them saw, day by day."

PREFACE

TO

THE FIRST EDITION.

IT is proper that I should state the circumstances under which the present volume is offered to the public. The substance of it formed the matter of a course of lectures delivered. about a year since in the University of Dublin. In selecting the subject of North American slavery I was influenced in the first instance by considerations of a purely speculative kind—my object being to show that the course of history is largely determined by the action of economic causes. To causes of this description, it seemed to me, the fortunes of slavery in North America—its establishment in one half of the Union and its disappearance from the other— were directly to be ascribed ; while to that institution, in turn, the leading differences in the character of the Northern and Southern people, as well as that antagonism of interests between the two sections which has issued in a series of political conflicts extending over half a century, were no less distinctly traceable. The course of events, however, since I first took up the subject, has given to it an interest far other than speculative, and has rendered conclusions, of which the value (if they possessed any) was little more than scientific, directly applicable to problems of immediate and momentous interest. Under these circumstances I have been induced to extend considerably the original plan of my investigations, and to give the whole subject a popular and practical treatment, in the hope of contributing something to the elucidation of a question of vast importance, not only to America, but to the whole civilized world.

The rapid movement of events, accompanied by no less rapid fluctuations in public opinion, during the progress of the work, will explain, and, it is hoped, will procure indulgence for, some obvious imperfections. Some topics, it is probable, will be found to be treated with greater fulness, and some arguments to be urged with greater vehemence, than the present position of affairs or the present state of public feeling may appear to require. For example, I have been at some pains to show that the question at issue between North and South is not one of tariffs—a thesis prescribed to me by the state of the discussion six months ago, when the affirmative of this view was pertinaciously put forward by writers in the interest of the South, but

which, at the present time, when this explanation
of the war appears to have been tacitly abandoned,
cannot but appear a rather gratuitous task.

In a certain degree, indeed, the same remark
applies to the main argument of the work; for,
in spite of elaborate attempts at mystification, the
real cause of the war and the real issue at stake
are every day forcing themselves into prominence
with a distinctness which cannot be much longer
evaded. Whatever we may think of the tendencies
of democratic institutions, or of the influence of
territorial magnitude on the American character,
no theory framed upon these or upon any other
incidents of the contending parties, however inge-
niously constructed, will suffice to conceal the fact,
that it is slavery which is at the bottom of this
quarrel, and that on its determination it depends
whether the Power which derives its strength from
slavery shall be set up with enlarged resources and
increased prestige, or be now once for all effectually
broken. This is the one view of the case which
every fresh occurrence in the progress of events
tends to strengthen; and it is this which it is the
object of the present work to enforce.

But, although the development of the movement
may have deprived the following speculations of
some of that novelty which they might have possessed when they were first delivered, still it is hoped

that they will not be without their use—that, while
they will assist honest enquirers to form a sound
judgment upon a question which is still the subject
of much designed and much unconscious misrepre-
sentation, they may possess a more permanent interest, as illustrating by a striking example the value
of a fruitful but little understood instrument of
historical inquiry— that which investigates the
influence of material interests on the destinies of
mankind.

THE SLAVE POWER,

ITS

CHARACTER, CAREER, AND DESIGNS.

CHAPTER I.

INTRODUCTORY.

THE CASE STATED.

THOSE who have followed the discussions in this country on the American contest are aware that the view taken of that event by the most influential organs of the English press has, during the period which has elapsed since its commencement, under-gone considerable modification. The first announce-ment by South Carolina of its intention to secede from the Union was received in this country with simple incredulity. There were no reasons, it was said, for secession. What the constitution and laws of the United States had been on the eve of Mr. Lincoln's election, that they were on its morrow. It was absurd to suppose that one half of a nation should separate from the other because a first magis-trate had been elected in the ordinary constitutional course. The agitation for secession was therefore

pronounced to be a political feint intended to cover
a real movement in some other direction. But
when the contest had passed beyond its first stages,
when the example set by South Carolina was followed by the principal States of the extreme South
with a rapidity and decision shewing evident concert, when the treacherous seizure of Fort Moultrie
in Charleston harbour gave further significance to
the votes of the conventions, when lastly the attack
on Fort Sumpter awoke the North, as one man, to
arms, belief in the reality of the movement could no
longer be withheld, and speculation was directed to
the causes of the catastrophe. The theory at first
propounded was nearly to this effect. Commercial
and fiscal differences were said to be at the bottom
of the movement. The North fancied she had an
interest in protection; the South had an obvious
interest in free trade. On this and other questions
of less moment North and South came into collision,
and the antagonism thus engendered had been
strengthened and exacerbated by a selfish struggle
for place and power—a struggle which the constitution and political usages of the Americans rendered
more rancorous and violent than elsewhere. But in
the interests of the two sections, considered calmly
and apart from selfish ends, there was nothing, it
was said, which did not admit of easy adjustment,
nothing which negotiation was not far more compe-

tent to deal with than the sword. As for slavery, it was little more than a pretext on both sides, employed by the leaders of the South to arouse the fears and hopes of the slaveholders, and by the North in the hope of attracting the sympathies of Europe and hallowing a cause which was essentially destitute of noble aims. The civil war was thus described as having sprung from narrow and selfish views of sectional interests (in which, however, the claims of the South were coincident with justice and sound policy), and sustained by passions which itself had kindled; and the combatants were advised to compose their differences, and either return to their political partnership, or agree to separate and learn to live in harmony as independent allies.

With the progress of events these views have undergone some change, principally in excluding more completely than at first from the supposed causes of the movement the question of slavery, and in bringing more prominently into view the right of nations to decide on their own form of political existence as identified with the cause of the South. "It is a struggle," said the Foreign Minister, "for empire on the one side and for independence on the other." "The watchword of the South," said the *Times*,* "is Independence, of the North Union, and in these two war-cries the real issue is contained."

* September 19, 1861.

That there is much plausibility in this view of
the American crisis for those who have no more
knowledge of American history than is possessed by
the bulk of educated men in this country needs not be
denied. Superficial appearances, perhaps we should
say the facts most immediately prominent, give it
some support. The occasion on which secession
was proclaimed was the election of a Republican
president, who, far from being the uncompromising
champion of abolition, had declared himself ready
to maintain the existing *régime* of slavery with the
whole power of the Federal government. On the
retirement of the Southern representatives and senators from Congress, the Republican party became
supreme in the legislature ; and in what way did
they employ this suddenly acquired power ? In
passing a law for the abolition of slavery in the
Union ? or even in repealing the odious Fugitive
Slave Law ? Nothing of the kind ; but in passing
the Morrill tariff—in enacting a measure by which
they designed to aggrandize the commercial population of the North at the expense of the South.

Since the breaking out of hostilities, again, some of
the most salient acts of the drama have only tended
to confirm the view which these occurrences would
suggest. When slaves have escaped to the Federal
army, instead of being received by the general with
open arms as brothers for whose freedom he is

fighting, they have been placed upon the footing of property, and declared to be contraband of war. When a Federalist general, transcending his legitimate powers, issues a proclamation declaring that slaves shall be free, it is not a proclamation of freedom to slaves as such, but only to the slaves of "rebels," while no sooner is this half-hearted act of manumission known at head-quarters than it is disavowed and over-ruled.

All this, and more to the same purpose, may be urged, as it has been urged, in favour of the view of the American crisis taken by some leading organs of the English press; yet I venture to say that never was a historical theory raised on a more fragile foundation; never was an explanation of a political catastrophe propounded in more daring defiance of all the great and cardinal realities of the case with which it professed to deal.

One is tempted to ask, whether those who thus expound American politics suppose the present crisis to be an isolated phenomenon in American history, disconnected from all the past; or, to look at the question from another point of view, whether they imagine that the coincidence of the political division of parties with the geographical division of slave and free states is an accident—that, to borrow the expression of Jefferson, "a geographical line coinciding with a marked principle" has no significance. It seems almost trifling with the reader to remind him that the present outbreak is but the crowning result, the inevitable climax of the whole past history of American politics—the catastrophe foreseen with more or less distinctness by all the leading statesmen of America, from Washington to Webster and Clay, which was the constant theme of their forebodings, and to escape or defer which was the great problem of their political lives. And equally superfluous does it seem to mention what was the grand central question in that history—the question to which all others were subordinate, and around which all political divisions ranged themselves.*

* In opposition to the views propounded by the most influential organs of opinion in England, and in support of what I may venture to call the obvious (though little recognized) account of the war, I am glad to be able to quote the high authority of two leading French Reviews, the *Revue des Deux Mondes*, and the *Revue Nationale:*—

"Il faut aimer à discuter contre l'évidence pour se persuader que la question de l'esclavage n'est point la cause principale de la crise actuelle. Dans ce conflit qui depuis trente ans va toujours en s'aggravant et qui vient enfin d'aboutir à la guerre civile, quelle question va toujours en grandissant et finit par dominer tout le reste, sinon cette redoutable question de l'esclavage ? Ils n'ont pas lu les discours de Calhoun, de Webster, de Seward, de Douglas, de Clay, de Sumner, ceux qui croient que la question de l'esclavage n'a dans la politique américaine qu'une importance secondaire. Ils oublient que toute la Virginie s'est levée en armes contre John Brown et ses vingt-cinq compagnons. Voici un fait d'ailleurs : quels sont les belligérans ? D'un côté les états sans esclaves, de l'autre

Never surely was the unity of a national drama better preserved. From the year 1819 down to the present time the history of the United States has been one record of aggressions by the Slave Power,

les états à esclaves, et l'on prétendrait que la question de l'esclavage est étrangère à la guerre ! Entre les états du nord et ceux du sud il y a des états frontières, les *border states*, qui, sans être des états libres, contiennent moins d'esclaves que les états cotonniers. Chose étrange ! la fidélité de ces états à l'Union est précisément en raison inverse du nombre de possesseurs d'esclaves ; la Virginie, qui a des esclaves se rallie au mouvement sécessioniste ; la partie occidentale de cet état, oasis sans esclaves, séparée du reste par une chaine des Alleghanys, reste fidèle à l'Union et lui donne des soldats. Le nord du Delaware, qui n'a plus d'esclaves, renferme à peine un sécessioniste ; le sud, qui en a un grand nombre, contient beaucoup d'adversaires de l'Union. Le sud et l'est du Maryland sont remplis d'esclaves, et en conséquence de sécessionistes ; l'ouest du Maryland, où l'on voit très peu de noirs non affranchis, est presque unanime pour l'Union. Les six mille esclaves de Baltimore appartiennent à l'aristocratie de cette ville, et l'on sait que cette aristocratie "n'est retenue dans l'obéissance que par des mesures de rigueur. Le Tennessee occidental, abandonné au travail servile, est un centre de rébellion ; le Tennessee oriental, où le travail libre l'emporte de beaucoup, est sympathique à l'Union. Le Kentucky ne fait pas exception à ce règle : dans les comtés du nord et de l'est, où il y a peu d'esclaves, il y a peu de sécessionistes ; dans les autres, où ils sont nombreux, on se prononce pour la 'neutralité,' ce qui n'est qu'une forme de la trahison. Dans le Missouri, la ligne de démarcation est nettement établie entre le travail libre et le travail servile. Les Allemands détestent l'esclavage, et forment le noyau le plus fidèle de l'état ; les unionistes anglo-saxons sont plutôt en faveur de la neutralité, tandis que les maîtres d'esclaves sont en armes contre l'Union. Il y a quelques sympathies pour l'Union jusque dans le Texas occidental, parce qu'on y voit peu

feebly, and almost always unsuccessfully, resisted by
the Northern States, and culminating in the present
war. At the time of the revolution, as is well known,
slavery was regarded by all the great founders of
the Republic, whether Northern or Southern men,
as essentially an immoral system : it was, indeed,
recognized by the Constitution, but only as an ex-

d'esclaves et beaucoup d'Allemands. Quel est l'état sécessioniste
par excellence ? C'est la Caroline du sud, qui contient relativement
plus d'esclaves que tous les autres états. Dira-t-on encore que le
défense de l'esclavage n'est pas la cause des sécessionistes ? S'il
resta des doutes dans quelques esprits, qu'on écoute donc le propre
témoignage des gens du sud."—*Revue des Deux Mondes,* 1re *Nov.,*
1861.

In an article by M. Pressensé, in the *Revue Nationale,* the point
is put with equal perspicuity and force :—" Je sais qu'on s'efforce
d'en dissimuler la gravité, et que d'un certain côté on essaye de
la réduire à un simple conflit constitutionnel, à une question de
droit politique, à l'interprétation du contrat qui lie entre eux les
divers Etats de la confédération puissante dont les gigantesques
progrès étonnaient naguère le monde.   Mais cette explication
mesquine de la crise actuelle de l'Amérique du Nord n'est qu'un
sophisme destiné à excuser une lâcheté.   On essaye de donner ainsi
le change à la conscience publique, qui ne comprendrait pas et ne
permettrait pas que l'on hésitât en Europe entre le Nord et le
Sud, une fois que la question de l'esclavage serait nettement posée
entre eux.   Ceux qui trouvent leur intérêt à incliner vers le Sud se
plaisent à rabaisser le conflit américain à des proportions misé-
rables qui mettent la conscience hors de cause ; mais cela est moins
facile que cela ne semble commode, et ils ont beau faire, la vraie
situation se dessine toujours mieux."

The same view is sustained by Le Comte Agénor De Gasparin
with remarkable eloquence in his work, ' *Un Grand Peuple qui se
relève.*'

ceptional practice, a local and temporary fact. In
the unsettled territory then belonging to the Union
it was by a special ordinance prohibited. Even
in 1819, although in the interval the Slave Power
had pushed its dominion and pretensions far beyond
their original limits, the claim was scarcely advanced
for slavery to rank as an equal with free institutions
in any district where it was not already definitively
established, and certainly no such claim was acknowledged. Of this the Missouri Compromise affords
the clearest proof, since, regarded as a triumph
by the slaveowners, it only secured the admission
of slavery to Missouri on the express condition
that it should be confined for the future to the
territory south of a certain parallel of latitude. But
what has been the career of the Slave Power since
that time ? It is to be traced through every questionable transaction in foreign and domestic politics
in which the United States has since taken part—
through the Seminole war, through the annexation
of Texas, through the Mexican war, through filibustering expeditions under Walker, through attempts
upon Cuba, through the Fugitive Slave Law of 1850,
through Mr. Clay's compromises, through the repudiation of the Missouri Compromise so soon as the
full results of that bargain had been reaped, through
the passing of the Nebraska Bill and the legislative
establishment of the principle of " Squatter Sove-

reignty," through the invasion of Kansas, through
the repudiation of " Squatter Sovereignty" when
that principle had been found unequal to its purposes, and lastly, through the Dred Scott decision
and the demand for protection of slavery in the Territories—pretensions which, if admitted, would have
converted the whole Union, the Free States no less
than the Territories, into one great domain for slavery.
This has been the point at which the Slave Power,
after a series of successful aggressions, carried on
during forty years, has at length arrived. It was on
this last demand that the Democrats of the North
broke off from their Southern allies—a defection
which gave their victory to the Republicans, and
directly produced the civil war. And now we are
asked to believe that slavery has no vital connexion
with this quarrel, but that the catastrophe is due to
quite other causes—to incompatibility of commercial interests, to uncongeniality of social tastes, to
a desire for independence, to anything but slavery.

But we are told that in this long career of aggression the extension of slavery has only been
employed by the South as a means to an end, and
that it is in this end we are to look for the key to
the present movement. " Slavery," it seems, " is but
a surface question in American politics."* The seem-
ing aggressions were in reality defensive movements

* *Saturday Review*, Nov. 9th, 1861.

forced upon the South by the growing preponderance of the Free States ; and its real object, as well in its former career of annexation and conquest, as in its present efforts to achieve independence, has been constantly the same—to avoid being made the victim of Yankee rapacity, to secure for itself the development of its own resources unhindered by protective laws.*

Let us briefly examine this theory of the secession movement. And, first, if free trade be the object of the South, why, we may ask, has it not employed its power to accomplish this object during its long period of predominance in the Union ? It has been powerful enough to pass and repeal the Missouri Compromise, to annex Texas, to spend 40,000,000 dollars of Federal money in a war for the recapture of slaves, to pass the Fugitive Slave Law, to obtain the Dred Scott decision : if it has been able to accomplish these results, to lead the North into foreign complications in which it had no interest, and to force upon it measures to which it was strongly averse, is it to be supposed that it could not, had it so desired, have carried a free trade tariff ? Yet not only has the South not attempted this during its long reign, it has even co-operated effectively in the passing of protective measures—nay, these enthusiastic free

* Mr. Yancey's letter to the *Daily News*, January 25, 1862.

traders have not hesitated, when the opportunity offered, to profit by protective measures. With the exception of the Morrill tariff, Congress never passed a more highly protective law than the tariff of 1842 ; and this tariff was supported by a large number of Southern statesmen ; and, not only so, but gave effective protection to Southern products —to the sugar of Louisiana, the hemp of Kentucky, and the lead of Missouri, as well as to the manufactures of New England.*

Again, if free trade be the real object of the South, how does it happen that, having submitted to the tariffs of 1832,† 1842, and 1846, it should have resorted to the extreme measure of secession while under the tariff of 1857—a comparatively

* "Protection," says Mr. Rawlins, "was inaugurated at the very birth of the Union. The preamble of the first revenue law ever passed by Congress thus ran: 'Whereas, it is necessary for the support of Government, for the discharge of the debts of the United States, *and the encouragement and protection of manufactures,* that duties be laid on goods, wares, and merchandise imported.' The great apostle of protection was Mr. Clay of Kentucky; and Southern Legislatures have always advocated a moderate adoption of this policy."—*American Disunion, p. 23.*

† I say "having submitted to the tariff of 1832," because, although it is true that South Carolina threatened to rise in rebellion against this measure, she stood alone in her projected revolt. Far from receiving any general sympathy in the South, it was through the instrumentality of a Southern State (Virginia), employed by a Southern President (Jackson), that the threatened movement was suppressed.

free-trade law ? From 1842 down to 1860 the tendency of Federal legislation was distinctly in the
direction of free trade. The most liberal tariff the
Union ever enjoyed since 1816 was the tariff of
1857, and it was while this tariff was in force that
the plot .of secession was hatched, matured, and
carried into operation. But there are some who
would have us believe that it was the Morrill tariff
which produced the revolt; and this is the most
incomprehensible portion of the whole case ; since
there is nothing more certain than that secession
had been resolved upon, and the plot for its accomplishment traitorously prepared, before the Morrill
tariff was brought forward, and even before the
bargain with Pennsylvania was struck, in fulfilment
of which it was introduced. It is indeed well
known that it was the absence from Congress of the
Southern senators while carrying out the programme
of secession, which alone rendered possible the passing of this measure. If free trade were the prime
object of the South, why did its senators withdraw
from their posts precisely at the time when their
presence was most required to secure their cherished
principle ? Nay, if this was their game, why did
they not apply to Mr. Buchanan to veto the Bill—
Mr. Buchanan, the creature and humble tool of the
Slave Party ? We are asked by this theory to
believe that the South has had recourse to civil war,

has incurred the risk of political annihilation, to accomplish an object for the effectual attainment of which its ordinary constitutional opportunities afforded ample means.*

But the difficulties of this theory do not end here. If the secession movement be a revolt against protective tariffs, why is it confined to the Southern States ? The interest of the Cotton States in free exchange with foreign countries is not more obvious than that of Ohio, Indiana, Illinois, and Wisconsin. No class in these States has anything to gain by protective measures : nothing is produced in them which is endangered by the freest competition with the rest of the world : an artificial enhancement of European manufactures is to them as pure an injury as it is to South Carolina or Alabama: yet all these States are ranged on the side of the North in this contest, and resolute for the suppression of the revolt.

* The writer in the *Revue des Deux Mondes* from whom I have already quoted suggests (pp. 156–157) that the conduct of the Southern senators in permitting the passing of the Morrill tariff was deliberately contrived with a view to make political capital out of the sentiments which they calculated on its exciting in England— an explanation which is countenanced by the fact that Mr. Toombs, representative of Georgia, who now holds a command in the army of Jefferson Davis, was in the Senate when the Morrill tariff was submitted to that assembly, and voted for the new law. If this was their object, never was plot more skilfully contrived or more successful.

It is, however, by the watch word of "independence," still more than by that of free trade, that
the partisans of the South in this country have
sought to enlist our sympathies in favour of that
cause. We are told of the naturalness, the univer-
sality, the strength of the desire for self-government.
We are reminded of the peculiar power of this
passion among the Anglo-Saxon race. The act of
the original thirteen States in severing their connexion with the mother country is dwelt upon ; and
we are asked why the South should not also be
permitted to determine for itself the mode of its
political existence ? "It threatens none, demands
nothing, attacks no one, but wishes to rule itself,
and desires to be ' let alone :'" why should this
favour be denied it ? Now let it at once be conceded that the right to an independent political
existence is the most sacred right of nations : still
even this right must justify itself by reference to
the ends for which it is employed. The demand
of a robber or murderer for "independence" is
not a claim which we are accustomed to respect ;
and it does not appear how our obligations are
altered if the demand proceed from a robber
or murderer nation—if national independence be
sought solely and exclusively as a means of carrying out designs which are nothing less than robbery
and murder on a gigantic scale. I am assuming

that these crimes are involved in the extension
of slavery, and that the extension of slavery is
the end for which the Southern Confederacy has
engaged in the present war. These assumptions
I hope to make good hereafter ; but meanwhile,
it may be asked, if the extension of the domain
of slavery be not the object for which the South
seeks independence, what is that object ? Let those
who have undertaken the defence of that body
explain to us in what way the legitimate development of the Southern States, within their proper
limits, was hindered by Federal restraints ? If they
had grievances to complain of, why did they not let
the world know them ? Why did they resist all the
efforts of the Northern States to extract from them a
categorical statement of what they sought? " That,"
says an able writer, " was precisely what it was impossible to obtain from the representatives and senators of the extreme South. They steadily refused to
make known, even under the form of an ultimatum,
the conditions on which they would consent to remain in the Union. Their invariable response was
that, it was too late; their constituents would acquiesce in no arrangement."* Before then we allow
ourselves to be carried away by the cry of the South
for independence, it is material to ascertain the purpose for which independence is desired. It is im-

* *Annuaire des Deux Mondes* (1860), p. 618.

portant to distinguish between (to quote the words of the eminent man whose name has been prefixed to this volume) " the right to rebel in defence of the power to tyrannize," and " the right to resist by arms a tyranny practised over ourselves."

The causes and character of the American contest are not for Englishmen questions of merely speculative interest. On the view which we take of this great political crisis will depend, not alone our present attitude towards the contending parties, but in no small degree our future relations with a people of our own race, religion and tongue, to whom has been committed the task, under whatever permanent form of polity, to carry forward in the other hemisphere the torch of knowledge and of civilization. We may, according as we act from sound knowledge of the real issues which are at stake, or in ignorance of them, do much to promote or to defeat important human interests bound up with the present contest, and to increase or to diminish the future influence for good of this country. It would indeed be a grievous misfortune if, in one of the great turning points of human history, Great Britain were found to act a part unworthy of the position which she occupies and of the glorious traditions which she inherits.

The present essay is intended as a contribution towards the diffusion of sound ideas upon this subject. The real and sufficient cause of the present

position of affairs in North America appears to the
writer to lie in the character of the Slave Power—
that system of interests, industrial social and political, springing from slavery, which for the greater
part of half a century has directed the career of the
American Union, and which now, embodied in the
Southern Confederation, seeks admission as an equal
member into the community of civilized nations. In
the following pages an attempt will be made to
resolve this system into its component elements, to
trace the connexion of the several parts with each
other, and of the whole with the foundation on
which it rests, and to estimate generally the prospects which it holds out to the people who compose
it, as well as the influence it is likely to exercise on
the interests of other nations ; and, if I do not
greatly mistake the purport of the considerations
which shall be adduced, their effect will be to show
that this Slave Power constitutes the most formidable
antagonist to civilized progress which has appeared
for many centuries, representing a system of society
at once retrograde and aggressive, a system which,
containing within it no germs from which improvement can spring, gravitates inevitably towards barbarism, while it is impelled by exigencies, inherent in its
position and circumstances, to a constant extension
of its territorial domain. The vastness of the interests at stake in the American contest, regarded under

this aspect, appears to me to be very inadequately conceived in this country ; and the purpose of the present work is to bring forward this view of the case more prominently than has yet been done.

But it is necessary here to guard against a misapprehension. The view that the true cause of the American contest is to be found in the character and aims of the Slave Power, though it connects the war ultimately with slavery, as its radical cause, by no means involves the supposition that the motive of the North in taking up arms has been the abolition of slavery. Such certainly has not been its motive, and, if we keep in view its position as identified with legal government and constitutional rights in the United States, we shall see that this motive, even had it existed, could scarcely, at least in the outset, have been allowed to operate. Let us recall for a moment the mode in which the crisis developed itself. It must be remembered—what seems now almost to be forgotten—that the war was commenced by the South—commenced for no other reason, on no other pretext, than because a Republican president was elected in the ordinary constitutional course. If we ask why this was made the ground for revolt, I believe the true answer, as I have just intimated, is to be found in the aims of the Slave Power,—aims which were inconsistent with its remaining in the Union while the Government was carried on upon the principle of restricting the extension of its domain. So long as it was itself the dominant party, so long as it could employ the powers of the Government in propagating its peculiar institution and consolidating its strength, so long it was content to remain in the Union; but from the moment when, by the constitutional triumph of the Republicans, the government passed into the hands of a party whose distinctive principle was to impose a limit on the further extension of slavery, from that moment its continuance in the Union was incompatible with its essential objects, and from that moment the Slave Power resolved to break loose from Federal ties. The war had thus its origin in slavery : nevertheless the proximate issue with which the North had to deal was not slavery, but the right of secession. For the constitution having recognised slavery within the particular states, so long as the South confined its proceedings within its own limits, the Government which represented the constitution could take no cognizance of its acts. The first departure from constitutional usage by the South was the act of secession,* and it was on the ques-

---

* I am aware that this has been denied by some English advocates of the South, in their zeal for the cause more Southern than the Southerns; no less an authority than Mr. Buchanan—though not a Southern, the elect of the South—having declared that

tion, therefore, of the right to adopt this course that the North was compelled to join issue.

The contest, thus springing from slavery, and involving, as will be shewn, consequences of the most momentous kind in connexion with the future well-being of the human race in North America, wore the appearance, to persons regarding it from the outside, of a struggle upon a point of technical construction—a question of law which it was sought to decide by an appeal to arms. It was not un-

secession was unconstitutional. It would be foreign to my purpose here to enter into an argument on the constitutional question. I will therefore only say that after having carefully studied, so far as I know, all that has been written on both sides by competent persons, I have been quite unable to discover any other ground on which the claim of secession can be placed than that ultimate one —the right which in the last resort appertains to all people to determine for themselves their own form of government. How far the case of the South will stand the test when tried by this principle, I have intimated my opinion in the text.

Since the above note was written I have had the advantage of reading Mr. Rawlins' work, "*American Disunion*," in which the constitutional question is discussed. A more complete refutation of all that has been written in support of the Southern claim it would be difficult to conceive. Not only is every argument in Mr. Spence's chapter on this question effectually disposed of, but his authorities are turned against himself; and it has been shown that quotations which have been adduced in support of the constitutional right of secession, have only to be slightly extended in order to show that their authors were in reality opposed to it. The knowledge and logical power exhibited in this unpretending volume are not more remarkable than is the perfect fairness of mind which characterizes it throughout.

natural, then, that the people of this country, who
had but slight acquaintance with the antecedents
of the contest or with the facts of the case, should
wholly misconceive the true nature of the issues
at stake, and, disconnected as the quarrel seemed
to have become from the question of slavery, should
allow their sympathies, which had originally gone
with the North, to be carried, under the skilful
management of Southern agency acting through the
press of this country, round to the Southern side.*
Nevertheless, had the cause of the North, regarded
even from this point of view, been fairly put before
the English people, it is difficult to believe that it
would not have been recognized as founded, at
least in its first phase, in reason and justice.
When the South forced on a contest by attacking
the Federal forts, what was Mr. Lincoln to do ?
Before acquiescing in its demand for separation,
was he not at least bound to ascertain that that
demand represented the real wish of the Southern
people ?   But, after war had been proclaimed, or
rather commenced, by the South, how was this to
be done otherwise than by accepting the challenge ?
Was the Government at once to lower the standard
of law before that of revolution without even
inquiring by whom the revolution was supported ?
But in truth the President's case was much stronger

* *See* APPENDIX A.

than this.   The Government was in possession of evidence which at least rendered it very probable that at this time the separatists were in a minority in the South, even in those places where they were believed to be strongest.   At the presidential election which had just been held, the votes for the unionist candidates in the states of the extreme South exceeded those for the candidate who represented the secession ; in the intermediate states, the unionist votes formed two-thirds of the constituency ; in Missouri, three-fourths.*   Will it be said that, with such facts before him, which were surely a safer criterion of Southern feeling than the votes of conventions obtained under mob-terrorism, Mr. Lincoln should at once have acquiesced in the demand for secession, and quietly permitted the consummation of a conspiracy, which, for deliberate treachery, betrayal of sacred trusts, and shameless and gigantic fraud, has seldom been matched ?   To have done so, would have been to have written himself down before the world as incompetent—

* See *Annuaire des Deux Mondes*, 1860, p. 608 ; also the extract from the *Commonwealth* of Frankfort (Kentucky), p. 606, and that from the Charlestown *Mercury*, p. 609, from which it appears that on the eve of the presidential election, some of the leading journals of the South regarded the secession movement as the work of a body of noisy demagogues, whose views found no response among the majority of the people.

nay, as a traitor to the cause which he had just sworn to defend.

The right of secession became thus by force of circumstances the ostensible ground of the war; and with the bulk of the Northern people it must be admitted it was not only the ostensible but the real ground; for it is idle to claim for the North a higher or more generous principle of conduct than that which itself put forward. The one prevailing and overpowering sentiment in the North, so soon as the designs of the South were definitively disclosed, was undoubtedly the determination to uphold the Union, and to crush the traitors who had conspired to dissolve it. In this country we had looked for something higher; we had expected, whether reasonably or not, an anti-slavery crusade. We were disappointed; and the result was, as has been stated, a re-action of sentiment which has prevented us from doing justice to that which was really worthy of admiration in the Northern cause. I say " worthy of admiration "; for the spectacle which the North presented at the opening of the war was such as I think might well have called forth this feeling. It was the spectacle of a people, which, having long bent its neck before a band of selfish politicians, and been dragged by them through the mire of shameless transactions, had suddenly recovered the consciousness of its power and responsibilities, and, shaking itself free from their spell, stood erect before the men who had enthralled its conscience and its will. A community, the most eager in the world in the chase after gain, forgot its absorbing pursuit; parties, a moment before arrayed against each other in a great political contest, laid aside their party differences; a whole nation, merging all private aims in the single passion of patriotism, rose to arms as a single man : and this for no selfish object, but to maintain the integrity of their common country and to chastise a band of conspirators, who, in the wantonness of their audacity, had dared to attack it. The Northern people, conscious that it had risen above the level of ordinary motives, looked abroad for sympathy, and especially looked to England. It was answered with cold criticism and derision. The response was perhaps natural under the circumstances, but undoubtedly not more so than the bitter mortification and resentment which that response evoked.

The prevailing idea that inspired the Northern rising was, I have said, the determination to uphold the Union. Still it would be a great mistake to suppose that this idea represented the whole significance of the movement, even so far as this was to be gathered from the views of the North. While loyalty to the Union pervaded and held together all

classes, another sentiment—the sentiment of hostility
to slavery—though less widely diffused, was strongly
entertained by a considerable party, and came more
directly into collision than the unionist feeling
with the real aims of the seceders. "The abolitionists," conventionally so known, formed indeed a
small band. With them slavery was not an evil
merely, but a sin, and, as such, to be got rid of at
any cost—even, were it necessary, at that of national
dissolution. In strict consistency with this view
they had, while the South was yet dominant, repudiated the constitution, branding it as "a league
with death and a covenant with hell," and advocated
separation, as, in the condition of affairs which then
prevailed, the only practicable escape from the con-
taminating influence of the sin which they denounced.
But the triumph of the Republican party wrought
an immediate change in the policy of the abolitionists ; and, from being the advocates of separation,
they now threw themselves with ardour into a war
for the maintenance of the Union. For this they
have been reproached with inconsistency. In truth,
however, they have merely changed their tactics to
meet a change in the position of affairs. From their
original aim they have never swerved, and they now
support the war as the most effectual means of
advancing that aim by breaking with slavery for
ever. With true instinct they feel that, secession

having been undertaken for the purpose of extending slavery, the most effectual means to defeat that
purpose is to defeat secession. The anti-slavery
feeling, however, prevails far beyond the bounds
of the party known as " abolitionists "; though
it is important to observe that, on passing these
bounds, the sentiment changes its character. By
the mass of the Republicans slavery is regarded as
a great evil, but their objection to it rests not on
moral, but on social and political grounds. Had
the South been content to maintain its institution
within the limits of its proper domain, slavery in the
present state of public morality in the North, would
have had nothing to apprehend from any considerable Northern party ; but the aggressive tendencies
of the Slave Power having brought it into collision
with important interests in the Free States, a political and social antagonism has been developed—an
antagonism which, as distinguished from the high
moral ground taken by the abolitionists proper,
forms the basis of anti-slavery feeling, such as it
exists among the mass of the Republican party.
The anti-slavery policy, therefore, of these two sections rests upon distinct grounds ; but the course
of events tends constantly to bring them into closer
relations. They have now begun to act habitually
together, and for practical purposes may be regarded as constituting a single party. Now it is these

men, and not the mere unionists, whose opinions form the natural antithesis to the aims of the seceders.   Between these and the South there can be no compromise; and, conformably to the law which invariably governs revolutions, they are the party who are rapidly becoming predominant in the North.   Already the anti-slavery feeling is fast gaining on the mere unionist feeling, and bids fair ultimately to supersede it.   In the anti-slavery ranks are now to be found men who but a year ago were staunch supporters of slavery.   Anti-slavery orators are now cheered to the echo by multitudes who but a year ago hooted and pelted them : they have forced their way into the stronghold of their enemies, and William Lloyd Garrison lectures in New York itself with enthusiastic applause.   The anti-slavery principle thus tends constantly, under the influences which are in operation, to become more powerful in the North ; and it is this fact which justifies the view of those who have predicted that it is only necessary the war should continue long enough in order that it be converted into a purely abolition struggle.

These considerations will enable the reader to perceive how, while the North has arisen to uphold the Union in its integrity, slavery is yet the true cause of the war, and that the real significance of the war is its relation to slavery.   I think, too, they

must be held to afford a complete justification of
the North in its original determination to maintain
the Union. But this is scarcely now the practical
question. There was, at the first, reason to believe
that a very considerable element of population
favourable to the Union existed in the South.
While this was the case, it was no less than the duty
of the Federal government to rescue these citizens
from the tyranny of a rebel oligarchy. But do
grounds for that supposition still exist ? Before the
war broke out, it is well known that something like
a reign of terror prevailed in the South for all who
fell short of the most extreme standard of pro-slavery
opinion. The rigour of that reign, as we know
from recent revelations,* has not been relaxed since
the war commenced, and must no doubt have produced a very considerable emigration of loyal citizens. The infectious enthusiasm of the war will probably have operated to make many converts; and,
under the influences of both these causes, the South,
or at least that portion of the South which has led
the way in this movement, has probably by this
time been brought to a substantial unanimity of
opinion, a conclusion which is strongly confirmed
by the absence of any sign of disaffection to the

* See the speeches of Southern refugees at a meeting held in
New York in October, 1862. See also *The Experience of an Impressed
New Yorker.* London : Trubner.

Confederation among its population.* Under these circumstances what is the policy to which Europe, in the interests of civilization, should give its moral support ? This country has long made up its mind as to the impossibility of forcibly reconstructing the Union ; perhaps it has also satisfied itself of the undesirableness of this result. Of neither of these opinions is the writer prepared to contest the the soundness. But this being conceded, an all-important question remains for decision. On what conditions is the independence of the South to be established ? For the solution of this question in the interests of civilization, a knowledge of the character and designs of the power which represents the South is requisite, and it is this which it is the aim of the present work to furnish. Meanwhile, however, it may be said that the definitive severance of the Union is perfectly compatible with either the accomplishment of the original design of the seceders —the extension of slavery, or the utter defeat of that design, according to the terms on which the separation takes place ; and that therefore the sever-ance of the Union by no means implies the defeat of

---

* Since the above passage was written some unionist demonstra-tions in the Border states following on the success of the Northern armies, have shown that the unanimity is not as complete as the writer imagined : still he does not conceive that what has occurred is at all calculated to affect the general scope of his reasoning.

the North or the triumph of the South. The Southern leaders may be assumed to know their own objects, and to be the best judges of the means which are necessary to their accomplishment ; and we may be certain that no arrangement which involves the frustration of these objects will be acquiesced in until after a complete prostration of their strength. If this be so, it is important to ascertain what the objects of the South are. For if these objects be inconsistent with the interests of civilization and the happiness of the human race (and I shall endeavour to show that this is the case), then no settlement of the American dispute which is not preceded by a thorough humbling of the slave party should be satisfactory to those who have human interests at heart. This is the cardinal point of the whole question. The designs of the seceders are either legitimate and consistent with human interests, or the contrary. If they are legitimate, let this be shown, and let us in this case wish them God speed ; if they are not, and if the Southern leaders may be taken to know what is essential to their own ends, then we may be sure that nothing short of the effectual defeat of the South in the present war will secure a settlement which shall be consistent with what the best interests of mankind require.

CHAPTER II.

THE ECONOMIC BASIS OF SLAVERY.

BEFORE proceeding to an examination of the social and political system which has been reared upon the basis of slavery in North America, it will be desirable to devote some consideration to the institution itself in its industrial aspects. The political tendencies of the Slave Power, as will hereafter be seen, are determined in a principal degree by the economic necessities under which it is placed by its fundamental institution; and in order, therefore, to appreciate the nature of those tendencies, a determination of the conditions requisite for the success of slavery, as an industrial system, becomes indispensable.

The form in which it will be most convenient to discuss this question will be in connexion with the actual position of slavery in the American continent. As is well known, the system formed originally a common feature in all the Anglo-Saxon settlements in that part of the world, existing in the northern no less than the southern colonies, in New England no less than in Virginia. But before much time had elapsed from their original foundation, it became evident that it was destined to occupy very different positions among these rising communities. In the colonies north of Delaware Bay slavery rapidly fell into a subordinate place, and gradually died out ; while in those south of that inlet its place in the industrial system became constantly more prominent, until ultimately it has risen to a position of paramount importance in that region, overpowering every rival influence, and moulding all the phenomena of the social state into conformity with its requirements.   The problem, then, which I propose to consider is the cause of this difference in the fortunes of slavery in these different portions of American soil.

Several theories have been advanced in explanation of the phenomenon.   One of these attributes it to diversity of character in the original founders of the communities in question ;* for, though proceeding from the same country and belonging to the same race, the Anglo-Saxon emigrations to North America, according as they were directed to the north or south of that continent, were in the main drawn from different classes of the mother nation. Massàchusetts and the other New England States were colonized principally from the *élite* of the mid-

---

* See Stirling's *Letter from the Slave States*, p. 64, where greater importance is attributed to this circumstance than it appears to me to deserve; and compare Olmsted's *Seaboard States*, pp. 181–183, 220, 221.

dle and lower classes—by people who, being accustomed to labour with their own hands, would feel less the need of slaves ; and who, moreover, owing to their political views, having little to hope for in the way of assistance from the country they had quitted, would have little choice but to trust to their personal exertions. On the other hand, the early emigration to Virginia, Maryland, and the Carolinas was for the most part composed of the sons of the gentry, whose ideas and habits but ill fitted them for a struggle with nature in the wilderness. Such emigrants had little disposition to engage personally in the work of clearance and production ; nor were they under the same necessity for this as their brethren in the North ; for, being composed in great part of cavaliers and loyalists, they were favourites with the government at home, and, for many years after the establishment of the settlements, received from its paternal care, not merely capital in the shape of constant supplies of provisions and clothing, but labourers in the shape of convicts, indented servants, and slaves. In this way the colonists of the Virginian group were relieved from the necessity of personal toil, and in this way, it is said, slavery, which found little footing in the North, and never took firm root there, became established in the Southern States.

This explanation, however, carries us but a short

way towards the point we have in view. It explains the more rapid extension of slavery in early times in the colonies which were in their origin most patronized by the home government, but it does not explain why slavery, which had, though not extensively, been introduced into the Northern colonies, should not have subsequently increased ; much less does it afford any explanation of its ultimate extinction in the North. It is certain the New Englanders were not withheld from employing slaves by moral scruples, and, if the system had been found suitable to the requirements of the country, it is to be presumed that they would have gradually extended its basis, and that, like their neighbours, especially since the treaty of Utrecht had secured for English enterprise the African slave-trade, they would have availed themselves of this means of recruiting their labour market.

Another and more generally accepted solution refers the phenomenon in question to the influence of climate and the character of the negro race. The European constitution, we are told, cannot endure a climate in which the negro can toil, thrive, and multiply, and the indolence of the negro is such that he will only work under compulsion. If it were not, therefore, for negro slavery, the world must have gone without those commodities which are the peculiar product of tropical climes. Mankind, in effect, says this theory, has had to choose between maintaining slavery and abandoning the use of cotton, tobacco, and sugar, and the instincts of humanity have succumbed before the more powerful inducements of substantial gain.*

It would, perhaps, be too much to say that this view of the causes which have maintained slavery in the Southern districts of North America is absolutely destitute of foundation, but there can be no hesitation in saying that, as a theory, it utterly fails to account for the facts which it is sought to explain.

* See *The South Vindicated* pp. 113–114, by the Hon. James Williams, late American Minister to Turkey, where this thesis is stoutly maintained in the face of the most flagrant facts. "Philanthropists," says Mr. Williams, "should bear in mind that the greater part of that soothing beverage prepared from the coffee bean, which is alike the cheap luxury of the rich, and the solace of the humble and the poor of every land, is the produce of slave labour." Again, "the cane sugar and syrups, which from their cheapness have become accessible to the poor, and which may be found in every cottage in America, and to a great extent throughout the world, are *alone* made accessible to them through the instrumentality of slave labour." It would appear from the latter statement that the writer had never heard of sugar being produced by free labour in the Mauritius and West India islands. The former assertion, that "the greater part" of the coffee consumed in the world is raised by slave labour may be true, but is nothing to the purpose, so long as a very considerable quantity is raised efficiently and profitably by free labour. And, on the whole, it will be found that every other statement advanced by Mr. Williams in support of his position, is open to one or other of the above objections,—either it is not pertinent, or it is not true.

The climate of the oldest of the Slave States—Virginia, Maryland, Delaware, North and South Carolina —is remarkably genial and perfectly suited to the industry of Europeans;* and, though the same is not true in the same degree of the Gulf States, yet it is a fact that these regions' also afford examples of free European communities increasing in numbers under a semi-tropical climate, and rising to opulence through the labour of their own hands. In Texas a flourishing colony of free Germans, among whom no slave is to be found, engage in all the occupations of the country, and are only prevented by their distance from the great navigable rivers, and the want of other means of communication, from applying themselves extensively to that very cultivation—the growing of cotton—which the complacent reasoners whose theory we are considering choose to regard as the ordained function of the negro race.†

"If we look," says Mr. Weston, "to the origin of the European races which inhabit this country, Georgia and Alabama and Tennessee are more like

* Olmsted's *Seaboard Slave States.*

† "The Southern parts of the Union," says Tocqueville, "are not hotter than the south of Italy and of Spain ; and it may be asked why the European cannot work as well there as in the two latter countries. If slavery has been abolished in Italy and in Spain without causing the destruction of the masters, why should not the same thing take place in the Union? I cannot believe that

their mother countries than New England is.   The
Irishman and Englishman and German find in Mis-
souri and Texas a climate less dissimilar to that at
home, than they do in Wisconsin and Minnesota.
The heats of summer are longer and steadier at the
South, but not more excessive than at the North.
Labour in the fields is performed by whites, and
without any ill consequences in the extreme South.
Nearly all the heavy out-door work in the city of
New Orleans is performed by whites. . . . The
practical experience of mankind is a sufficient answer
to fanciful rules, which, applied on the other side of
the Atlantic, would surrender to the African, Spain,
France, and Italy, and drive back their present inhabitants to the shores of the Baltic. The three
thousand years of recorded civilization in the regions
which environ the Mediterranean on all its sides,
prove that no part of the continental borders of the
Gulf of Mexico, and none of the islands which separate it from the ocean, need be abandoned to the
barbarism of negro slavery.   The European stock is
found everywhere, from Texas to Patagonia, and in

Nature has prohibited the Europeans in Georgia and the Floridas,
under pain of death, from raising the means of subsistence from the
soil; but their labour would unquestionably be more irksome and
less productive to them than that of the inhabitants of New England.   As the free workman thus loses a portion of his superiority
over the slave in the Southern States, there are fewer inducements
to abolish slavery."

every part of that whole extent is more vigorous
and prolific than any other race, indigenous or imported.   Isothermal lines are not uniform with
parallels of latitude ; vertical suns are qualified by
ocean breezes and mountain heights ; and America,
even at the equator, offers to man salubrious
abodes."*

But still more fatally does the theory halt upon
the other limb of the argument—the incorrigible
indolence of the negro.   Whatever plausibility there
may have been in this oft repeated assertion in times
when the negro was only known as a slave or as a
pariah in the land where his existence was scarcely
tolerated, it is perfectly futile to advance such statements now in the face of the facts which recent
observations have revealed to us.   "We, in the
United States," says Mr. Sewell, "have heard of
abandoning properties in the West Indies, and, without much investigation, have listened to the planters'
excuse—the indolence of the negro, who refuses to
work except under compulsion.   But I shall be able
to show that, in those colonies where estates have
been abandoned, the labouring classes, instead of
passing from servitude to indolence and idleness,
have set up for themselves, and that small proprietors since emancipation have increased a hundred-
fold.   .   .   .   .   It is a fact which speaks vol-

* *Progress of Slavery*, pp. 160, 161.

umes that, within the last fifteen years, in spite of
the extraordinary price of land and the low rate of
wages, the small proprietors of Barbadoes holding
less than five acres have increased from 1100 to
3537. *A great majority of these proprietors were
formerly slaves, subsequently free labourers, and
finally landholders.* This is certainly an evidence of
industrious habits, and a remarkable contradiction
to the prevailing idea that the negro will work only
under compulsion. That idea was formed and fos-
tered from the habits of the negro as a slave ; his
habits as a freeman, developed under a wholesome
stimulus and settled by time, are in striking contrast
to his habits as a slave. I am simply stating a truth
in regard to the Barbadian creole, which here, at
least, will not be denied. I have conversed on the
subject with all classes and conditions of people, and
none are more ready to admit than the planters
themselves, that the free labourer in Barbadoes is a
better, more cheerful, and more industrious workman than the slave ever was under a system of compulsion." And, again, of an island very differently
circumstanced from Barbadoes the same author
writes :—" I have taken some pains to trace the
creole labourers of Trinidad from the time of emancipation, after they left the estates and dispersed,
to the present day; and the great majority of them
can, I think, be followed, step by step, not downward

in the path of idleness and poverty, but upward
in the scale of civilization to positions of greater
independence."* This testimony of a perfectly un-
impassioned witness, coming after ten years' further
experience in corroboration of the evidence given
by Mr. Bigelow in 1850, ought to set this question
at rest. There is not a tittle of evidence to show
that the aversion of the negro to labour is naturally
stronger than that of any other branch of the human
family.† So long as he is compelled to work for the

* Sewell's *Ordeal of Free Labour in the West Indies*, pp. 34–35,
39–40. And for evidence to the same effect respecting the Jamaican
negroes, see pp. 198, 202, &c. Yet in the face of this evidence,
which has just been corroborated in all its particulars by the independent and unimpeachable testimony of Mr. Edward Bean Underhill (quoted below), an advocate of slavery repeats to English
readers—and so far as I have seen, repeats without rebuke—the
stale calumny, that the negro will only work under the lash:—
" Too late it was discovered that the African would not work without a master! No stimulants of pride or ambition could move his
soul to rise above the level which it would seem that the God of
nature has assigned to him."—*South Vindicated*, p. 163.

† " Considérons," says M. De Gasparin, " ces jolies chaumières,
ces mobiliers propres et presque élégants, ces jardins, cet air général
de bien-être et de civilisation ; interrogeons ces noirs dont l'aspect
physique s'est déjà modifié sous l'influence de la liberté, ces noirs
dont le nombre décroissait rapidement à l'époque de l'esclavage et
commence au contraire à s'accroître depuis l'affranchissement; ils
nous parleront de leur bonheur. Les uns sont devenus propriétaires
et travaillent pour leur propre compte (ce n'est pas un crime,
j'imagine); les autres s'associent pour affermer de grandes plantations
ou portent peut-être aux usines des riches planteurs les cannes

exclusive benefit of a master, he will be inclined to evade his task by every means in his power, as the white man would do under similar circumstances ; but emancipate him, and subject him to the same motives which act upon the free white labourer, and there is no reason to believe he will not be led to exert himself with equal energy.

A circumstance more influential in determining the history of slavery in America than either origin or climate is pointed at by Tocqueville in his re- mark, that the soil of New England " was entirely opposed to a territorial aristocracy." " To bring that refractory land into cultivation, the constant and interested exertions of the owner himself were necessary ; and, when the ground was prepared, its produce was found to be insufficient to enrich a master and a farmer at the same time. The land was then naturally broken up into small portions which the proprietor cultivated for himself." Such a country, for reasons which will presently be more fully indicated, was entirely unsuited to cultivation by slave labour; but what I wish here to remark

récoltées chez eux; ceux-ci sont marchands, beaucoup louent leurs bras comme cultivateurs. Quels que soient les torts d'un certain nombre d'individus, l'ensemble des nègres libres a mérité ce témoig- nage rendu en 1857 par le gouverneur de Tabago : ' Je nie que nos noirs de la campagne aient des habitudes de paresse. Il n'existe pas dans le monde une classe aussi industrieuse.' "—*Un Grand Peuple qui se relève*, p. 312.

MERITS AND DEFECTS OF SLAVE LABOUR.   43

is, that this fact, important as it is with reference
to our subject, is yet insufficient in itself to afford
the solution which we seek ; for, though it would
account for the disappearance of slavery from the
New England States, it fails entirely when applied to
the country west and south of the Hudson, which is
for the most part exceedingly fertile, but in which,
nevertheless, slavery, though extensively introduced,
has not been able to maintain itself. To understand,
therefore, the conditions on which the success of a
slave *régime* depends, we must advert to other considerations than any which have yet been adduced.

The true causes of the phenomenon will appear,
if we reflect on the characteristic advantages and
disadvantages which attach respectively to slavery
and free labour, as productive instruments, in connexion with the external conditions under which
these forms of industry came into competition in
North America.

The economic advantages of slavery are easily
stated : they are all comprised in the fact that the
employer of slaves has absolute power over his
workmen, and enjoys the disposal of the whole fruit
of their labours.* Slave labour, therefore, admits of

* Which advantages, the economists of the South appears to
think comprise all advantages. "Without entering into a comparison of the present nominal price of labour in this and other
countries, it is sufficient to say that, whatever the price may be, none
can produce any given article as cheap with hired labour as he who

the most complete organization, that is to say, it may be combined on an extensive scale, and directed by a controlling mind to a single end, and its cost can never rise above that which is necessary to maintain the slave in health and strength.

On the other hand, the economical defects of slave labour are very serious. They may be summed up under the three following heads:—it is given reluctantly; it is unskilful; it is wanting in versatility.

It is given reluctantly, and consequently the industry of the slave can only be depended on so long as he is watched. The moment the master's eye is withdrawn, the slave relaxes his efforts. The cost of slave labour will therefore, in great measure, depend on the degree in which the work to be performed admits of the workmen being employed in close proximity to each other. If the work be such that a large gang can be employed with efficiency within a small space, and be thus brought under the eye of a single overseer, the expense of superintendence will be slight ; if, on the other hand, the nature of the work requires that the workmen should be dispersed over an extended area, the number of overseers, and therefore, the cost of the labour which requires this supervision,

owns it himself."—De Bow's *Industrial Resources,* vol. ii. p. 112. As if the condition of efficiency, not to mention the cost of support, might not turn the scale.

will be proportionately increased.   The cost of
slave labour thus varies directly with the degree
in which the work to be done requires dispersion
of the labourers, and inversely as it admits of their
concentration.   Further, the work being performed
reluctantly, fear is substituted for hope, as the
stimulus to exertion.   But fear is ill calculated to
draw from a labourer all the industry of which
he is capable.   " Fear," says Bentham, " leads the
labourer to hide his powers, rather than to show
them ; to remain below, rather than to surpass
himself. . . . . By displaying superior capacity,
the slave would only raise the measure of his
ordinary duties ; by a work of supererogation he
would only prepare punishment for himself."   He
therefore seeks, by concealing his powers, to reduce
to the lowest the standard of requisition.   " His
ambition is the reverse of that of the free man ;
he seeks to descend in the scale of industry, rather
than to ascend."

Secondly, slave labour is unskilful, and this, not
only because the slave, having no interest in his
work, has no inducement to exert his higher faculties, but because, from the ignorance to which he
is of necessity condemned, he is incapable of doing
so.   In the Slave States of North America, the
education of slaves, even in the most rudimentary
form, is proscribed by law, and consequently their

intelligence is kept uniformly and constantly at the very lowest point. " You can make a nigger work," said an interlocutor in one of Mr. Olmsted's dialogues," " but you cannot make him think." He is therefore unsuited for all branches of industry which require the slightest care, forethought, or dexterity. He cannot be made to co-operate with machinery; he can only be trusted with the coarsest implements; he is incapable of all but the rudest forms of labour.*

But further, slave labour is eminently defective in point of versatility. The difficulty of teaching the slave anything is so great, that the only chance of turning his labour to profit is, when he has once learned a lesson, to keep him to that lesson for life.

---

* " The reason was, that the negro could never be trained to exercise judgment; he cannot be made to use his mind; he always depends on machinery doing its own work, and cannot be made to watch it. He neglects it until something is broken or there is great waste. We have tried rewards and punishments, but it makes no difference. It's his nature, and you cannot change it. All men are indolent and have a disinclination to labour, but this is a great deal stronger in the African race than in any other. In working niggers, we must always calculate that they will not labour at all except to avoid punishment, and they will never do more than just enough to save themselves from being punished, and no amount of punishment will prevent their working carelessly and indifferently. It always seems on the plantation as if they took pains to break all the tools and spoil all the cattle that they possibly can, even when they know they'll be punished for it."— Olmsted's *Seaboard Slave States*, pp. 104, 105.

Where slaves, therefore, are employed there can be no variety of production. If tobacco be cultivated, tobacco becomes the sole staple, and tobacco is produced, whatever be the state of the market, and whatever be the condition of the soil.* This peculiarity of slave labour, as we shall see, involves some very important consequences.

Such being the character of slave-labour, as an industrial instrument, let us now consider the qualities of the agency with which, in the colonization of North America, it was brought into competition. This was the labour of peasant proprietors, a productive instrument, in its merits and defects, the exact reverse of that with which it was called upon to compete. Thus, the great and almost the sole excellence of slave labour is, as we have seen, its capacity for organization ; and this is precisely the circumstance with respect to which the labour of peasant proprietors is especially defective. In a community of peasant proprietors, each workman labours on his own account, without much reference to what his fellow-workmen are doing. There is no commanding mind to whose guidance the whole labour force will yield obedience, and under whose control it may be directed by skilful combinations to the result which is desired. Nor does this system afford room for classification and economical distri-

---

* Olmsted's *Seaboard Slave States*, pp. 337 to 339.

bution of a labour force in the same degree as the
system of slavery.   Under the latter, for example,
occupation may be found for a whole family of
slaves, according to the capacity of each member, in
performing the different operations connected with
certain branches of industry.   Thus, in the culture
of tobacco, the women and children may be employed in picking the worms off the plants, or gathering
the leaves as they become ripe, while the men are
engaged in the more laborious tasks.   But it is
otherwise when the cultivator is a small proprietor.
His children are at school, and his wife finds enough
to occupy her in her domestic duties : he can, therefore, command for all operations, however important
or however insignificant, no other labour than his
own, or that of his grown-up sons—labour which
would be greatly misapplied in performing such
manual operations as I have described.   His team
of horses might be standing idle in the stable,
while he was gathering tobacco leaves or picking
worms, an arrangement which would render his
work exceedingly costly.   The system of peasant
proprietorship, therefore, does not admit of combination and classification of labour in the same degree as
that of slavery.   But if in this respect it lies under
a disadvantage as compared with its rival, in every
other respect it enjoys an immense superiority.
The peasant proprietor, appropriating the whole

produce of his toil, needs no other stimulus to exertion. Superintendence is here completely dispensed with. The labourer is under the strongest conceivable inducement to put forth, in the furtherance of his task, the full powers of his mind and body ; and his mind, instead of being purposely stinted and stupified, is enlightened by education, and aroused by the prospect of reward.*

Such are the two productive agencies which came into competition on the soil of North America. If we now turn to the external conditions under which the competition took place, we shall, I think, have no difficulty in understanding the success of each respectively in that portion of the Continent in which it did in fact succeed.

The line dividing the Slave from the Free States marks also an important division in the agricultural capabilities of North America. North of this line, the products for which the soil and climate are best adapted are cereal crops, while south of it the prevailing crops are tobacco, rice, cotton, and sugar ; and these two classes of crops are broadly distinguished in the methods of culture suitable to each.* The cultivation of the one class, of which cotton may be taken as the type, requires for its efficient conduct that labour should be combined and organ-

* See *North America, its Agriculture and Climate*, by Robert Russell, chapter viii.

ized on an extensive scale.*   On the other hand, for
the raising of cereal crops this condition is not so
essential.   Even where labour is abundant and that
labour free, the large capitalist does not in this
mode of farming appear on the whole to have any
preponderating advantage over the small proprietor,
who, with his family, cultivates his own farm, as the
example of the best cultivated states in Europe
proves.   Whatever superiority he may have in the
power of combining and directing labour seems to
be compensated by the greater energy and spirit
which the sense of property gives to the exertions of
the small proprietor.   But there is another essential
circumstance in which these two classes of crops
differ.   A single labourer, Mr. Russell tells us,† can
cultivate twenty acres of wheat or Indian corn,
while he cannot manage more than two of tobacco,
or three of cotton.   It appears from this that tobacco and cotton fulfil that condition which we
saw was essential to the economical employment
of slaves—the possibility of working large numbers
within a limited space; while wheat and Indian corn,
in the cultivation of which the labourers are dispersed over a wide surface, fail in this respect.   We
thus find that cotton, and the class of crops of which
cotton may be taken as the type, favour the employment of slaves in the competition with peasant pro-

* Russell's *North America*, pp. 141.   † Ibid. p. 141, 164.

prietors in two leading ways : first, they need extensive combination and organization of labour—
requirements which slavery is eminently calculated
to supply, but in respect to which the labour of
peasant proprietors is defective; and secondly, they
allow of labour being concentrated, and thus minim-
ize the cardinal evil of slave labour—the reluctance with which it is yielded. On the other hand,
the cultivation of cereal crops, in which extensive
combination of labour is not important, and in
which the operations of industry are widely diffused,
offers none of these advantages for the employment of slaves,* while it is remarkably fitted to
bring out in the highest degree the especial excel-

* The same observation had been made by Tocqueville, who
in the following passage has suggested a further reason for the
unsuitableness of slave labour for raising cereal crops :—" It has
been observed that slave labour is a very expensive method of
cultivating corn. The farmer of corn land, in a country where
slavery is unknown, habitually retains a small number of labourers
in his service, and at seed-time and harvest he hires several additional hands, who only live at his cost for a short period. But the
agriculturist in a slave state is obliged to keep a large number of
slaves the whole year round, iu order to sow his fields and to gather
in his crops, although their services are only required for a few
weeks ; but slaves are unable to wait until they are hired, and to
subsist by their own labour in the mean time like free labourers :
in order to have their services they must be bought. Slavery,
independently of its general disadvantages, is therefore still more
inapplicable to countries in which corn is cultivated than to those
which produce crops of a different kind."—*Democracy in America*,
vol. ii. p. 233.

lencies of the industry of free proprietors. Owing to these causes it has happened that slavery has been maintained in the Southern States, which favour the growth of tobacco, cotton, and analogous products, while, in the Northern States, of which cereal crops are the great staple, it from an early period declined and has ultimately died out. And, in confirmation of this view, it may be added that wherever in the Southern States the external conditions are especially favourable to cereal crops, as in parts of Virginia, Kentucky, and Missouri, and along the slopes of the Alleghanies, there slavery has always failed to maintain itself. It is owing to this cause that there now exists in some parts of the South a considerable element of free labouring population.

These considerations appear to explain the permanence of slavery in one division of North America, and its disappearance from the other; but there are other conditions essential to the economic success of the institution besides those which have been brought into view in the above comparison, to which it is necessary to advert in order to a right understanding of its true basis. These are high fertility of the soil, and a practically unlimited extent of it.

The necessity of these conditions to slavery will be apparent by reflecting on the unskilfulness and want of versatility in slave labour to which we have already referred.

When the soils are not of good quality, cultivation needs to be elaborate; a larger capital is expended; and with the increase of capital the processes become more varied, and the agricultural implements of a finer and more delicate construction. With such implements slaves cannot be trusted, and for such processes they are unfit.* It is only, therefore, where the natural fertility of the soil is so great as to compensate for the inferiority of the cultivation,† where nature does so much as to leave little for art, and to supersede the necessity of the more difficult contrivances of industry, that slave labour can be turned to profitable account.‡

Further, slavery, as a permanent system, has need not merely of a fertile soil, but of a practically unlimited extent of it. This arises from the defect of

* *See* APPENDIX B.

† Mr. Russell (pp. 164, 165) states that the soil on which the sea-island cotton is raised is "poor, consisting for the most part of light sand;" but this is scarcely an exception to the statement in the text. The peculiar qualities of the soil in question, and the high price which its products are consequently enabled to command, render it, in an economic sense, "a fertile soil," however it may be designated by an agriculturist as "poor."

‡ In a debate in the House of Lords last session on the annexation of St. Domingo by Spain, it was stated by the Duke of Newcastle that, in reply to the remonstrances of the British government relative to the apprehended introduction of slavery into that island, the Spanish government had referred to the great fertility of the soil of St. Domingo, *which renders slavery unnecessary* ; in which reasoning his grace, as well as Lord Brougham, appeared to acquiesce.

slave labour in point of versatility. As has been already remarked, the difficulty of teaching the slave anything is so great—the result of the compulsory ignorance in which he is kept, combined with want of intelligent interest in his work—that the only chance of rendering his labour profitable is, when he has once learned a lesson, to keep him to that lesson for life. Accordingly where agricultural operations are carried on by slaves, the business of each gang is always restricted to the raising of a single product.* " In Brazil," says M. Elisée Reclus, " the proprietors carefully refrain from imposing on their slaves agricultural labours which demand the intelligence and versatility which are only to be found amongst the free. They know instinctively that the cultivation of wheat, of maize, of the numerous roots and plants which

---

* " The culture [of tobacco] being once established [in Virginia] there were many reasons," says Mr. Olmsted, " growing out of the social structure of the colony, which for more than a century kept the industry of the Virginians confined to this one staple. These reasons were chiefly the difficulty of breaking the slaves, or training the bond servants to new methods of labour; the want of enterprise or ingenuity in the proprietors to contrive other profitable occupations for them; and the difficulty or expense of distributing the guard or oversight, without which it was impossible to get any work done at all, if the labourers were separated, or worked in any other way than side by side, in gangs, as in the tobacco fields. Owing to these causes, the planters kept on raising tobacco with hardly sufficient intermission to provide themselves with the gross-

constitute the agricultural flora, requires the concurrence of many minds, skilful to foresee and prompt to decide. Now what of all this could they expect from their slaves—bodies without souls—deprived by servitude of all power of initiative, and resembling in their movements inanimate machines ? The planters are thus obliged to employ their negroes exclusively in the production of a few commodities, and can only make their labour profitable by keeping up an invariable routine."* Whatever crop may be best suited to the character of the soil and the nature of slave industry, whether cotton, tobacco, sugar, or rice, that crop is cultivated, and that alone. Rotation of crops is thus precluded by the conditions of the case. The soil is tasked again and again to yield the same product, and the inevitable result follows.

est animal sustenance, though often by reason of the excessive quantity raised, scarcely anything could be got for it." .. "Tobacco is not now considered peculiarly and excessively exhaustive : in a judicious rotation, especially as a preparation for wheat, it is an admirable fallow-crop, and, under a scientific system of agriculture, it is grown with no continued detriment to the soil. But in Virginia it was grown without interruption or alteration, and the fields rather deteriorated in fertility."—*Seaboard Slave States*, pp. 237, 238; and see De Bow's *Industrial Resources of the South-West*, vol. ii. pp. 117–118, where the same fact—the over-production of particular staples under a system of plantation industry—is dwelt upon, and deplored.

* *Revue des Deux Mondes*, 15 Juillet, 1862, p. 393.

After a short series of years its fertility is completely exhausted, the planter—" land-killer" he is called in the picturesque nomenclature of the South*—abandons the ground which he has rendered worthless, and passes on to seek in new soils for that fertility under which alone the agencies at his disposal can be profitably employed.

This point being a fundamental one, it is important to observe that, with reference to it—whatever may be said by reckless partisans of the South in this country—there is absolutely no difference of opinion among the highest authorities in the United States, whether Northern or Southern. As to the tendency of the system of slave cultivation, as practised in the South, to exhaust the soil, and as to the fact of an extensive exhaustion of the soil throughout the plantation districts, the testimony of Mr. De Bow is not less clear and decided than that of Mr. Olmsted:—"The great error of Southern agriculture is the general practice of exhausting culture—the almost universal deterioration of the productive power of the soil—which power is the main and essential foundation of all agricultural wealth.." . . . " This unprofitable procedure, which would be deemed the most marvellous folly in re-

* " Many of the most intelligent men of this generally intelligent class, are ready enough to accept and to apply to themselves and their fellow-planters the name of ' land-killers.' "—De Bow's *Industrial Resources*, vol. iv. p. 43.

gard to any other kind of capital invested, is precisely that which is still generally pursued by the
cultivators of the soil in all the cotton-producing
states, and which prevailed as generally, and much
longer in my own country, and which, even now, is
more usual there than the opposite course of fertil-
izing culture. The recuperative powers of nature
are indeed continually operating, and to great effect,
to repair the waste of fertility caused by the destructive industry of man, and but for this natural and
imperfect remedy, all these Southern States (and
most of the Northern [States of the South] likewise) would be already barren deserts in which
agricultural labours would be hopeless of reward,
and civilized men could not exist."* " I can
show you with sorrow," says another Southern
authority, "in the older portions of Alabama, and
in my native county of Madison, the sad memo-
rials of the artless and exhausting culture of cotton. Our small planters, after taking the cream
off their lands, unable to restore them by rest,
manures, or otherwise, are going further west and
south in search of other virgin lands, which they
may and will despoil and impoverish in like man-

* De Bow's *Industrial Resources*, vol. iv. p. 34. The extract is
from " a paper read by Edwin Ruffin, Esq., of Virginia, the justly
celebrated American agriculturist, at the late fair of the South
Carolina Institute in Charleston, S. C., which we [Mr. De Bow]
had the pleasure of attending."

ner.   Our wealthier planters, with greater means
and no more skill, are buying out their poorer
neighbours, extending their plantations, and adding
to their slave force.   The wealthy few, who are able
to live on smaller profits, and to give their blasted
fields some rest, are thus pushing off the many who
are merely independent. . . In traversing that
county one will discover numerous farm-houses,
once the abode of industrious and intelligent freemen, now occupied by slaves, or tenantless, deserted,
and dilapidated; he will observe fields, once fertile,
now unfenced, abandoned, and covered with those
evil harbingers—fox-tail and broom-sedge; he will
see the moss growing on the mouldering walls of
once thrifty villages; and will find ' one only master
grasps the whole domain' that once furnished happy
homes for a dozen families.   Indeed, a country in
its infancy, where, fifty years ago, scarce a forest
tree had been felled by the axe of the pioneer, is
already exhibiting the painful signs of senility and
decay apparent in Virginia and the Carolinas ; the
freshness of its agricultural glory is gone, the vigour
of its youth is extinct, and the spirit of desolation
seems brooding over it."*   Even in Texas, before it
had yet been ten years under the dominion of this

* Address of the Hon. C. C. Clay, jun., a slaveholder and advocate of slavery, reported by the author in *De Bow's Review,* and
quoted by Olmsted, *Seaboard Slave States,* p. 576.

devastating system, Mr. Olmsted tells us that the
spectacle so familiar and so melancholy in all the
older Slave States was already not unfrequently
seen by the traveller—" an abandoned plantation
of ' worn-out' fields with its little village of dwellings, now a home only for wolves and vultures."*

Such have been fruits of the slave cultivation
on the continent. But it seems to be commonly
supposed that the history of the West Indies teaches
us a different lesson. The notion appears to be
widely entertained that these islands furnish the
example of a career of continuous prosperity enjoyed under slavery, extending over some two hundred years, and only interrupted by the fatal gift
of emancipation. There cannot be a greater mistake than this. Slavery in the West Indies has
been attended with precisely the same effects which
have followed it elsewhere. So entirely is this the
case that the feature in their history which most
forcibly arrests the philosophic observer is the

---

* To complete the review of the effects of·slave cultivation on
the continent of America, I may refer to the experience of Brazil as
given by a well-informed writer in the *Revue des Deux Mondes* :—
" Combien d'années ne faudrait-il pas au travail libre avant qu'il
pût rendre leur antique fertilité aux plantations appauvries par
cette culture brutale que les Brésiliens décorent du nom de *lavoura
grande !* car "l'institution patriarcale" "utilise la terre et l'homme
avec la même barbarie, et ne leur rend jamais rien en échange de
services : elle brûle le sol où elle passe."—*Revue des Deux Mondes,*
15 Juillet, 1862, p. 394.

uniformity with which—diversified as have been
the fortunes of those islands in other respects—
they have passed through the ordinary cycle of
slave-holding communities. " Before we pass on-
wards," says Mr. Merivale, summing up the results of his survey of the industrial history of the
West Indies, " let us pause for a moment to reflect
on the remarkable uniformity with which events
have succeeded each other in the economical history
of the West Indies in general. At each epoch in that
history we see the same causes producing almost
identical effects. The opening of a fresh soil, with
freedom of trade, gives a sudden stimulus to settlement and industry; the soil is covered with free
proprietors, and a general but rude prosperity prevails. Then follows a period of more careful cultivation, during which estates are consolidated,
gangs of slaves succeed to communities of freemen,
the rough commonwealth is formed into a most
productive factory. But fertility diminishes; the
cost of production augments: slave labour, always
dear, becomes dearer through the increased difficulty
of supporting it: new settlements are occupied, new
sources of production opened: the older colonies,
unable to maintain a ruinous competition, even
with the aid of prohibitions, descend after a period
of suffering and difficulty into a secondary state, in
which capital, economy, and increased skill make

up, to a certain extent only, for the invaluable
advantages which they have lost. Thus we have
seen the Windward Islands maintaining at one
period a numerous white population; afterwards,
importing numerous slaves, and supplying almost
all the then limited consumption of Europe. We
have seen Jamaica rise on their decay, and go
through precisely the same stages of existence. We
have seen how St. Domingo, in its turn, greatly
eclipsed Jamaica; but St. Domingo was cut off by
a sudden tempest, and never attained to the period
of decline. Lastly, we have seen the Spanish colonies of Cuba and Porto Rico, after so many centuries of comparative neglect and rude productiveness,
start all at once into the first rank among exporting
countries, and flourish like the exuberant crops of
their own virgin soil, while our islands, still rich in
capital, but for the most part exhausted in fertility
and deficient in labour, were struggling by the aid
of their accumulated wealth against the encroaching
principle of decay. The life of artificial and anti-
social communities may be brilliant for a time; but
it is necessarily a brief one, and terminates either
by rapid decline, or still more rapid revolution,
when the laboriously-constructed props of their
wealth give way, as they sometimes do, in sudden
ruin."*

* *Colonization and the Colonies*, new edition, p. 92, 93.

It appears, therefore, that the experience of history confirms the deductions of reason. Slave cultivation, wherever it has been tried in the new world, has issued in the same results. Precluding the conditions of rotation of crops or skilful management, it tends inevitably to exhaust the land of a country, and consequently requires for its permanent success not merely a fertile soil but a practically unlimited extent of it.*

To sum up, then, the conclusions at which we have arrived, the successful maintenance of slavery, as a system of industry, requires the following conditions :—1st. Abundance of fertile soil ; and, 2nd. a crop the cultivation of which demands combination and organization of labour on an extensive scale, and admits of its concentration. It is owing to the presence of these conditions that slavery has

---

* Olmsted's *Texas*, p. xiv. If there be any fact upon which all competent witnesses to the condition of the Slave States are agreed it is the rapid deterioration of the soil under slave cultivation. On this point, as I have shown, English, French, and American writers, the opponents and advocates of slavery, are at one. Yet a writer in the *Saturday Review* (Nov. 2, 1861) does not hesitate, on his own unsupported authority, to characterize this belief as "a popular fallacy." If it be a fallacy, it is certainly not only a popular but a plausible one, since it has succeeded in deceiving Miss Martineau, Olmsted, Russell, Stirling, and every writer of the least pretension to authority on the subject, no matter what his leanings. It is for the reader to make his choice between their united testimony and the closet experience of a Saturday Reviewer.

maintained itself in the Southern States of North America, and to their absence that it has disappeared from the Northern States.

CHAPTER III.

INTERNAL ORGANIZATION OF SLAVE COMMUNITIES.

THE explanation offered in the last chapter of the success and failure of slavery in different portions of North America resolved itself into the proposition, that in certain cases the institution was found to be economically profitable while it proved unprofitable in others. From this position—the profitableness of slavery under given external conditions—the inference is generally made by those who advocate or look with indulgence on the system, that slavery must be regarded as conducive to at least the material well-being of countries in which these conditions exist; and these conditions being admittedly present in the Slave States of North America, it is concluded that the abolition of slavery in those states would necessarily be attended with a diminution of their wealth, and by consequence, owing to the mode in which the interests of all nations are identified through commerce, with a corresponding injury to the material interests of the rest of the world. In this manner it is attempted to enlist the selfish feelings of mankind in favour of the institution; and it is not impossible that many persons, who would be disposed to condemn it upon moral grounds, are thus led to connive at its existence. It will, therefore, be desirable, before proceeding further with the investigation of our subject, to ascertain precisely the extent of the admission in favour of the system which is involved in the foregoing explanation of its success.

And, in the first place, it must be remarked that the profitableness which has been attributed to slavery is profitableness estimated exclusively from the point of view of the proprietor of slaves. Profitableness *in this sense* is all that is necessary to account for the introduction and maintenance of the system (which was the problem with which alone we were concerned), since it was with the proprietors that the decision rested. But those who are acquainted with the elementary principles which govern the distribution of wealth, know that the profits of capitalists may be increased by the same process by which the gross revenue of a country is diminished, and that therefore the community as a whole may be impoverished through the very same means by which a portion of its number is enriched. The economic success of slavery, therefore, is perfectly consistent with the supposition that it is prejudicial to the material well-being of the country where it is established. The argument, in short, comes to this : the interests of slave-masters—or rather that which slave-masters believe to be their interests—are no more identical with the interests of the general population in slave countries in the matter of wealth, than in that of morals or of politics. That which benefits, or seems to benefit, the one in any of these departments, may injure the other. It follows, therefore, that the economic advantages possessed by slavery, which were the inducement to its original establishment and which cause it still to be upheld, are perfectly compatible with its being an obstacle to the industrial development of the country, and at variance with the best interests, material as well as moral, of its inhabitants.

Further, the profitableness which has been attributed to slavery does not even imply that the system is conducive to the interests (except in the narrowest sense of the word) of the class for whose especial behoof it exists Individuals and classes may always be assumed to follow their own interests according to their lights and tastes; but that which their lights and tastes point out as their interest will vary with the degree of their intelligence and the character of their civilization. When the intelligence of a class is limited and its civilization low, the view it will take of its interests will be correspondingly narrow and sordid. Extravagant and undue importance will be attached to the mere animal pleasures. A small gain obtained by coarse and obvious methods will be preferred to a great one which requires a recourse to more refined expedients; and the future well-being of the race will be regarded as of less importance than the aggrandisement of the existing generation.

But our admissions in favour of slavery require still further qualification. The establishment of slavery in the Southern States was accounted for by its superiority in an economic point of view over free labour, in the form in which free labour existed in America at the time when that continent was settled. Now, the superiority of slave over free labour to which its adoption was originally owing, is by no means to be assumed as still existing in virtue of the fact that slavery is still maintained. Of two systems one may at a given period be more profitable than the other, and may on this account be established, but may afterwards cease to be so, and yet may nevertheless continue to be upheld, either from habit, or from unwillingness to adopt new methods, or from congeniality with tastes which had been formed under its influence. It is a difficult and slow process under all circumstances to alter the industrial system of a country ; but the difficulty of exchanging one form of free industry for another is absolutely inappreciable when compared with that which we encounter when we attempt to substitute free for servile institutions.

It is therefore quite possible—how far the case is actually so I shall afterwards examine—that the persistent maintenance of the system at the present day may be due less to its economical advantages than to the habits and tastes it may have engendered, and to the enormous difficulty of getting rid of it.   Since the settlement of the Southern States a vast change has taken place in the American continent.   Free labour, which was then scarce and costly, has now in many of the large towns become superabundant; and it is quite possible that, even with external conditions so favourable to slavery as the southern half of North America undoubtedly presents, free labour would now, on a fair trial, be found more than a match for its antagonist. Such a trial, however, is not possible under the present *régime* of the South.   Slavery is in possession of the field, and enjoys all the advantages which possession in such a contest confers.

The concession then in favour of slavery, involved in the explanation given of its definitive establishment in certain portions of North America, amounts to this, that *under certain conditions of soil and climate, cultivation by slaves may for a time yield a larger net revenue than cultivation by certain forms of free labour*.   This is all that needs to be assumed to account for the original establishment of slavery. But the maintenance of the institution at the present day does not imply even this quantum of advantage in its favour; since, owing to the immense difficulty of getting rid of it when once established on an extensive scale, the reasons for its continuance (regarding the question from the point of view of the slaveholders) may, where it has obtained a firm footing, prevail over those for its abolition, even though it be far inferior as a productive instrument to free labour. The most, therefore, that can be inferred from the existence of the system at the present day is that it is self-supporting.

Having now cleared the ground from the several false inferences with which the economic success of slavery, such as it is, is apt to be surrounded, I proceed to trace the consequences, economic social and political, which flow from the institution.

The comparative anatomist, by reasoning on those fixed relations between the different parts of the animal frame which his science reveals to him, is able from a fragment of a tooth or bone to determine the form, dimensions, and habits of the creature to which it belonged ; and with no less accuracy, it seems to me, may a political economist, by reasoning on the economic character of slavery and its peculiar connexion with the soil, deduce its leading social and political attributes, and almost construct, by way of *a priori* argument, the entire system of the society of which it forms the founda-

tion. A brief consideration of the economic principles on which, as we have seen in a former chapter,
slavery supports itself, will enable us to illustrate
this remark.

It was then seen that slave labour is, from the
nature of the case, unskilled labour ; and it is evident that this circumstance at once excludes it from
the field of manufacturing and mechanical industry.*
Where a workman is kept in compulsory ignorance,
and is, at the same time, without motive for exerting
his mental faculties, it is quite impossible that he
should take part with efficiency in the difficult and
delicate operations which most manufacturing and
mechanical processes involve. The care and dexterity which the management of machinery requires
is not to be obtained from him, and he would often
do more damage in an hour than the produce of his
labour for a year would cover. Nor is it for economic reasons only that the slave is shut out from
this department of industry. A still more potent
reason for his exclusion is to be found in the social
and political consequences which would follow his
admission to this field. The conduct of manufacturing industry on a great scale always brings with
it the congregation in towns of large masses of
workmen. The danger incident to this, where the
workmen are slaves, is too obvious to need being

* *See* APPENDIX C.

pointed out. Discussion, mutual understanding, combination, secret or open, for the purpose of redressing what is or seems to be amiss, would be the certain consequences. Where, indeed, freedom prevails, such consequences become sources of harmony and strength ; but is it to be supposed that slave-masters will consent to encounter the free development of the principle of association among their thralls ? The thing is inconceivable. Manu-facturing industry, where slavery exists, could only be carried on at the constant risk of insurrection,* and this must effectually prevent it in such societies from ever attaining any considerable growth.† And no less plain is it that slavery is unsuited to the functions of commerce ; for the soul of commerce is the spirit of enterprise, and this is ever found wanting in communities where slavery exists : their prevailing characteristics are subjection to routine

* " Hundreds of slaves in New Orleans must be constantly re-flecting and saying to one another, 'I am as capable of taking care of myself as this Irish hod-carrier, or this German market-gardener; why can't I have the enjoyment of my labour as well as they ? I am capable of taking care of my own family as much as they of theirs ; why should I be subject to have them taken from me by those other men who call themselves our owners ? Our children have as much brains as the children of these white neighbours of ours, who not long ago were cooks and waiters at the hotels; why should they be spurned from the school-rooms ?' "—Olmsted's *Sea-board Slave States*, p. 591.

† " Cheap living and low wages—cheap cotton, coal, and iron con-

and contempt for money-making pursuits. More-over, the occupations of commerce are absolutely prohibitive of the employment of servile labour. A mercantile marine composed of slaves is a form of industry which the world has not yet seen. Mutinies in mid-ocean and desertions the moment the vessel touched at foreign ports would quickly reduce the force to a cipher. These are obstacles which no natural instinct for commerce is sufficient to overcome. They have proved as fatal to its success in Southern, as in Northern, America, in Brazil as in the Confederate States. In both, notwithstanding the temptation of a vast range of coast line and excellent harbours, the descendants of races who in former ages and elsewhere have shewn a marvellous aptitude for maritime pursuits, have abandoned their natural career, and have permitted the whole external commerce of the country to pass into foreign hands.*

stitute the great elements of success in the introduction, and pro-secution of the cotton manufacture. No country in the world possesses these elements in a degree .equal to the Southern and South Western sections of the United States."—De Bow's *Industrial Resources.* Yet, in spite of these advantages, the writer is obliged to admit that, " in looking into the history of the South and South West since the earliest settlement, we find that almost the entire labour of the country has been applied to agriculture." The experi-ment is thus a crucial one. In Brazil we find a similar result; of the whole enslaved population, it seems that five-sixths are engaged in agriculture.—*Revue des Deux Mondes,* 15 *Juillet,* 1862, p. 386.

* " Une statistique officielle constate qu'en 1859, 11,698 Brésiliens

Slavery, therefore, excluded by these causes from the field of manufactures and commerce, finds its natural career in agriculture ; and, from what has been already established respecting the peculiar qualities of slave labour, we may easily divine the form which agricultural industry will assume under a servile *régime*. The single merit of slave labour as an industrial instrument consists, as we have seen, in its capacity for organization—its susceptibility, that is to say, of being adjusted with precision to the kind of work to be done, and of being directed on a comprehensive plan towards some distinctly conceived end. Now to give scope to this quality, the scale on which industry is carried on must be extensive, and to carry on industry on an extensive scale large capitals are required. Large capitalists will therefore have, in slave communities, a special and peculiar advantage over small capitalists beyond that which they enjoy in countries where labour is free. But there is another circumstance which renders a considerable capital still more an indispensable condition to the successful conduct of industrial operations in slave countries. A capitalist

et 8,339 étrangers payaient patente pour avoir le droit d'exercer un commerce, une industrie ou un métier ; mais si l'on défalque du nombre des nationaux 1,309 notaires, 626 avocats et 8,371 aubergistes, on voit que l'industrie brésilienne proprement dite compte, dans l'empire même, cinq fois moins de représentans que l'industrie étrangère."—*Revue des Deus Mondes*, 15 Juillet, p. 394.

who employs free labour needs for the support of
his labour force a sum sufficient to cover the amount
of their wages during the interval which elapses
from the commencement of their operations until
the sale of the produce which results from them.
But the capitalist employing slave labour requires
not merely this sum—represented in his case by the
food, clothing, and shelter provided for his slaves
during the corresponding period—but, in addition
to this, a sum sufficient to purchase the fee-simple
of his entire slave force. For the conduct of a given
business, therefore, it is obvious that the employer
of slave labour will require a much larger capital
than the employer of free labour. The capital of
the one will represent merely the current outlay ;
while the capital of the other will represent, in
addition to this, the future capabilities of the productive instrument   The one will represent the
interest, the other the principal and interest, of the
labour employed.   Owing to these causes large capitals are, relatively to small, more profitable, and are,
at the same time, absolutely more required in countries of slave, than in countries of free, labour. It
happens, however, that capital is in slave countries a
particularly scarce commodity, owing partly to the
exclusion from such countries of many modes of
creating it—manufactures and commerce for example—which are open to free communities, and

partly to what is also a consequence of the institution
—the unthrifty habits of the upper classes. We
arrive therefore at this singular conclusion, that,
while large capitals in countries of slave labour
enjoy peculiar advantages, and while the aggregate
capital needed in them for the conduct of a given
amount of industry is greater than in countries
where labour is free, capital nevertheless in such
countries is exceptionally scarce. From this state of
things result two phenomena which may be regarded
as typical of industry carried on by slaves—the magnitude of the plantations and the indebtedness of the
planters. Wherever negro slavery has prevailed in
modern times, these two phenomena will be found to
exist. They form the burden of most of what has
been written on our West Indian Islands while
under the *régime* of slavery ; they are reproduced in
Cuba and Brazil ;* and they are not less prominently the characteristic features of the industrial sys-

---

* "Une grande partie du sol du Brésil est distribuée en vastes
domaines dont les limites, souvent indécises, sont marquées par des
forêts, des fleuves ou des montagnes. En outre il existe un nombre
considérable de *sesmarias* qui recouvrent une superficie d'une demi-
lieue, d'une lieue, même de trois et de cinq lieues, et qui, n'ayant
jamais été mises en culture par leurs propriétaires, devraient faire
retour au domaine public pour être cadastrées et mises en vente.
Le gouvernement a souvent revendiqué ces *sesmarias;* mais partout
où les intérêts de la *grande culture* sont en jeu, les planteurs
coalisés savent fort bien empêcher ce qui pourrait nuire à la constitution féodale de leur société."—*Revue des Deux Mondes*, p. 404-5.

tem of the Southern States. "Our wealthier planters," says Mr. Clay, "are buying out their poor
neighbours, extending their plantations, and adding
to their slave force. The wealthy few, who are able
to live on smaller profits, and to give their blasted
fields some rest, are thus pushing off the many who
are merely independent." At the same time these
wealthier planters are, it is well known, very generally in debt, the forthcoming crops being for the
most part mortgaged to Northern capitalists, who
make the needful advances, and who thus become the
instruments by which a considerable proportion of
the slave labour of the South is maintained. The
tendency of things, therefore, in slave countries is to
a very unequal distribution of wealth. The large
capitalists, having a steady advantage over their
smaller competitors, engross, with the progress of
time, a larger and larger proportion of the aggregate wealth of the country, and gradually acquire
the control of its collective industry. Meantime,
amongst the ascendant class a condition of general
indebtedness prevails.

But we may carry our deductions from the
economic character of slavery somewhat further.
It has been seen that slave cultivation can only
maintain itself where the soil is rich, while it produces a steady deterioration of the soils on which it
is employed. This being so, it is evident that in

countries of average fertility but a small portion
of the whole area will be available for this mode of
cultivation, and that this portion is ever becoming
smaller, since, as the process of deterioration proceeds, more soils are constantly reaching that condition in which servile labour ceases to be profitable.   What, then, is to become of the remainder—
that large portion of the country which is either naturally too poor for cultivation by slaves, or which
has been made so by its continued employment?
It will be thought, perhaps, that this may be worked
by free labour, and that by a judicious combination
of both forms of industry the whole surface of the
country may be brought to the highest point of
productiveness.   But this is a moral impossibility :
it is precluded by what, we shall find, is a cardinal feature in the structure of slave societies—
their exclusiveness.   In free countries industry is
the path to independence, to wealth, to social distinction, and is therefore held in honour ; in slave
countries it is the vocation of the slave, and becomes
therefore a badge of degradation.   Idleness, which
in free countries is regarded as the mother of all
vices, becomes in the land of the slave the preroga-
tive of a caste and is transformed into a title of
nobility.*   The free labourer, consequently, who

* A writer in De Bow's Review tells us of "a large class of
persons in New Orleans who violate nature's laws by making
negroes of themselves"—*i. e.* working.

respects his calling and desires to be respected, instinctively shuns a country where industry is discredited, where he cannot engage in those pursuits by which wealth and independence are to be gained without placing himself on a level with the lowest of mankind. Free and slave labour are, therefore, incapable of being blended together in the same system. Where slavery exists it excludes all other forms of industrial life. " The traveller," says Tocqueville, " who floats down the current of the Ohio, may be said to sail between liberty and servitude. Upon the left bank of the stream the population is sparse ; from time to time one descries a troop of slaves loitering in the half-desert fields ; the primæval forest recurs at every turn ; society seems to be asleep, man to be idle, and nature alone offers a scene of activity and of life. From the right bank, on the contrary, a confused hum is heard which proclaims the presence of industry ; the fields are covered with abundant harvests ; the elegance of the dwellings announces the taste and activity of the labourer ; and man appears to be in the enjoyment of that wealth and contentment which is the reward of labour. Upon the left bank of the Ohio labour is confounded with the idea of slavery, upon the right bank it is identified with that of prosperity and improvement ; on the one side it is degraded, on the other it is honoured ; on the former territory

no white labourers can be found, for they would be
afraid of assimilating themselves to the negroes ; on
the latter no one is idle, for the white population
extends its activity and its intelligence to every
kind of employment.   Thus the men whose task it
is to cultivate the rich soil of Kentucky are ignorant
and lukewarm ; whilst those who are enlightened
either do nothing, or pass over into the State of
Ohio, where they may work without dishonour."*

" If there is little hope that in an agricultural community, in which the slave system is established, the
mass of the white population can be advanced to a
position of competence and independence ; there is
quite as little hope of the growth, from any elements
which such a population affords, of towns, of the

* _Democracy in America_, vol. ii. pp. 222, 223.   " The negroes,"
says Mr. Olmsted, " are a degraded people—degraded not merely
by position, but actually immoral, low-lived ; without healthy ambition ; but little influenced by high moral considerations ; and, in
regard to labour, not at all affected by regard for duty.   This is
universally recognized, and debasing fear, not cheering hope, is in
general allowed to be their only stimulant to exertion. . . Now,
let the white labourer come here from the North or from Europe—
his nature demands a social life—shall he associate with the poor,
slavish, degraded, low-lived, despised, unambitious negro, with
whom labour and punishment are almost synonymous ? or shall he
be the friend and companion of the white man,. in whose mind
labour is habitually associated with no ideas of duty, responsibility,
comfort, luxury, cultivation, or elevation and expansion either of
mind or estate, as it is where the ordinary labourer is a free man
—free to use his labour as a means of obtaining all these and all

mechanic arts, or of manufacturing and commercial interests. Capacity of labour, which is everywhere only the result of use and habit, is not called into existence, and a savage indolent contentment with the coarsest subsistence extinguishes all desire of advancement. Cuba, with a large non-slaveholding white population, relies upon Europe and the Northern States for engineers, machinists, and ordinary mechanics, and upon Spain for even petty shopkeepers. . . . . . Throughout the South towns are built up only by Northern and European immigration, and without it there would be scarcely any manifestation of civilization. Mills, railroads, cotton presses, sugar boilers, and steam-

else that is to be respected, honoured or envied in the world? Associating with either or both, is it not inevitable that he will be rapidly demoralized—that he will soon learn to hate labour, give as little of it for his hire as he can, become base, cowardly, faithless— 'worse than a nigger'? . . . When we reflect how little the great body of our working men are consciously much affected by moral considerations in their movements, one is tempted to suspect that the Almighty has endowed the great transatlantic migration with a new instinct, by which it is unconsciously repelled from the demoralizing and debilitating influence of slavery, as migrating birds have sometimes been thought to be from pestilential regions. I know not else how to account for the remarkable indisposition to be sent to Virginia which I have seen manifested by poor Irishmen and Germans, who could have known, I think, no more of the evils of slavery to the whites in the Slave States, than the slaves themselves know of the effect of conscription in France, and who certainly could have been governed by no considerations of self-respect."

boats, are mainly indebted for their existence in the Southern States to intelligence and muscle trained in free communities."*

Agriculture, therefore, when carried on by slaves, being by a sure law restricted to the most fertile portions of the land, and no other form of systematic industry being possible where slavery is established, it happens that there are in all slave countries vast districts, becoming, under the deteriorating effects of slave industry, constantly larger, which are wholly surrendered to nature, and remain for ever as wilderness. This is a characteristic feature in the political economy of the Slave States of the South, and is attended with social consequences of the most important kind. For the tracts thus left, or made, desolate become in time the resort of a promiscuous horde, who, too poor to keep slaves and too proud to work, prefer a vagrant and precarious life spent in the desert to engaging in occupations which would associate them with the slaves whom they despise. In the Southern States no less than four millions of human beings are now said to exist in this manner in a condition little removed from savage life, eking out a wretched subsistence by hunting, by fishing, by hiring themselves out for occasional jobs, by plunder. Combining the restlessness and contempt for

* Weston's *Progress of Slavery*, pp. 47, 48.

regular industry peculiar to the savage with the
vices of the *prolétaire* of civilized communities, these
people make up a class at once degraded and dangerous, and, constantly reinforced as they are by all that
is idle, worthless, and lawless among the population
of the neighbouring states, form an inexhaustible preserve of ruffianism, ready at hand for all the worst
purposes of Southern ambition.   The planters complain of these people for their idleness, for corrupting
their slaves, for their thievish propensities; but they
cannot dispense with them ; for, in truth, they perform an indispensable function in the economy of
slave societies, of which they are at once the victims
and the principal supports.   It is from their ranks
that those filibustering expeditions are recruited
which have been found so effective an instrument in
extending the domain of the Slave Power ; they
furnish the Border Ruffians who in the colonization
struggle with the Northern States contend with
Freesoilers on the Territories ; and it is to their
antipathy to the negroes that the planters securely
trust for repressing every attempt at servile insurrection.   Such are the " mean whites" or " white
trash" of the Southern States.*   They comprise
several local subdivisions, the " crackers," the " sand-

---

* " ' Mean' is an Americanism for ' poor ' or ' shabby.' They
speak here of a ' mean' hotel, a ' mean' dinner, &c."—Stirling's
Letters from the Slave States.   These contemptuous terms, with their

hillers," the " clay-eaters," and many more. The class is not peculiar to any one locality, but is the invariable outgrowth of negro slavery wherever it has raised its head in modern times. It may be seen in the new state of Texas* as well as in the old settled districts of Virginia, the Carolinas, and Georgia ; in the West India Islands† no less than on the Continent. In the States of the Confederacy it comprises, as I have said, four millions of human beings—about seven-tenths of the whole white population.‡

The industry of the Slave States, we have seen, is exclusively agricultural ; and the mode of agriculture pursued in them has been represented as partial, perfunctory, and exhaustive. It must, however, be admitted that, to a certain extent, this description is applicable to the industrial condition of all new countries, and will find illustrations in the

connotation, have, it would seem, passed into the vocabulary of the negroes. " Massa, dey'm pore trash. Dat's what de big folks call 'em, and it am true ; dey'm long way lower down dan de darkies."
—*Among the Pines.* J. R. Gilmore : New York.

* Olmsted's *Texas*, p. xvii. ; note.

† Merivale's *Colonization and the Colonies*, p. 83 ; note, new ed.

‡ " For all practical purposes," says Mr. Stirling, summing up the results of an extensive observation of the Southern States, and writing with the facts beneath his eyes, " for all practical purposes we may still regard Southern society as consisting of aristocratic planters and ' white trash'."—*Letters from the Slave States.* For a full discussion of this question, see APPENDIX D.

western regions of the Free States ; and it may therefore occur to the reader that the economical conditions which I have described are rather the consequence of the recent settlement of the societies where they prevail than specific results of the system of slavery. But it is easy to show that this view of the case is fallacious, and proceeds from confounding what is essential in slave industry with an accidental and temporary feature in the industrial career of free communities. The settlers in new countries, whether they be slaveholders or free peasants, naturally fix in the first instance on the richest and most conveniently situated soils, and find it more profitable to cultivate these lightly, availing themselves to the utmost of the resources which nature offers, than to force cultivation on inferior soils after the manner of high farming in old countries. So far the cases are similar. But here lies the difference. The labour of free peasants, though of course more productive on rich than on inferior soils, is not necessarily confined to the former ; whereas this is the case with the labour of slaves. Accordingly, therefore, as free peasants multiply, after the best soils have been appropriated, the second best are taken into cultivation ; and as they multiply still more, cultivation becomes still more general, until ultimately all the cultivable portions of the country are brought within the domain of industry. This has been the course of industrial progress throughout the settled portions of the Northern States, but it has been otherwise in the South. As slaves multiply, their masters cannot have recourse to inferior soils : they must find for them new soils : the mass of the country, therefore, remains uncultivated, and the population increases only by dispersion. Again, although the mode of cultivation pursued by free peasants in new lands is generally far from what would be approved of by the scientific farmers of old countries, still it does not exhaust the soil in the same manner as cultivation carried on by slaves. " I hold myself justified," says Mr. Olmsted, " in asserting that the natural elements of wealth in the soil of Texas will have been more exhausted in ten years, and with them the rewards offered by Providence to labour will have been more lessened, than without slavery would have been the case in two hundred. . . . After two hundred years' occupation of similar soils by a free labouring community, I have seen no such evidences of waste as in Texas I have after ten years of slavery. . . . Waste of soil and injudicious application of labour are common in the agriculture of the North ; . . . but nowhere is the land with what is attached to it now less promising and suitable for the residence of a refined and civilized people than it was before the operations, which have been attended with the alleged waste, were commenced." The same is not true of Virginia or the Carolinas, or of any other district where slavery has predominated for a historic period. "The land in these cases is positively less capable of sustaining a dense civilized community than if no labour at all had been expended upon it."* "Examples," says Mr. De Bow, "may be found in our own country of states having become poorer by a steady perseverance in an unwise application of their labour. Such is the case in the Atlantic states south of the Potomac, as I think will be granted by every intelligent and candid individual who is acquainted with the country, and I think it will be admitted that these states are poorer than they were twenty years ago. There is a small increase in the number of labourers, and there may have been something gained in skill ; but the great source of all wealth in an agricultural country—the soil—has been greatly deteriorated and diminished, and it may be affirmed without the fear of successful contradiction, that no country, and more especially an agricultural one, can increase in wealth while the soil is becoming more and more exhausted every year, for it is most clear that sooner or later an absolute state of exhaustion must be the result, and no wealth that could be acquired by the sale of those products, the

* Olmsted's *Texas*, p. xiv.

growth of which had caused this state of things, could compensate for the loss of the soil."* The superficial and careless mode of agriculture pursued by free peasants in new countries is, in short, accidental and temporary, the result of the exceptional circumstances in which they are placed, and gives place to a better system as population increases and inferior soils are brought under the plough; but the superficiality and exhaustiveness of agriculture carried on by slaves are essential and unalterable qualities, rendering all cultivation impossible but that which is carried on upon the richest soils, and not to be remedied by the growth of population, since to this they are an effectual bar.†

My position is, that in slave communities agriculture is substantially the sole occupation, while this single pursuit is prematurely arrested in its development, never reaching those soils of secondary quality which, under a system of free industry would, with the growth of society, be brought under

* *Industrial Resources, &c.*, vol. ii. p. 108, and see also vol. iv. pp. 34, 35.

† The reader will be curious to know how the upholders of the system reconcile their admiration for it with the full admission of results such as I have described. The following passage will show: —" In as much as my remarks would seem to ascribe the most exhausting system of cultivation especially to the slave-holding states, the enemies of the institution of slavery might cite my opinions, if without the explanation which will now be offered, as indicating that slave labour and exhausting tillage were necessarily connected as

cultivation ; and of this statement the industrial history of the Free and Slave States forms one continued illustration. The state of Virginia, for example, is the longest settled state in the Union, and for general productive purposes, one of the most richly endowed. It possesses a fertile soil, a genial climate ; it is rich in mineral productions—in iron, in copper, in coal—the coal fields of Virginia being amongst the most extensive in the world, and the coal of superior quality ; it is approached by one of the noblest bays ; it is watered by numerous rivers, some of them navigable for considerable distances, and most of them capable of affording abundance of water power for manufacturing purposes.* With such advantages, Virginia, a region as large as England, could not fail, in a career of two hundred and fifty years, under a system of free industry, to become a state of great wealth, population, and power. Her mineral and manufacturing, as well as her agricultural, resources would be

cause and effect. I readily admit that our slave labour has served greatly to facilitate our exhausting cultivation ; but only because it is a great facility—far superior to any found in the non-slave-holding states—for all agricultural operations. Of course, if our operations are exhausting of fertility, then certainly our command of cheaper and more abundant labour enables us to do the work of exhaustion, as well as all other work, more rapidly and effectually.— De Bow's *Industrial Resources*, vol. iv. p. 38.

* Olmsted's *Seaboard Slave States*, pp. 165, 166 ; and Art. Virginia, vol. iii. of De Bow's *Industrial Resources*.

brought into requisition ; her population would increase with rapidity, and become concentrated in
large towns ; her agriculture would be extended
over the whole surface of the country.   But what is
the result of the experiment under slavery ?   After
a national life of two hundred and fifty years the
whole free population is still under one million
souls.*   Eight-tenths of her industry are devoted
to agriculture ; and the progress which has been
made in this, the principal pursuit, may be estimated by the significant fact, that the average price
per acre of cultivated land in Virginia is no more
that eight dollars.   Contrast this with the progress
made in fifty years by the free state of Ohio—a
state smaller in area than Virginia, and inferior in
variety of resources.   Ohio was admitted as a state
into the Union in 1802, and in 1850 its population
numbered nearly two millions.†   Like Virginia it
is chiefly agricultural, though not from the same
causes, Ohio being from its resources and internal
position adapted in a peculiar manner to agriculture, while the resources of Virginia would fit it
equally for manufactures or commerce ; but, while

* The actual numbers were in 1850 :—

Whites	...	...	894,800
Free coloured		...	54,333
Total free		...	949,133

† The actual numbers were, 1,980,329.

the average price of cultivated land per acre in
Virginia, after an agricultural career of two hundred and fifty years, is eight dollars, the average
price in Ohio, after a career of fifty years, is twenty
dollars.* The contrast will of course only become
more striking, if, instead of a free state of fifty
years' growth, we take one more nearly on a par
in the duration of its career with the slave state
with which it is compared. New Jersey, for example, was founded about the same time as Virginia.
Its climate, Mr. Olmsted tells us, differs impercept-
ibly from that of Virginia, owing to its vicinity
to the ocean, while its soil is decidedly less fertile ;
but such progress has been made in bringing that
soil under cultivation that, against eight dollars per
acre—the average price of land in Virginia—there
is to be set in New Jersey an average of forty-four
dollars.† Let us take another example. New York
and Massachusetts are also, in relation to Virginia,

* " It certainly was a great temptation to me, while I was enjoying
the delightful January climate of Virginia, to be offered any amount
of land which I was certain could be easily made to produce, under
good tillage, twenty-five or thirty bushels of wheat to the acre,
within twenty-four hours of New York by rail, and forty-eight by
water-carriage, at exactly one fortieth of the price, by the acre, at
which I could sell my New York farm."—Olmsted's *Seaboard Slave
States,* p. 174.

† Olmsted's *Seaboard Slave States,* p. 171. In connexion with
this question Mr. Weston (*Progress of Slavery*) gives the following

contemporary states. In agricultural resources they are greatly its inferiors, the soil of Massachusetts in particular being sterile and its climate harsh. What then has been the relative progress made by these three states in bringing their respective soils under cultivation ? In Virginia, 26¼ per cent. of her whole area had, in 1852, been brought under tillage ; in New York, 41 per cent. ; and in Massachusetts, 42½ per cent. But these facts do not convey their full lesson till we add that, in bringing 26¼ per cent. of her soil under cultivation, Virginia employed eight-tenths of her industrial population, while New York and Massachusetts, in bringing under cultivation much larger proportions of their areas, employed but six- and four-tenths of their

striking statistics, p. 17 :—" The following were the prices per acre in the states and counties named, and the per-centage of slaves in Kentucky and the counties named :—

	Value per acre.	Per cent. of slaves.
Ohio	19·99	
Indiana	10·66	
Illinois	7·99	
Kentucky	9·03	22
Ohio counties adjoining Kentucky ...	32·34	
Kentucky counties adjoining Ohio ...	18·27	10
Indiana counties adjoining Kentucky ...	11·34	
Kentucky counties adjoining Indiana ...	10·44	21
Illinois counties adjacent to Kentucky ...	4·65	
Kentucky counties adjacent to Illinois ...	4·54	18"

respective populations.*   It thus appears that Virginia, with great agricultural resources and a population almost wholly devoted to agriculture, has been far outstripped in her own peculiar branch of industry by states of inferior resources, and whose industry has been largely or principally devoted to other pursuits.   The same comparison might be continued throughout the other Free and Slave States with analogous results.   The general truth is, that in the Free States, where external circumstances are favourable, industry is distributed over many occupations—manufactures, mining, commerce, agriculture ; while in the Slave States, however various be the resources of the country, it is substantially confined to one—agriculture, and this one is prematurely arrested, never reaching that stage of development which in countries where labour is free is early attained.

" If one acquainted with the present condition of the southwest, were told that the cotton-growing district alone had sold the crop for fifty millions of dollars per annum for the last twenty years, he

* These facts are given in an "Address to the Farmers of Virginia," by the *Virginia State Agricultural Society*, which after having been twice read, approved, and adopted, was finally rejected on the ground that "there were admissions in it which would feed the fanaticism of the abolitionists ;" but "no one argued against it on the ground of the falsity or inaccuracy of its returns."   It is quoted at length by Olmsted, *Seaboard Slave States*, pp. 167–170.

would naturally conclude that this might be the richest community in the world. He might well imagine that the planters all dwell in palaces, upon estates improved by every device of art, and that their most common utensils were made of the precious metals ; that canals, turnpikes, railways, and every other improvement designed either for use or for ornament, abounded in every part of the land ; and that the want of money had never been felt or heard of in its limits. He would conclude that the most splendid edifices dedicated to the purposes of religion and learning were everywhere to be found, and that all the liberal arts had here found their reward, and a home. But what would be his surprise when told, that so far from dwelling in palaces, many of these planters dwell in habitations of the most primitive construction, and these so inartificially built as to be incapable of protecting the inmates from the winds and rains of heaven ; that instead of any artistical improvement, this rude dwelling was surrounded by cotton fields, or probably by fields exhausted, washed into gullies, and abandoned ; that instead of canals, the navigable streams remain unimproved, to the great detriment of transportation ; that the common roads of the country were scarcely passable ; that the edifices erected for the accommodation of learning and religion were frequently built of logs, and covered with boards ; and that the fine arts were but little encouraged or cared for. Upon receiving this information, he would imagine that this was surely the country of misers—that they had been hoarding up all the money of the world, to the great detriment of the balance of mankind. But his surprise would be greatly increased when informed, that, instead of being misers and hoarders of money, these people were generally scarce of it, and many of them embarrassed and bankrupt. Upon what principle could a stranger to the country account for this condition of things ?"*

The reader is now in a position to understand the kind of economic success which slavery has achieved. It consists in the rapid extraction from the soil of a country of the most easily obtained portion of its wealth by a process which exhausts the soil, and consigns to waste all the other resources of the country where it is practised. To state the case with more particularity—by proscribing manufactures and commerce, and confining agriculture within narrow bounds ; by rendering impossible the rise of a free peasantry; by checking the growth of population—in a word, by blasting every germ from which national well-being and general civilization may spring—at this cost, with the further condition of encroaching, through a reckless system of culture,

* De Bow's *Industrial Resources*, vol. ii. pp. 113, 114.

on the stores designed by Providence for future generations, slavery may undoubtedly for a time be made conducive to the pecuniary gain of the class who keep slaves. Such is the net result of advantage which slavery, as an economic system, is capable of yielding. To the full credit of all that is involved in this admission the institution is fairly entitled.

The constitution of a slave society, it has been seen, is sufficiently simple : it resolves itself into three classes, broadly distinguished from each other, and connected by no common interest—the slaves on whom devolves all the regular industry, the slaveholders who reap all its fruits, and an idle and lawless rabble who live dispersed over vast plains in a condition little removed from absolute barbarism. Besides these, indeed, there is in certain Southern districts a class of peasant farmers—a hardy and industrious race ; but these form no part of the economy of slave society. They are in no sense the growth of slavery, but a foreign element obtruded on the system from without, marring its symmetry, and impairing its strength. Wherever they exist, there a centre of weakness to the cause of slavery exists, and of loyalty to that of freedom. Thus the real constituents of slave society resolve themselves into the three classes I have described ; and of these the Slave Power is the political representative. What the nature of that power is, now that we have ascertained the elements out of which it springs, we can have little difficulty in determining. When the whole wealth of a country is monopolized by a thirtieth part of its population, while the remainder are by physical or moral causes consigned to compulsory poverty and ignorance; when the persons composing the privileged thirtieth part are all engaged in pursuits of the same kind, subject to the influence of the same moral ideas, and identified with the maintenance of the same species of property—in a society so constituted, political power will of necessity reside with those in whom centre the elements of such power—wealth, knowledge, and intelligence—the small minority for whose exclusive benefit the system exists.* The polity of such a society must thus, in essence, be an oligarchy, whatever be the particular mould in which it is cast. Nor is this all. A society so organized tends to develop with a peculiar intensity the distinctive vices of an oligarchy. In a country of free labour, whatever be the form of government to which it is subject, the pursuits of industry are various. Various interests, therefore, take root, and parties grow up which, regarding national questions form various points of view, become centres of opposition, whether against the undue pretensions of any one of their number, or against those of a single

* See APPENDIX E.

ruler. It is not so in the Slave States. That variety of interests which springs from the individual impulses of a free population does not here exist. The elements of a political opposition are wanting. There is but one party,* but one set of men who are capable of acting together in political concert. The rest is an undisciplined rabble. From this state of things the only possible result is that which we find—a despotism, in the last degree unscrupulous and impatient of control, wielded by the wealthy few. Now it is this power which for half a century has exercised paramount sway in the councils of the Union. It is the men educated in the ideas of this system who have filled the highest offices of State, who have been the representatives of their country to European powers, and who, by their position and the influence they have commanded, have given the tone to the public morality of the nation. The deterioration of the institutions and of the character of the people of the United States is now very com-

* There is one exception to this statement. Between the breeding and working states a difference of interest has been developed which has resulted in the formation of two parties within the Slave States. But (as will hereafter be shown) this difference of interest has never been sufficient to produce any serious discordance among the politicians of the South. The sympathies which bind the breeding and working states together are far stronger than any interests which separate them; and in the main they have always acted as a single party.

monly taken for granted in this country. The fact
may be so ; so far as the South is concerned I believe, and shall endeavour to prove, that it unquestionably *is* so. But it is very important that we
should understand to what cause this deterioration
is due. There are writers who would have us believe that it is but the natural result of democratic
institutions working through the Federal system ;
and for this view a plausible case may be easily
made out. Democratic institutions have admittedly
exercised a powerful influence in forming the American character and determining the present condition of the United States. It is only necessary,
therefore, to bring this point strongly into view in
close connexion with all that is most objectionable
in the public morals, and all that is most discredit-
able in the recent history, of the Union, keeping
carefully out of sight the existence in the political
system of institutions the reverse of democratic, and
avoiding all reference to the cardinal fact, that it is
these and not the democratic institutions of the
North which, almost since its establishment, have
been the paramount power in the Union,—to leave
the impression that everything which has been made
matter of reproach in transatlantic politics has
been due to democracy and to democracy alone.
According to this method of theorising, the abstrac-
tion of Florida, the annexation of Texas, the filibus-

tering expeditions of Lopez and Walker, the attempts upon Cuba, have no connexion with the aggressive ambition of the Slave Power : they are only proofs of the rapacious spirit of democracy armed with the strength of a powerful federation. It is, indeed, quite astounding to observe the boldness with which this argument is sometimes handled. One would have thought that an advocate of the Southern cause would at least have shown some hesitancy in alluding to an attack made by a Southern bully, on the floor of the Senate house, upon one of the most accomplished statesmen of the North. That attack was in all its circumstances plainly branded with the marks of its origin. It was committed by a slave-holder, acting as the champion of slaveholders, in revenge of an anti-slavery speech; it was charac-terized by that mingled treachery, cowardice, and brutality which are only to be found in societies reared in the presence of slavery ; it was adopted and applauded by the whole people of the South, recognized by testimonials, and rewarded by gifts : yet this act is deliberately put forward as an exam-ple of the "irreverence for justice" which is pro-duced by democratic institutions, and is employed to prepossess our minds in favour of the Southern cause !* The present writer is far from being an

* Spence's *American Union,* pp. 65-6, 74-5. Mr. Spence states the act, omitting to mention the occasion, or whether the actors were

admirer of democracy as it exists in the Northern States ; but, whatever be the merits or demerits of that form of government, it is desirable that it should be judged by its own fruits, and not by the fruits of a system which is its opposite—a system which, in place of conferring political power on the majority of the people, gives it, free from all control, to a small minority whose interests are not only not identical with those of their fellow-citizens,

Northern or Southern men ; but, in the same paragraph, having alluded to the case of Mr. Sickles, he adds that the man "who committed a deliberate and relentless murder in open day . . . . is now a Brigadier-General in the Northern army." Is the mention of the criminal's origin in one case, and its suppression in the other, an accident ?

In a later portion of the volume a still more striking instance occurs of Mr. Spence's candour. "A French writer, Raymond, comments upon the singular fact that whilst between England and France but one serious quarrel has occurred since 1815, there have arisen during the same period twelve or thirteen most serious difficulties between the United States and ourselves. . . . We have had minor wars with China, conducted on the principle of throwing open to the world every advantage obtained by ourselves. On one occasion we invited the co-operation of the American Government, but in vain, and every opportunity was seized to thwart our policy. Even the Chinese know they may expect to see the flag of any other power in union with our own, but never that of America. There was, indeed, a moment when our men were falling under a murderous fire, that for once an American was heard to declare that ' blood was thicker than water.' It would ill become us to forget the noble conduct of Commodore Tatnall on that occasion. He was a Southerner, and is now a 'traitor and a rebel'" (pp. 294-296). Let the reader note the art with which the facts are here manipulated.

but are directly opposed to theirs. Democracy, beyond all doubt, has been a powerful influence in moulding the character of the Americans in the Northern States : it would be absurd to deny this ; but it would be no less absurd, and would be still more flagrantly in defiance of the most conspicuous facts of the case, to deny that that character has also been profoundly modified by the influence of Southern institutions, acting through the Federal

We are asked to refuse our sympathies to the North, because, since 1815 we have had frequent difficulties with the United States (which the North now represents)—the circumstance that during almost the whole of this period the Government of the United States was in the hands of Southern statesmen being suppressed as of no importance in the case. On the other hand, a single instance in which a Southerner has performed an act of a friendly nature towards Great Britain is brought prominently forward as a ground for giving our sympathies to the South. It is evident that the contrast thus instituted between the friendly conduct of Commodore Tatnall—a Southerner—and the hostile spirit which had just been commented on as manifested by the Government of the Union, can, taken in connexion with the general tenor of the argument, have no other effect than to leave readers unacquainted with the facts (a rather numerous class unfortunately in this country) under the impression that, as the friendly demonstration was the act of a Southerner, so the hostile manifestations proceeded from the North. The spirit evinced in this passage, which is merely a specimen of the main argument of the work from which it is taken, is all the more remarkable in a writer who in his preface bespeaks the confidence of his readers on the ground that " personal considerations and valued friendships incline him without exception to the Northern side," which he has been compelled reluctantly to abandon by " convictions forced upon the mind by facts and reasonings."

government in the persons of Southern men—institutions which I repeat are the reverse of democratic.
It is the Slave Power, and not the democracy of the
North, which for half a century has been dominant
in the Union.*   It is this Power which has directed
its public policy ; which has guided its intercourse
with foreign nations, conducted its diplomacy, regu-
lated its internal legislation, and which, by working
on its hopes and fears through the unscrupulous
use of an enormous patronage, has exercised an un-
bounded sway over the minds of the whole people.
Whatever other agencies may have contributed to
shape the course of American politics, this at least
has been a leading one ; and whatever be the political character of the citizens, for that character this
system must be held in a principal degree responsible.†

* "As our Norman kinsmen in England, always a minority, have
ruled their Saxon countrymen in political vassalage up to the present day, so have we, the 'slave oligarchs,' governed the Yankees
till within a twelvemonth. We framed the constitution, for seventy
years moulded the policy of the government, and placed our own
men, or 'northern men with Southern principles,' in power. On
the 6th of November, 1860, the puritans emancipated themselves
and are now in violent insurrection against their former owners.
This insane holiday freak will not last long, however; for, dastards
in fight, and incapable of self-government, they will inevitably
again fall under the control of a superior race. A few more Bull
Run thrashings will bring them once more under the yoke as docile
as the most loyal of our Ethiopian 'chattels.'"—*Louisville Courier.*

† "Alors que subsistait triomphante aux Etats-Unis l'alliance

To sum up in a few words the general results of the foregoing discussion :—the Slave Power—that power which has long held the helm of government in the Union—is, under the forms of a democracy, an uncontrolled despotism, wielded by a compact oligarchy. Supported by the labour of four millions of slaves, it rules a population of four millions of whites—a population ignorant, averse to systematic industry, and prone to irregular adventure. A system of society more formidable for evil, more menacing to the best interests of the human race, it is difficult to conceive.

entre le parti démocratique et le parti esclavagiste, la doctrine dite de Monroe, arrangée par d'audacieux commentateurs, avait déterminé des actes assez nombreux qui avaient blessé profondément l'Europe. Cette alliance, qui viciait la politique intérieure des Etats-Unis non moins que leur politique étrangère, a pendent une suite d'années dominé le pays : c'est elle qui surtout dictait les choix dans les élections à la présidence ; mais il était infaillible que le sentiment public se réveillerait dans la grande république américaine de manière à rendre l'ascendant aux principes de progrès et de liberté. C'est ce qui a eu lieu dans l'élection du président Lincoln."—M. Chevalier in the *Revue des Deux Mondes,* 15 Avril, 1862, p. 914.

CHAPTER IV.

TENDENCIES OF SLAVE SOCIETIES.

IN what direction is slave society, as presented in the States of the Confederation, moving ? Towards a higher civilization, or towards barbarism? On the answer to this question, I apprehend, will principally depend the degree of indulgence which we may be disposed to extend to modern slavery. If the form of society springing from the institution be found to be but an incident of a certain stage of human progress, a shell of barbarism from which nations gradually work themselves free with the development of their moral and material life, an evil which will disappear by a spontaneous process—we shall probably be disposed to regard the institution with considerable leniency, to deprecate schemes for its overthrow, and, perhaps, in certain cases, even to look with favour on plans for its extension. If, on the other hand, it appears that the system is essentially retrograde in its character, contrived so as to arrest and throw back the development, moral and material, of the people on whom it is imposed, and to hold them in a condition of permanent barbarism, the sentiments with which we

shall regard it, as well as our policy towards the
countries which uphold it, will be of a very different
kind.

Thus, to give the point a practical illustration, the
mode of dealing with Mexico is at present a most
perplexing question for European statesmen.   In
the present condition of that country—the prey of
contending factions, whose alternate excesses prevent the growth of steady industry, deter European
settlement, and deprive the world of the benefit
which its great natural resources are calculated to
confer—almost any change would be a change for
the better.   The establishment of an effective government of some kind, of a power capable of preserving the lives and properties of the inhabitants,
is a matter of prime necessity, without which the
first foundations of improvement cannot be laid.
Now the most obvious method of effecting this
purpose would be to hand the country over to the
Southern Confederation ;* and this arrangement
would entirely fall in with the views of the leaders
of that body.   But Mexico, whatever be the vices
of its political system, is a state in which labour
is free ; whereas, if annexed to the dominions of
the Southern Confederation, it would at once be-

---

* This is not a mere fanciful hypothesis. The plan has been
suggested in terms sufficiently unambiguous by the *Times*, in a
leading article, 31st July, 1861.

come the abode of slavery. Nevertheless it can
scarcely be doubted that this annexation would, in
the first instance, be attended with some advantages.
For the chieftains whose combined weakness and
violence now keep the country in constant agitation
there would be substituted a strong government—a
government incompatible, indeed, with freedom of
speech or writing, or with security of life or property for such as ventured to dissent from its principles, but still able to preserve order after a certain
fashion—able to protect slaveholders in the enjoyment of their property, and to prevent revolutions.
Under such a government productive industry might
be expected to start forward with vigour; those
products which are capable of being raised with
profit by slave labour, and amongst these cotton,
would be multiplied and cheapened in the markets
of the world; the position of Mexican bondholders
would be improved. Such would probably be the
immediate effect of the annexation. But what
would be its permanent consequences? To answer
this question we must resolve the problem with
which we started. We must determine the direction in which society in the Southern States is
moving. If the "peculiar institution" be essentially temporary and provisional in its character,
if it be not incompatible with the ultimate emancipation of those on whom it is imposed, as well

as with the continued progress of the people among whom it is established, then the permanent, as well as the immediate, consequences of the extension of Southern rule over Mexico, notwithstanding that it would be attended with the introduction of slavery into a country where labour is at present free, might perhaps be thought to be, on the whole, advantageous. But, if the institution of the South be a permanent thraldom, and if the form of society to which it gives birth be of a kind effectually to arrest the growth of the whole people amongst whom it is planted—under these conditions, to hand over Mexico to the Southern Confederacy would be nothing less than, for the sake of certain material advantages to be reaped by the present generation, to seal the doom of a noble country—a country which, under better auspices, might become a perennial source of benefits for all future time, and a new centre of American civilization.

It is therefore of extreme importance to ascertain the tendencies of these slave societies, and what prospects they hold out of future advancement to the people who compose them. And, in approaching this question, it at once occurs that slavery is not a new fact in the world. It prevailed, as we know, among all the nations of antiquity, of whom, nevertheless, some displayed great aptitude for intellectual cultivation, and attained a high degree of general civilization. It formed, at one time, an ingredient in the social system of all modern states, which, however, did not find it incompatible with a progressive career, and the last traces of slavery, in the mitigated form of serfdom, are but now disappearing from Europe. If slavery was not inconsistent with progressive civilization among the ancient Greeks, Romans, and Hebrews—if mediæval Europe contrived to work itself free from this vicious element of its social constitution, it will perhaps be asked why need we despair of progress for the States of the Confederation. Why are we to suppose that they, under the influence of the same causes which operated in ancient and mediæval society, should not, in the same gradual fashion, emáncipate their slaves, and ultimately reach the same level of general cultivation which those societies attained? Nay, it is possible there may be those who, while holding slavery to be, as a permanent *status*, noxious, may nevertheless regard it as not incapable of performing an useful function towards a people in a certain stage of their development, as a kind of probationary discipline suited to their preparation for a higher form of civilized existence, and may consider its maintenance in the Southern States at present as defensible upon this ground. Some such notion, it seems to me, is at the bottom of much of the indulgence, and even favour, with which the cause of the South has come to be regarded in this country;* and it is, therefore, worth while to consider how far this view of modern slavery is well-founded.

And here it may be advantageous to bear in mind the caution of Tocqueville. "When I compare the Greek and Roman republics with these American States; . . when I remember all the attempts which are made to judge the modern republics by the assistance of those of antiquity, and to infer what will happen in our time from what took place two thousand years ago, I am tempted to burn my books, in order to apply none but novel ideas to so novel a condition of society." The truth is, between slavery, as it existed in classical and mediæval times and the system which now erects itself defiantly in North America, there exist the most deep-reaching distinctions. I will mention three, which as it seems to me, are in themselves sufficient to take the case of modern slavery entirely out of the

* "Slavery," says a writer in the *Saturday Review*, "appears to die away, or at least its most horrible incidents disappear in proportion as the community in which it exists becomes older, more wealthy, and therefore more dense. . . . The best chance for the alleviation of the slave's condition lies in the increased wealth and prosperity of the South. In other words, its freedom to develop its own resources, without foreign intervention, is the slave's best hope. And it is agreed on all hands that a modified and alleviated slavery is a transitional state in which it is very difficult for the slave-owners long to halt."—*Nov. 2nd*, 1861.

scope of the analogies furnished by the former experience of mankind.

In the first place, there is the vital fact—the difference in race and colour between modern slaves and
their masters—a difference which had nothing corresponding to it in the slavery of former times.
The consequences flowing from this fact cannot be
better stated than in the language of Tocqueville.
" The slave, amongst the ancients, belonged to the
same race as his master, and he was often the superior
of the two in education and instruction.   Freedom
was the only distinction between them ; and when
freedom was conferred, they were easily confounded
together. . . . The greatest difficulty of antiquity
[in the way of abolition] was that of altering the
law ; amongst the moderns it is that of altering the
manners ; and, as far as we are concerned, the real
obstacles begin where those of the ancients left off.
This arises from the circumstance that, amongst the
moderns, the abstract and transient fact of slavery
is fatally united to the physical and permanent fact
of colour.   The tradition of slavery dishonours the
race, and the peculiarity of the race perpetuates the
tradition of slavery.   No African has ever voluntarily emigrated to the shores of the New World ;
whence it must be inferred, that all the blacks who
are now to be found in that hemisphere are either
slaves or freed-men.   Thus the negro transmits the

external mark of his ignominy to all his descendants. The law may cancel servitude, God alone can obliterate its brand.

" The modern slave differs from his master not only in his condition, but in his origin. You may set the negro free, but you cannot make him otherwise than an alien to the European. Nor is this all: we scarcely acknowledge the common features of mankind in this child of debasement whom slavery has brought amongst us. His physiognomy is to our eyes hideous, his understanding weak, his tastes low ; and we are almost inclined to look upon him as a being intermediate between man and the brutes. The moderns, then, after they have abolished slavery, have three prejudices to contend against, which are less easy to attack, and far less easy to conquer, than the mere fact of servitude : the prejudice of the master, the prejudice of race, and the prejudice of colour."*

* *Democracy in America*, vol. ii. pp. 215–217. It is only in the United States that the antipathy arising from colour appears to have come into play in its full force. In other slave countries the element of purely white blood in the population has been too small to determine absolutely public feeling. Thus in Brazil the number of pure whites is less than one eighth of the whole population. Accordingly "au Brazil ce n'est pas la couleur qui fait la honte, c'est la servitude." The result is that the facilities for emancipation are far greater here than in the slaveholding states of North America.— See *Revue des Deux Mondes*, 15 Juillet, 1862, pp. 386–388.

But, secondly, the immense development of international commerce in modern times furnishes another
distinction between ancient and modern slavery,
which very intimately affects the question we are
discussing.

So long as each nation was in the main dependent
on the industry of its own members for the supply
of its wants, it is obvious that a strong motive
would be present for the cultivation of the intelligence, and the improvement of the condition, of the
industrial classes. The commodities which minister
to comfort and luxury cannot be produced without
skilled labour, and skilled labour implies a certain
degree of mental cultivation, and a certain progress
in social respect. To attain success in the more
difficult industrial arts, the workman must respect
his vocation, must take an interest in his task ;
habits of care, deliberation, forethought must be
acquired ; in short, there must be such a general
awakening of the faculties, intellectual and moral,
as, by leading men to a knowledge of their rights
and of the means of enforcing them, inevitably
disqualifies them for the servile condition.* Now,
this was the position in which the slave-master
found himself in the ancient world. He was, in

* "Whenever a slave is made a mechanic, he is more than half
freed, and soon becomes, as we too well know, and all history attests,
with rare exceptions, the most corrupt and turbulent of his class."
—De Bow's *Industrial Resources*, vol. iii., p. 34.

the main, dependent on the skill of his slaves for obtaining whatever he required. He was, therefore, naturally led to cultivate the faculties of his slaves, and by consequence to promote generally the improvement of their condition. *His* progress in the enjoyment of the material advantages of civilization depended directly upon *their* progress in knowledge and social consideration. Accordingly the education of slaves was never prohibited in the ancient Roman world, and, in point of fact, no small number of them enjoyed the advantage of a high cultivation. " The youths of promising genius," says Gibbon, " were instructed in the arts and sciences, and almost every profession, liberal and mechanical, might be found in the household of an opulent senator." The industrial necessities of Roman society (and the same was true of society in the middle ages) in this way provided for the education of at least a large proportion of the slave population; and education, accompanied as it was by a general elevation of their condition, led, by a natural and almost inevitable tendency, to emancipation.*

---

* " The only fair analogy," says Mr. Congreve, " to the slavery of Greece and Rome is to be found in that which is still prevalent in Asia, where the evils of West Indian or American slavery are wholly unknown, and the relation of master and slave is accepted by both, as being, in Aristotle's words, at once light and for the common interest." On the other hand, " if we seek for an analogy in ancient times to modern slavery," we may find one in " the

But in the position of slavery in North America there is nothing which corresponds to this. Owing to the vast development in modern times of international trade, modern slaveholders are rendered independent of the skill, and therefore of the intelligence and social improvement, of their slave population. They have only need to find a commodity which is capable of being produced by crude labour, and at the same time in large demand in the markets of the world; and by applying their slaves to the production of this, they may, through an exchange with other countries, make it the means of procuring for themselves whatever they require. Cotton and sugar, for example, are commodities which fulfil these conditions: they may be raised by crude labour, and they are in large demand throughout the world. Accordingly Alabama and Louisiana have only to employ their slaves in raising these products, and they are enabled through their means to command the industrial resources of all commercial nations. With-

latifundia of the Roman nobles, or what may be termed the corn plantations of Sicily. The population there was slave, and there was no check to the misuse of their power by the agents or masters who superintended them. And there was no intercourse, no sense of connexion to soften the inherent hardships of their condition. They revolted once and again, and there was danger lest their revolt should spread, lest throughout the Roman world the slave population should feel that it had a common cause."—Congreve's *Politics of Aristotle*, p. 496.

out cultivating one of the arts or refinements of civilization, they can possess themselves of all its material comforts. Without employing an artisan, a manufacturer, a skilled labourer of any sort, they can secure the products of the highest manufacturing and mechanical skill. " In one way or other," says Mr. Helper,* putting the point strikingly, though from the protectionist point of view, " we are more or less subservient to the North every day of our lives. In infancy we are swaddled in Northern muslin ; in childhood we are humoured with Northern gew-gaws ; in youth we are instructed out of Northern books ; at the age of maturity we sow our ' wild oats' on Northern soil ; . . . in the decline of life we remedy our eyesight with Northern spectacles, and support our infirmities with Northern canes ; in old age we are drugged with Northern physic ; and, finally, when we die, our inanimate bodies, shrouded in Northern cambric, are stretched upon the bier, borne to the grave in a Northern carriage, entombed with a Northern spade, and memorized with a Northern slab !" Yet all these products of manufacturing and mechanical skill the States which consume them are able to command through the medium of a commodity which is raised by the crudest servile labour. The resources of slavery have in this

* *Impending Crisis*, p. 27.

way been indefinitely increased in modern times.
Its capabilities have been multiplied, and, without
submitting to the slightest alleviation of its harshest features, it can adapt itself to all the varying
wants of human society.

But the consequences of the increased capabilities
of slavery do not end in merely negative results.
Whatever inducements may exist *for* cultivating
the intelligence of slaves, there are always very
weighty reasons *against* conferring this boon. Accordingly, the former not coming into play in
modern times, the latter have operated with unre-
stricted force. The merest rudiments of learning
are now rigorously proscribed for the negroes in
the Slave States of North America ; and the
prohibition is enforced, both in the persons of the
teachers and the taught, with penalties of extraordinary severity.*   " The only means by which the

* The following are some extracts from the laws of some of the
Southern States upon this subject. In South Carolina an act was
passed in 1834, which provides as follows :—" If any person shall
hereafter teach any slave to read or write, or shall aid in assisting
any slave to read or write, or cause or procure any slave to be
taught to read or write, such person, if a free white person, upon
conviction thereof, shall for every such offence against this act be
fined not exceeding one hundred dollars, and imprisoned not more
than six months ; or if a free person of colour, shall be whipped
not exceeding fifty lashes, and fined not exceeding fifty dollars ;
and if a slave, shall be whipped, not exceeding fifty lashes ; and
if any free person of colour or a slave shall keep any such school

ancients maintained slavery were fetters and death ;
the Americans of the South of the Union have discovered more intellectual securities for the duration
of their power.   They have employed their despotism and their violence against the human mind.   In
antiquity, precautions were taken to prevent the
slave from breaking his chains ; at the present day
measures are adopted to deprive him even of the
desire of freedom.   The ancients kept the bodies of
their slaves in bondage, but they placed no restraint
upon the mind and no check upon education ; and
they acted consistently with their established principle, since a natural termination of slavery then
existed, and one day or other the slave might be set

or other place of instruction for teaching any slave or free person of
colour to read or write, such person shall be liable to the same fine,
imprisonment and corporal punishment as are by this act imposed
and inflicted on free persons of colour and slaves for teaching slaves
to read or write."   In Virginia, according to the code of 1849,
" every assemblage of negroes for the purpose of instruction in reading or writing shall be an unlawful assembly.   Any justice may
issue his warrant to any officer or other person, requiring him to
enter any place where such assemblage may be, and seize any negro
therein ; and he or any other justice may order such negro to be
punished with stripes."   " If a white person assemble with negroes
for the purpose of instructing them to read or write, he shall be
confined to jail not exceeding six months, and fined not exceeding
one hundred dollars."   In Georgia in 1829 it was enacted :—" If
any slave, negro, or free person of colour, or any white person, shall
teach any other slave, negro, or free person of colour to read or
write either written or printed characters, the said free person of

free, and become the equal of his master. But the
Americans of the South, who do not admit that the
negroes can ever be commingled with themselves,
have forbidden them to be taught to read and write
under severe penalties; and as they will not raise
them to their own level, they sink them as nearly as
possible to that of the brutes."*   The education of
slaves amongst the ancients prepared the way for
emancipation.   The prohibition of the education of
slaves amongst the moderns has naturally suggested
the policy of holding them in perpetual bondage;
and laws and manners have conspired to interpose
obstacles all but insuperable in the way of manumission.†   Thus the modern slave is cut off from

colour or slave shall be punished by fine and whipping, or fine or
whipping at the discretion of the court ; and if a white person so
offending, he, she, or they shall be punished with fine not exceeding
five hundred dollars, and imprisonment in the common jail, at the
discretion of the court." By the act of Assembly of Louisiana,
passed in March, 1830, " all persons who shall teach or cause to be
taught any slave in this state to read or write shall, on conviction
thereof, &c., be imprisoned not less than one or more than twelve
months." And in Alabama, "any person who shall attempt to
teach any free person of colour or slave to spell, read or write, shall
upon conviction, &c., be fined in a sum not less than 250 dollars
nor more than 500 dollars."

* *Democracy in America*, vol. ii. p. 246, 247.

† " In this respect also the condition of Brazil is more hopeful than
that of the Confederate States. " En effet, la loi brésilienne, moins
terrible que les codes noirs des états confédérés, n'enferme pas l'esclave dans un infranchissable cercle de servitude: elle ne l'empêche

the one great allevation of his lot—the hope of freedom.*

But there is yet another distinction between the slavery of modern times and slavery as it was known among the progressive communities of former ages, which deserves to be noticed—I mean the place which the slave trade fills in the organization of modern slavery. Trading in slaves was doubtless practised by the ancients, and with sufficient barbarity. But we look in vain in the records of antiquity for a traffic which in extent, in systematic character, and above all, in the function discharged by it as the common support of countries breeding

---

pas de se racheter par son travail et de secouer la poussière de ses habits pour s'asseoir à côté des hommes libres.   Bien plus, elle lui donne aussi la permission tacite de s'instruire, s'il en trouve le temps et le courage ; elle l'autorise à fortifier son intelligence en vue d'une libération possible, et ne condamne pas à la prison le blanc charitable qui lui enseigne l'art diabolique de la lecture."—*Revue des Deux Mondes,* 15 *Juillet,* 1862.

* " In Aristotle himself we find suggested one of the greatest alleviations of which slavery is susceptible. There ought to be held out to the slave, he says, the hope of liberty as the reward of his service. Thus, by a gradual infiltration, the slave population might pass into the free. It did so at Rome through the intermediate stage of freedom ; and the position of freed-men at Rome in the later republic, and even more under the empire, was such that the prospect of reaching it must have been a great inducement to the slaves to acquiesce in their present lot; and it would be an inducement which would have most weight with the highest class of slaves."—Congreve's *Politics of Aristotle,* p. 497.

and consuming human labour, which can with justice be regarded as the analogue of the modern
slave trade—of that organized system which has
been carried on between Guinea and the coast of
America, or of that between Virginia, the Guinea of
the New World, and the slave-consuming states of
the South and West.* This peculiar outgrowth
of the institution forms a characteristic feature in
modern slavery, and its consequences, in connexion
with the question which we are considering, are of a
very important kind.

The effects of the slave trade in aggravating a
hundredfold all the evils of servitude have often
been described. African slave-hunts, the horrors
of the middle passage, the misery of unhappy barbarians, accustomed to the wild freedom of their
native land, caught up and hurried away to a remote
continent, and compelled to toil for the rest of their
days under the whip of an alien taskmaster, have
often been dwelt upon. So, also, the story of human
beings, reared amidst the softening influences of civilization, who, so soon as they arrive at the maturity
of their physical power, are, like so many cattle,
shipped off to a distant region of tropical heat there

* M. Dureau de la Malle, in a critical examination of the loose
and rhetorical statements of ancient authors and their modern
critics, has dispelled much misconception respecting the extent of
the ancient commerce in slaves. See his *Econòmie Politique des
Romains*, tom. i., pp. 246–269.

to be worked to death—of husbands separated from their wives, children from their parents, brothers and sisters from each other—of exposure on the auction-block and transfer to new masters and strange climates—all this happening not to heathen savages, but to men and women capable of affection and friendship, and sensible to moral suffering,—this story, I say, is familiar to us all ; but my object at present is to direct attention, not so much to the barbarous inhumanity of the slave trade, whether foreign or domestic, as to what has not been so often noticed—the mode in which it operates in giving increased coherence and stability to the system of which it is a part. Now, it does this in two ways, by bringing the resources of salubrious countries to supplement the waste of human life in torrid regions ; and, secondly, by providing a new source of profit for slaveholders, which enables them to keep up the institution when, in the absence of this resource, it would become unprofitable and disappear.

While countries depended for the supply of servile labour upon the natural increase of their own slave population, there existed an obvious limit to the range of the system and to the hardships it was capable of inflicting. Where the character of the climate, or the nature of the work to be done, was such as to be seriously prejudicial to human life,

slavery, if recruited from within, could only exist
through great attention given to the physical requirements of the slaves.   Without this, it must
have become extinct by the destruction of its victims.
But, a commerce in slaves once established, these
natural restraints upon the fullest development of
slavery are effectually removed.   The rice-grounds
of Georgia or the swamps of the Mississippi may be
fatally injurious to the human constitution; but the
waste of human life, which the cultivation of these
districts necessitates, is not so great that it cannot be
repaired from the teeming preserves of Virginia and
Kentucky.   Considerations of economy, moreover,
which, under a natural system, afford some security
for humane treatment by identifying the master's
interest with the slave's preservation, when once
trading in slaves is practised, become reasons for
racking to the uttermost the toil of the slave; for,
when his place can at once be supplied from foreign
preserves, the duration of his life becomes a matter
of less moment than its productiveness while it lasts.
It is accordingly a maxim of slave management, in
slave-importing countries, that the most effective
economy is that which takes out of the human
chattel in the shortest space of time the utmost
amount of exertion it is capable of putting forth.
" It is in tropical culture, where annual profits often
equal the whole capital of plantations, that negro

life is most recklessly sacrificed. It is the agriculture of the West Indies, which has been for centuries
prolific of fabulous wealth, which has engulfed millions of the African race. It is in Cuba, at this
day, whose revenues are reckoned by millions, and
whose planters are princes, that we see, in the
servile class, the coarsest fare, the most exhausting
and unremitting toil, and even the absolute destruction of a portion of its numbers every year, by
the slow torture of overwork and insufficient sleep
and rest. In our own country, is it in Maryland
and Virginia that slaves fare the worst, or is it in
the sugar regions of Louisiana and Texas, where
the scale of profits suggests the calculation of using
them up in a given number of years as a matter of
economy? Is it not notorious, that the states upon
the Gulf of Mexico, in which forced labour is most
productive to those who own it, are made use of by
the northern slave states, not merely as markets in
which to dispose of slaves as a matter of profit, but
as a Botany Bay, furnished to their hands, to which
their slaves are sent by way of punishment?"* The
slave trade thus affords the means of extending the
institution in its harshest form to countries in which
without this support, it either could not have been
permanently maintained at all, or only in a very
mitigated form, sustaining the waste of human life

* *Progress of Slavery*, pp. 132, 133.

in tropical regions from the hardier and healthier populations of barbarous countries and of temperate climes.*

But the benefits of commerce are reciprocal, and if slavery receives a new impulse from the slave trade in the warm regions of the South, it acquires increased stability in more temperate countries through the same cause.   We have already seen the tendency of slave labour to exhaust the soil, and the rapidity with which this process proceeds, reducing to the condition of wilderness districts which fifty years before were yet untouched by the hand of cultivation.   Now, this would seem to promise that the reign of slavery, if ruinous, should at least be brief, and we might expect that, when the soil had been robbed of its fertility, the destroyer would retire from the region which he had rendered desolate. And such would be the fate of slavery, were it depending exclusively on the soil for its support ; but, when trading in human beings is once introduced, a new source of profit is developed for the system, which renders it in a great degree independent of the resources of the soil.   It is this, the

* In this adaptation the slaveholders trace the finger of God. The Professor of Agricultural Chemistry in the University of Georgia remarks on the "providential" proportion between the untilled lands of the South, and the "unemployed power of human muscles in Africa:"—"I trace," he exclaims, "the growing demand for negro muscles, bones, and brains to the good providence of God."

profit developed by trading in slaves, and this alone,
which has enabled slavery in the older slave states
of North America to survive the consequences of its
own ravages.*   In Maryland and Virginia, perhaps
also in the Carolinas and Georgia, free institutions
would long since have taken the place of slavery,
were it not that just as the crisis of the system had
arrived, the domestic slave trade opened a door of
escape from a position which had become untenable.
The conjuncture was peculiar, and would doubtless
by Southern theologians be called providential. The
progress of devastation had reached the point at
which slave cultivation could no longer sustain
itself—the contingency predicted by Roanoke,
when, instead of the slave running away from
his master, the master should run away from his
slave.   A considerable emigration of planters had
actually taken place, and the deserted fields were
already receiving a new race of settlers from the
regions of freedom.†   The long night of slavery
seemed to be passing away, and the dawn of a

* " Were it not for the Southern demand for the surplus labourers
of Kentucky, Maryland and Virginia, the institution of slavery could
not exist many years in these states ; for if no check were put to
the natural increase of the negroes, their numbers would depress
the value of property in the same manner as the poor-rates do in
England."—Russell's *North America*, p. 156.

† See APPENDIX F.

brighter day to have arrived,* when suddenly the auspicious movement was arrested. A vast extension of the territory of the United States, opening new soils to Southern enterprise, exactly coincided with the prohibition of the external slave trade, and both fell in with the crisis in the older states. The result was a sudden and remarkable rise in the price of slaves. The problem of the planter's position was at once solved, and the domestic slave trade com-

* The following comment of Mr. De Bow upon the course of events referred to in the text sets in a striking light the point of view from which the whole question is regarded by the Southern slaveholder. " As the lands become more and more exhausted in the older and more northern parts of the slaveholding districts, slave labour will become less and less valuable ; it will therefore press south and southwest, and their places will be filled by white labourers, thus insensibly narrowing the limits of the slave district, until the whole of this population will be crowded into a comparatively small area in the extreme South. *This result of all others should be avoided if possible by the slaveholders.*" . . . . " As the country fills up with a more crowded population in the non-slaveholding states, free labour by degrees will press upon the northern limits of the slaveholding states, and gain a footing within its borders. *This will be a different race from the Southern non-slaveholder ; these will be people who are inured to habits of industry and enterprise; they will bring the means to purchase the worn-out fields, and they will go to work to restore them to fertility by their own industry and skill ; they will not use slave labour, and all the land thus purchased and occupied will be so much taken from the occupation of slaves ;* for it may be safely assumed that when the slaves have once progressed South, they will never return to the North again."—De Bow's *Industrial Resources, &c.* vol. ii., p. 120.

menced. Slavery had robbed Virginia of the best riches of her soil, but she still had a noble climate— a climate which would fit her admirably for being the breeding place of the South. A division of labour between the old and the new states took place. In the former the soil was extensively exhausted, but the climate was salubrious ; in the latter the climate was unfavourable to human life spent in severe toil, but the soil was teeming with riches. The old states, therefore, undertook the part of breeding and rearing slaves till they attained to physical vigour, and the new that of using up in the development of their virgin resources the physical vigour which had been thus obtained.

The charge of breeding slaves for the market is one which the citizens of Virginia, more especially when resident in Europe, are apt indignantly to deny ;* and, in a certain sense, the denial may not be wholly destitute of foundation. It is perhaps true that in no particular instance is a slave brought into the world for the purpose, distinctly conceived

---

* And there are people here who would have us take such denials as conclusive on the question. For such the following anecdote, told by Mr. Olmsted, may have its use :—" While calling on a gentleman occupying an honourable official position at Richmond, I noticed upon his table a copy of Professor Johnson's *Agricultural Tour in the United States*. Referring to a paragraph in it, where some statistics of the value of the slaves raised and annually exported from Virginia were given, I asked if he knew how these

beforehand, of being sold to the South.   Neverthe-.
less it is absolutely certain that the whole business
of raising slaves in the Border states is carried on
with reference to their price, and that the price of
slaves in the Border states is determined by the
demand for them in the Southern markets.   " Nowhere," said Henry Clay, " in the farming portion of the United States would slave labour
be generally employed, if the proprietors were
not tempted to raise slaves by the high price
of the Southern markets which keeps it up in their
own."   Of the truth of this remark an illustration
was afforded in 1829, when a law having been
passed by the state legislature of Louisiana inter-
posing obstacles to the introduction of slaves into
that state, within two hours after this was known
the price of slaves on the breeding grounds
of the North fell 25 per cent.*   Again, at a later
epoch, when the efforts of the Border slaveholders
to establish slavery in California had failed, what

had been obtained, and whether they were reliable.   ' No,' he
replied ; ' I don't know anything about it ; but if they are anything
unfavourable to the institution of slavery, you may be sure they are
false.'   This is but an illustration, in extreme, of the manner in
which I find a desire to obtain more correct and *definite* information,
on the subject of slavery, is usually met, by gentlemen otherwise of
enlarged mind and generous qualities."—*Seaboard Slave States,* p. 56.

  * This fact was stated by Judge Upshur in the Convention of
Virginia.

was the comment on this failure made by a candidate for the governorship of Virginia,* then on an electioneering tour through the state ?—that, but for this, the price of an able-bodied negro would have risen to 5,000 dollars—in other words, that the closing of the Californian mines to slave labour represented a loss to that state of 4,000 dollars per head on every first class Virginian slave.   Such is the aspect under which the extension of the domain of slavery is regarded in Virginia—a point of view somewhat hard to reconcile with the air of injured virtue assumed by the 'Old Dominion' in its repudiation of the internal slave trade.†

Indeed it would be futile to deny—nor is it denied by the more outspoken of the Southern politicians‡—that the markets of the South form the

* Mr. Wise, who was subsequently elected.

† " Very revolting exhibitions are constantly taking place here [Richmond] in selling negroes for the South.   With the exception of New Orleans, this is the greatest market for slaves in the United States.   The numerous offices of agents or dealers lead us to reflect that there must be much laceration of feelings in the way in which families are broken up and separated.   So long as slavery exists in Virginia, the exportation of the natural increase of the negroes will take place ; for, were it prohibited, the institution would be soon uprooted.   As an example of the large inland traffic in slaves, it may be mentioned that one of the engineers on the North Carolina railroad stated, that on one occasion he had taken 600 slaves south in one train."—Russell's *North America*, p. 157.

‡ " It is not the *domestic* demand for slave labour which has ever

main support of slavery in the older Slave States. Of the extent to which the trade is carried, and the important interests depending on it, some notion may be formed from its effects on the census. For the purpose of exhibiting these I shall compare the population returns of the three principal Border states,—Virginia, Maryland and Kentucky,—with those of three working states in the extreme south-west,—Arkansas, Mississippi, and Louisiana.

PER CENTAGE INCREASE OF POPULATION IN THE DECADE ENDING 1850.

	Whites.	Slaves.
Virginia	20·77	5·21
Maryland	31·34	0·70
Kentucky	28·99	15·75
Arkansas	110·16	136·26
Mississippi	65·13	58·74
Louisiana	61·23	45·32

It will be seen from the above that, while in the former group of states the white population has progressed with, on the whole, tolerable regularity,

graduated their price here, but the *foreign* demand. Their labour is infinitely more productive on the sugar, and rice, and cotton plant-ations of the South and West, than it can ever be rendered in Virginia, and consequently their value here must very much depend on the demand there. No man could, from mere pecuniary consi-derations, afford to give five hundred dollars for a slave, to be worked on an ordinary Virginia plantation."—Mr. Brodnax in the Virginia Legislature.

the slave population has, in two of them, scarcely advanced at all, and in the third at a rate far short of that attained by the white population. On the other hand, in the latter group—a group composed of states in which it is perfectly notorious that plantation labour is far severer than in the former —the slave population has in one instance increased with much greater rapidity than the whites, and in another at almost the same rate. Even in Louisiana the increase of the slave population has not fallen greatly behind that of the whites, although the circumstances of that state might well lead us to expect this result, being, as it is, the seat of a great commercial city with a large and rapidly growing white population, and its prevailing industry—the cultivation of sugar—being, as is well known, enormously destructive of slave life.

But we may bring out the same fact by another and still more striking comparison. From a series of tables,* in which the inhabitants, free and slave, are classed according to their ages, I have constructed the following statement :—

* pp. xlii.–xliv.

RATIO OF WHITE TO SLAVE POPULATION (MALE)—100 BEING TAKEN TO REPRESENT THE FORMER.

	Between the ages of 1 and 5 years.		Between the ages of 10 and 15 years.		Gain per cent. of slave on white population.	Loss per cent. of slave in relation to white population.	Between the ages of 10 and 15 years.		Between the ages of 20 and 30 years.		Gain per cent. of slave on white population.	Loss per cent. of slave in relation to white population.
	White.	Slave.	White.	Slave.			White.	Slave.	White.	Slave.		
Virginia	100	56	100	56	—	—	100	56	100	52	—	7.1
Maryland	100	24	100	27	12.5	—	100	27	100	20	—	26.
Kentucky	100	28	100	30	7.1	—	100	30	100	27	—	10.
Arkansas	100	27	100	28	3.6	—	100	28	100	32	14.3	—
Mississippi	100	103	100	98	—	4.8	100	98	100	110	12.2	—
Louisiana	100	92	100	94	2.1	—	100	94	100	91	—	3.

The significance of these proportions cannot easily be mistaken. Take, for example, Virginia. It appears that up to fifteen years of age the two populations maintain exactly their relative position, but after twenty—after the period of physical maturity has been reached—after the full-grown slave has been exported—the slave population of a sudden drops. The case of Maryland is still more striking. The slave population here gains rapidly upon the white between the ages of five and fifteen, while after twenty it undergoes an immense reduction. In Kentucky the result is perfectly analogous. Compare this with the progress of the population in the three slave-consuming states in the South-West. The ratio of growth is here substantially reversed. In Arkansas and Mississippi the relative position of the two races up to the age of fifteen remains almost unchanged, but no sooner do we reach the age of twenty, than in those states of severe plantation labour the slave population exhibits, in relation to the whites, a large increase. Louisiana, indeed, in this, as in the former example, seems at first glance to weaken the argument; but in fact it strengthens it. The adult slave population, instead of gaining on the whites, slightly loses ground. But what does this prove? Only that to which every traveller in Louisiana testifies—the frightful destruction of slave life which

cane-crushing on the sugar plantations entails. Yet,
notwithstanding the inroads made on the slave population by this cause, and notwithstanding the
support given to the whites by the rapid growth
of New Orleans, the adult slave population in this
state almost—such is the activity of the slave dealer
—maintains its relative position.   Now these are
facts which no mere migration of population will
account for.   If a planter, with his family and its
following of slaves, removed from Virginia to Arkansas, the young and old of both races would go
together, and the proportion between the two populations would remain unchanged.   But where slave
dealing prevails in connexion with slave-breeding,
this cannot happen.   The slave is sold off as he
arrives at his maturity, and thus at this point the
proportion between the slave and free population
is disturbed.   The former falls behind ; the latter
gains.   In a word, that state of things is realized
which, we find from the census returns, actually
exists in the slave-breeding states of the South.*

* " A gentleman, with whom I was conversing on the subject of
the cost of slave labour, in answer to an inquiry—what proportion
of all the stock of slaves of an old plantation might be reckoned
upon to do full work ?—answered, that he owned ninety-six
negroes; of these, only thirty-five were field hands, the rest being
either too young or too old for hard work.   He reckoned his whole
force as only equal to twenty-one strong men, or *prime* field-
hands.'   But this proportion was somewhat smaller than usual, he

It is plain that nothing less than a regular and systematic traffic in human beings could produce such results as these in the vital statistics of a nation. As for the probable extent of this traffic, it would not be difficult to deduce this approximately from data furnished by the census; but it is unnecessary: the task has already been performed by unquestionably competent hands. In 1830 Professor Dew* estimated the trade of Virginia alone at an annual export of 6,000 slaves. But we have a later estimate from a still higher authority. In 1857 the subject of the domestic slave trade was referred to a special committee of the House of Representatives of South Carolina with a view to report upon its pro-

added, 'because his women were uncommonly good breeders; he did not suppose there was a lot of women anywhere that bred faster than his; he never heard of babies coming so fast as they did on his plantation; it was perfectly surprising; and every one of them, in his estimation, was worth two hundred dollars, as negroes were selling now, the moment it drew breath.'

" I asked what he thought might be the usual proportion of workers to slaves, supported on plantations, throughout the South. On the large cotton and sugar plantations of the more Southern States, it was very high, he replied; because their hands were nearly all bought and *picked for work;* he supposed, on these, it would be about one-half; but, on any old plantation, where the stock of slaves had been an inheritance, and none had been bought or sold, he thought the working force would rarely be more than one-third, at most, of the whole number."—*Seaboard Slave States,* pp. 57, 58.

* At one time President of William and Mary College, Williams-

bable extent, and the conclusion arrived at by this committee* was that for the decade of 1840 to 1850 the number of slaves exported from the Border states (of which nearly a half came from Virginia) was not less than 235,000. This will give an annual export of 23,500 slaves ; and, taking these at an average value of 700 dollars—which, considering that the bulk of them were slaves in the prime of life, would probably not be an over-estimate —we arrive at a sum of 16,450,000 dollars equivalent to about £3,290,000 sterling, as the annual value of the domestic slave trade. So extensive are the interests involved in this accursed traffic.

But it will here perhaps occur to the reader that this commerce may have its hopeful side—that the constant and copious drain of slaves of which we have here the proof, may, through the exhaustion of the negro population, issue ultimately in the extinction of slavery in the states from which it proceeds.

burgh. Of his treatise on slavery, in which this estimate occurs, Mr. De Bow says that " it entitles him to the lasting gratitude of the South ;" and Chancellor Harper of South Carolina characterizes the same work as "perhaps the most profound, original, and truly philosophical treatise which has appeared within the time of my recollection."

* A conclusion, it may here be remarked, which was not likely to be an over-estimate, since the purpose with which the Carolinian Committee was appointed was to establish a case for reopening the African slave trade on the ground of the insufficiency of the internal supply.

This view of the case is indeed not unfamiliar to those who in America have speculated upon this subject, whether they have been the opponents or the supporters of slavery :—by the former it has been put forward as a ground for tolerating, by the latter as one for restraining, the traffic.   On the occasion, for example, of the annexation of Texas, it was an argument employed by those who sought to reconcile the Northern states to this measure, that, through the new outlet which would thus be provided for slaves, a prospect would be opened of extinguishing slavery in the older states.*   On the other hand, the possibility of this consummation has aroused the apprehensions of the South ; and the more ardent apostles of slavery have denounced the practice of "emptying" the slaves of the Border States on the more Southern countries, as savouring of disloyalty to the institution,—sacrificing —so the point has been put—to mere pecuniary considerations the vital interests of a great system.†   In truth, however, these hopes and fears are alike without foundation.   A slave trade may, indeed,—as the figures which I have quoted prove that in point of fact it does—exercise a retarding influence on the growth of the slave population in the exporting states, and it is conceivable that it might even for a time

* Letter of the Hon. Robert J. Walker.
† See Spratt's *Philosophy of Secession.* (APPENDIX.)

effect a reduction of its numbers ; but to suppose
that a cause, which renders human beings more
valuable, should in the long run have the effect of
exhausting the supply, would be to show but a weak
faith in the reproductive powers of the human race,
and would involve assumptions which have been
amply refuted by the experience of this very trade.

Far from conducing in the slightest degree to the
decline of slavery in the older states, the inter-state
traffic has tended directly to establish it, and the
slave population of those states has increased steadily,
though slowly, under the drain.   A remarkable
proof of this position has been furnished by the
State of Delaware—the only one of the Border
states in which the sale or removal of slaves is
prohibited by law, and also the only one in which
slavery shows any tendency to expire.   A similar
lesson is taught by the history of Virginia.   Between
1830 and 1840 the number of slaves in that state
underwent an actual diminution ; but in 1844 came
the annexation of Texas, followed by an increased
demand for slaves for the South ; and in 1850 the
slave population in Virginia was found to have
increased.   The explanation of this is, of course, perfectly simple.   Slaves in the older states being of
little value for agricultural purposes, there is no
inducement to encourage their increase so long as
agriculture is the sole purpose to which they can be

turned ; but with the increase of the slave trade, their value increases, and they are, therefore, raised in greater numbers.   So that, although the slave trade restrains the growth of the negro population in the exporting states, it yet gives to the system in those very states a deeper root and firmer hold.   It invigorates the plant by pruning it.   The phenomenon need surprise no one who has attended to the ordinary facts of emigrating countries.   The immense emigration from the United Kingdom has produced scarcely a perceptible effect on its population ; and the experience of Spain and Portugal, when Spain and Portugal were colonizing countries, and that of Germany at the present day, bear testimony to the same fact—the power of population, so long as the means of subsistence do not fail, to sustain any practicable drain.   But an illustration still more apposite to our present purpose is furnished by cattle breeding.   It has never been found that the opening of new markets for cattle has any tendency to exhaust the breed in the countries which raise them ; and, so long as human beings are subjected to precisely the same influences as cattle, it is idle to expect a different result.   In each case the power of multiplication is the same, and where the same inducement is offered, a corresponding result may be expected to follow.

CHAPTER V.

INTERNAL DEVELOPMENT OF SLAVE SOCIETIES.

IT may be well here to trace briefly the salient
features of the system which in the previous chapter it has been attempted to describe. A race superior to another in power and civilization holds that
other in bondage, compelling it to work for its
profit. The enslaved race, separated broadly from
the dominant one in its leading physical and moral
attributes, is further distinguished from it by the
indelible mark of colour, which prevents the growth
of mutual sympathy and transmits to posterity the
brand of its disgrace. Kept in compulsory ignorance
and deprived of all motive for intelligent exertion,
this people can supply to its masters only the
crudest form of manual labour. It is thus rendered
unfit for every branch of industry which requires,
in any but the lowest forms, the exercise of care, intelligence, or skill, and is virtually restricted to the
pursuit of agriculture. In agriculture it can only
be turned to profitable account under certain special
conditions—in raising crops of a peculiar kind and
upon soils of more than average fertility; while
these by its thriftless methods it tends constantly

to exhaust.   The labour of the enslaved race is thus in practice confined to the production of a few leading staples ; but, through the medium of foreign trade, these few commodities become the means of furnishing its masters with all the conveniences and comforts of life—the product of intelligence and skill in countries where labour is free.   Further, it was seen that the defects of servile labour are best neutralized, and such advantages as it possesses best turned to account, where the scale of the operations is large,—a circumstance, which by placing a premium on the employment of large capitals, has gradually led to the accumulation of the whole wealth of the country in the hands of a small number of persons.   Four million slaves have thus come into the possession of masters less than one-tenth of their number, by whom they are held as chattel property ; while the rest of the dominant race, almost equalling the slaveholders and their slaves together, squat over the vast area which slave labour is too unskilful to cultivate, where, by hunting and fishing, by plunder or by lawless adventure, they eke out a precarious livelihood.   Three leading elements are thus presented by the economy of slave states—a few planters cultivating the richest soils, a multitude of slaves toiling for their profit, the bulk of the white population dispersed in a semi-savage condition over a vast territory.   In course of time the system begins to bear its fruit. The more fertile soils of the country, tasked again and again to render the same products, at length become exhausted, and refuse any longer to yield up their riches to servile hands ; but there are new soils within reach which the plough has not yet touched, regions of high fertility, pre-eminently fitted for the cultivation of slave products, bordering however on the tropics, and unfavourable to human life when engaged in severe toil. At this point a new phase of the system discloses itself. A division of labour takes place. A portion of the slaveholders with their slave bands move forward to occupy the new territory, while the remainder, holding to their old seats, become the breeders of slaves for those who have left them, and take, as their part, the repairing from their more healthy populations the waste of slave life produced by tropical toil. Thus, as the domain of slavery is extended, its organization becomes more complete, and the fate of the slave population more harsh and hopeless. Slavery in its simple and primitive form is developed into slavery supported by a slave trade—into slavery expansive, aggressive, destructive of human life, regardless of human ties,—into slavery in its most dangerous and most atrocious form ; and for the system thus matured a secure basis is afforded by the principles of population. Such is an outline of the economy of society in the Slave States of North America, as I have ventured to describe it; and the condition of facts which it discloses goes far, as it seems to me, to establish the conclusion that it is a structure essentially different from any form of social life which has hitherto been known among progressive communities, and one which, if allowed to proceed in its normal development undisturbed by intervention from without, can only conduct to one issue—an organized barbarism of the most relentless and formidable kind.

But it may be well to pursue this inquiry somewhat further. If the germs of a future civilization are contained in the social system which has been described, in what department of it are they to be found? Among the poor whites? Among the slaves? Among the slave masters?

The poor whites, as has been shown, are the natural growth of the slave system; their existence and character flowing necessarily from two facts— the slaves, who render the capitalists independent of their services,* and the wilderness, the constant feature of slave countries, which enables them to exist without engaging in regular work. There is no capital to support them as hired labourers, and

* "The rich," said General Marion, and in these few words he sketched the whole working of slavery, "have no need of the poor, because they have their own slaves to do their work."

they have the means of subsisting, in a semi-savage condition, without it. Under these circumstances by what steps are they to advance to an improvement of their condition ?

It will perhaps be thought that with a vast unappropriated territory around them the poor whites may be expected in time to become peasant proprietors, and to cultivate the districts which they now merely occupy. This is undoubtedly what would happen with an influx of Northern settlers. It is what has actually happened in certain districts of the South which have derived their population directly from free countries. But the mass of the white people in the Southern States lack for such a lot two indispensable requisites—capital and industry. Had they the latter, they might perhaps in time acquire the former; but regular industry is only known to them as the vocation of slaves, and it is the one fate which above all others they desire to avoid. They will for a time, indeed, when pressed for food, their ordinary resources of hunting or plunder failing them, hire themselves out for occasional services; but, so soon as they have satisfied the immediate need, they hasten to escape from the degradation of industry, and are as eager as Indians to return to their wilds.*

* Olmsted's *Seaboard Slave States*, pp. 348–350, and 505–506; Russell's *North America*, p. 296; and see a paper by Mr. Charles T. James on this subject published in De Bow's *Review*.

Another means of redemption is sometimes imagined for the "mean whites." It is thought that,
with the progress of population in the Slave States,
they will ultimately be forced into competition with
the slaves, and that, this competition once effectually
commenced, the whites once engaged in regular
industry, the superiority of free to servile labour
will become manifest, and will gradually lead to
the displacement of the latter. In this way, it is
anticipated, the problem of abolishing slavery, and
that of elevating the white population, may in the
natural course of events be effectually solved by the
same process. Unfortunately this cheering view is
entirely unsustained by any foundation of fact.
Population in slave communities follows laws of
growth of its own. It increases, it is true, but by
dispersion, not by concentration, and consequently
the pressure upon the poor white, which it is
assumed will force him into competition with the
slave, is never likely to be greater than at the present moment.* In fact it has now in many districts
reached the starvation point, but without producing
any of the effects which are anticipated from it.
But, again, the free labour of the South possesses
none of that superiority to slave labour, which is

---

* "The poor white man will endure the evils of pinching poverty
rather than engage in servile labour under the existing state of
things, even were employment offered him, which is not general."
—Mr. James in *De Bow's Review*.

characteristic of free labour when reared in free communities. This is a distinction which in economic
reasonings on slavery is frequently overlooked,*
but which it is all-important to bear in mind. The
free labourer reared in free communities, energetic,
intelligent, animated by the impulse of acquiring
property, and trained to habits of thrift, is the best
productive agent in the world, and, when brought
into competition with the slave, will, unless under
very exceptional circumstances (such as existed when
the continent was first settled), prove more than a
match for him. But the free labourer of the South,
blighted physically and morally by the presence of
slavery, and trained in habits more suited to savage
than to industrial life, easily succumbs in the competition. In fact the experiment is being constantly
tried in the Southern States, and always with the
same result.† On the relative merits of slave and

* See Appendix G.

† "The poor white people that had to labour for their living,"
said a Southern informant of Mr. Olmsted, "never would work
steadily at any employment. . . . . He had had to hire white
men to help him, but they were poor sticks and would be half the
time drunk, and you never know what to depend upon with them.
One fellow that he had hired, who had agreed to work for him all
through harvest, got him to pay him some wages in advance, (he
said it was to buy him some clothes with, so he could go to meeting,
Sunday, at the Court-House), and went off the next day, right in
the middle of harvest, and he never had seen him since. He had
heard of him—he was on a boat—but he didn't reckon he should
ever get his money again. Of course, he did not see how white

free labour—such free labour as the Slave States can produce—there is but one opinion among the planters. It is universally agreed that the labour of the "mean whites"* is more inefficient, more unreliable, more unmanageable than even the crude efforts of the slaves. If slavery in the South is to be displaced by free industry, it can never be through the competition of such free industry as this.

It does not appear, therefore, in what manner habits of regular industry can ever be acquired by the mass of the population of the Southern States while under a slave *régime*. The demoralization produced by the presence of a degraded class renders the white man at once an unwilling and an inefficient labourer ; and the external incidents of slavery afford him the means of existing without engaging in regular toil. The question has, in truth, passed beyond the region of speculation. For two

labourers were ever going to come into competition with negroes here, at all. You never could depend on white men, and you couldn't *drive* them any ; they wouldn't stand it. Slaves were the only reliable labourers—you could command them and *make* them do what was right."—*Seaboard Slave States*, pp. 83, 84. And it would seem that in factory work the whites have equally failed. " All overseers," says Mr. Gregg in *De Bow's Review*, " who have experience in the matter, give the decided preference to blacks as operatives." See also to the same effect De Bow's *Industrial Resources*, vol. ii., p. 127.

* And it may be added, of such free labourers as will consent to the degradation of living in a slave community. The following incident related by Mr. Olmsted will shew with what free immigrant

hundred years it has been submitted to the proof ;
and the poor whites of the South are as far now
from having made any progress in habits of regular
industry as they were at the commencement of the
period.

The result, then, at which we arrive is, that regular industry is not to be expected from the mass
of the free people of the Southern States while
slavery continues.   Let us for a moment reflect
upon some of the consequences involved in this
single fact.

And, first, it is evident that under these conditions
population in the Slave States must ever remain
sparse ; for density of population is the result of concentrated wealth, and concentrated wealth flows from
the steady pursuit of systematic industry.   What are
the facts ?   Over the whole area of the Slave States
the average density of population did not in 1850

labour in the South has to put up.   "The white hands are mostly
English or Welshmen.   One of them, with whom I conversed,
told me that he had been here several years ; he had previously
lived some years at the North.   He got better wages here than he
had earned at the North, but he was not contented, and did not
intend to remain.   On pressing him for the reason of his discontent,
he said, after some hesitation, that he had rather live where he
could be more free ; a man had to be too '*discreet*' here : if one
happened to say anything that gave offence, they thought no more
of drawing a pistol or a knife upon him, than they would of kicking
a dog that was in their way.   Not long since, a young English
fellow came to the pit, and was put to work along with a gang of

exceed 11.29 persons to the square mile. It is true a large portion of the region included in this average has but recently been acquired, and cannot be considered as having yet received its full complement of inhabitants. Let us, then, confine our observations to the older states. If population be capable of becoming dense under slave institutions, it should have realized this condition in Virginia. This state has been for two hundred and fifty years the seat of the Anglo-Saxon race, and the chosen field of industry: it abounds in natural advantages; its climate is remarkably salubrious. What, then, is the result of the experiment in Virginia? It appears from the census of 1850, that, after an industrial career of two hundred and fifty years, this country contained an average of 23 persons to the square mile! This, however, does not adequately represent the case; for of these 23 persons one-third

negroes. One morning, about a week afterwards, twenty or thirty men called on him, and told him that they would allow him fifteen minutes to get out of sight, and if they ever saw him in those parts again, they would 'give him hell.' They were all armed, and there was nothing for the young fellow to do but to move 'right off.'

'What reason did they give him for it?'

'They did not give him any reason.'

'But what had he done.'

'Why I believe they thought he had been too free with the niggers; he wasn't used to them, you see, sir, and he talked to 'em free like, and they thought he'd make 'em think too much of themselves.'"

on an average were slaves. Deducting these, the
density of population in Virginia—of population
among whom knowledge is not considered contraband, of population who are capable of mixing
together as fellow-citizens (which is the point essential to our argument)—the density of this population
is represented by the proportion of 15 persons to the
square mile ! But the peculiar feature of the case,
and that which places beyond question the true
solution of these phenomena, is the fact, that the
districts in the state which are most thickly populated are not those of the greatest natural fertility,
but the contrary. The richest districts—those in the
central and eastern divisions of the state*—which
are for the most part in the hands of wealthy planters,
and are cultivated with tobacco—are less densely
inhabited than the districts to the north-west, which
are less richly endowed by nature, but have become
the abode of a free farming population, mostly
immigrants from the Northern States. It is thus
scarcely an exaggeration to say (and it surely affords
a striking proof how completely the whole system of
slavery tends to thwart the purposes of nature) that
in slave countries density of population varies inversely with the natural richness of the country—
inversely, that is to say, with the means of supporting it. What is the explanation of this unparalleled

* Russell's *North America*, p. 154.

fact? Let Mr. De Bow answer. " The striking fact that those districts possessing naturally the best soils are almost stationary in population, while districts of inferior soils naturally are filling up, shows not only the exhausted state of the soil in the former, but proves that the character of slave labour and the system of cultivation adopted are unfriendly to density of population."* But, to return, it appears that, even including the more densely peopled free-labour districts, of Virginia, the average density of the white population in that state had not in 1856 exceeded the proportion of 15 persons to the square mile. Compare this with the progress of population in an area of the Free States naturally less favourable to the multiplication of people and not so long settled,—with the area comprised by Massachusetts, Rhode Island, Connecticut, New Jersey, New York, and Pennsylvania—and what do we find ? Population has here, in a shorter time, and under external conditions less favourable, reached an average density of 82 persons to the square mile. For equal areas in the Free and Slave States there are thus considerably more than five persons capable of taking part in the business of civilized life in the former for one in the latter. Population under slave institutions, in fact, only increases

* De Bow's *Review* for November, 1855. The passage occurs in an article on the agriculture of South Carolina, recommended by the editor as an able and valuable essay.

by dispersion. Fifteen persons to the square mile represent the maximum density which population under the most favourable circumstances is, with slavery, capable of attaining.* Now, this state of things is incompatible with civilized progress. Under such conditions social intercourse cannot exist ; popular education becomes impracticable ; roads, canals, railways, must be losing speculations ; in short, all the civilizing agencies of highest value are, by the very nature of the case, excluded. Among a people so dispersed, for example, how is popular education to be carried on ! Not to dwell upon the obstacles presented to the diffusion of knowledge by the mental habits of a people accustomed to the life of the "mean whites"—a life alternating between list-less vagrancy and the excitement of marauding expeditions—the mere physical difficulties of the problem—the task of bringing together from a popu-lation so dispersed the materials of a school—would be such as might well discourage the most determined zeal.† In point of fact, all attempts at conveying

* The density of population in Delaware, Maryland, and Ken-tucky is no doubt greater than this ; but it is because these states are occupied, over large districts, with a free labouring peasantry, because in fact in these districts slavery does not exist. This is the case also with Western Virginia, and doubtless, as I have remarked, raises the average of the whole country above what a purely servile *régime* would produce.

† "My experience has satisfied me that, unless our poor people can be brought together in villages, and some means of employment

education to the bulk of the people in the Southern States have proved costly failures.* Experiments have been made in some of the states, and always with the same result.† The moral and physical difficulties of the problem have proved insuperable ; and the mass of the people remains, and under the present social system ever must remain, entirely uninstructed.‡

Nor is this the only way in which sparseness of population operates unfavourably on the intellectual progress of a people. Scarcely less important than school teaching, as instruments of popular education, are the societies established for the mutual improvement of those who take part in them, such as mechanics' institutes, and literary and scientific asso-

afforded them, it will be utterly hopeless to undertake to educate them."—Mr. William Gregg before the South Carolina Institute; and see also De Bow's *Industrial Resources*, vol. ii., pp. 109, 110, where the same point is fully admitted.

* "The appropriation annually made by our legislature for our School Fund every one must be aware, so far as the country is concerned, has been little better than a waste of money. . . . While we are aware that the Northern and Eastern States find no difficulty in educating their poor, we are ready to despair of success in the matter, for even penal laws against the neglect of education would fail to bring many of our country people to send their children to school."—Address before the South Carolina Institute by Mr. William Gregg.

† See Reports of County School Commissioners quoted by Olmsted—*Seaboard Slave States*, pp. 292–296.

‡ See Appendix H.

ciations, of which such extensive use is made in this
country and in the Northern States.   But from this
efficacious mode of awakening intelligence, a people,
whose social institutions prevent it from attaining
greater concentration than is reached by the people
of the South, is entirely excluded.*

Lastly, how are the means of communication to
be developed under such conditions?† How are railways to be made profitable in a population of fifteen
persons to the square mile ?   Railways, no doubt,
have been made in the South, but with more advantage to the travellers than to the shareholders.   In

---

* Some statistics bearing upon this aspect of the question have
been given by Mr. Helper, which are sufficiently striking.   It
appears that the number of public libraries throughout the whole
of the Slave States are only 695 against 14,911 in the Free States;
or about 1 public library in the South to 21 in the North.   Again,
the number of volumes in public libraries in the Slave States is
649,577; while the number in public libraries in the Free States is
3,888,284 ; that is to say, in the proportion of about 1 to 6.—
(Helper's *Impending Crisis*, p. 337.)   Probably, were the quality of
the literature as well as the quantity given, the result would be
still more significant.

† "One topic of the President's Message may seem strange to
European readers.   It appears that, not only have the gains of the
Post-office increased, but its expenses have diminished through the
secession of the Confederate States.   It is conceivable that the
correspondence between the Northern soldiery and their families,
and the activity of business caused by such a war, might more than
compensate for the loss of the Southern letter writers *en masse ;*
but it is necessary to have known something of the conditions of
life in the Slave states to understand the diminution of expense.

South Carolina a train has been known to travel a hundred miles with a single passenger.*

The poor whites of the South seem thus, under an inexorable law, to be bound to their present fate by the same chain which holds the slave to his. Slavery produces distaste for industry. Distaste for industry, coexisting with a wilderness which is also the fruit of slavery, disperses population over vast areas as the one condition of its increase. Among such a people the requisites of progress do not exist ; the very elements of civilization are wanting.

If, then, society is to advance in the South, we must look somewhere else than among the mass of the white population for the motive principle which is to propel it. And where are we to look ? Southern society furnishes but two other elements— the slaves and their masters. What germ of hope

The fact is, the comparative barbarism of Southern society has prevented the postal service from being ever self-supporting there. Southern patriots have complained that everything about them was Northern, the railways, the steamers, the mail officers, coaches and bags ; and they might have added that the postal service itself was a boon—a gift from the North, bestowed through the machinery of government. In a country where the labouring class is anxiously kept ignorant of reading and writing, and where the sham middle class, the mean whites, are usually no less ignorant, the Post-office department can scarcely pay ; yet to many readers this will look like a new and strange disclosure of the state of Southern society."—*Daily News*, December, 1862.

* See Stirling's *Letters from the Slave States*, p. 265.

does either of these present? If civilization is to
spring up among the negro race, it will scarcely be
contended that this will happen while they are still
slaves ; and if the present ruling class are ever to
rise above the existing type, it must be in some
other capacity than as slaveholders. The whole
question therefore turns ultimately on the chances
of slave emancipation. Slave emancipation may, of
course, be forced upon the South by pressure from
without ; but the point which we have now to consider is the prospect of this result being attained in
the natural course of its internal development.

And first let us observe the inherent difficulty of
the problem. It was shown in a former chapter
that in the system of North American slavery, obstacles exist to the emancipation of the slave which
had no place among the ancients. It may now be
added that the difficulties of slave emancipation in
the present Slave States are far greater than those
which were successfully encountered in the Northern. Owing to causes already explained, slavery
had never taken very firm root in the North :
it was becoming, with the growth of society, constantly less profitable : the total number of slaves
formed but a small fraction of the whole population : above all, the Northern States had in the
markets of the South a ready means of ridding
themselves, at trifling loss, of a class which had

become an incumbrance.   For, to borrow the words
of Tocqueville, the overthrow of slavery in the
Northern States was effected " by abolishing the
principle of slavery, not by setting the slaves free."
The Northern people did not emancipate negroes
who were enslaved, but they provided for the future
extinction of slavery by legislating for the freedom
of their offspring.   The operation of this plan may
be readily supposed.   The future offspring of the
slave having by the law of a particular state been
declared free, the slave himself lost a portion of
his value in that state.   But in the South these
laws had no force, and consequently in the South
the value of the slave was unaltered by the change.
The effect, therefore, of the Northern measures of
abolition was, for the most part, simply to transfer
Northern slaves to Southern markets.   In this way,
by an easy process, without incurring any social
danger, and at slight pecuniary loss, the Northern
States got rid of slavery.   The problem of enfranchisement in the South is of a very different character.   Slavery, instead of being, as it always was
in the North, but one, and an unimportant one,
among many modes of industry, is there virtually
the sole industrial instrument; instead of comprising
an insignificant fraction of the whole population, it
comprises throughout the whole South one-third,
and in some states one-half : it numbers altogether

four millions of people : lastly, the South is wholly
without that easy means of shuffling off slavery
which its markets provided for the North.   The
two cases are thus wholly unlike, and the spontaneous disappearance of slavery from the Northern
section of the Union gives little ground to hope for
a similar result in the present Slave States.

And still less warranted are we in expecting a
policy of emancipation from the South by the history of British emancipation in the West Indies ;
for that event was not brought about in the natural
course of social improvement in those islands, but
was forced upon them by the mother nation, in
the face of the protests and remonstrances of their
ruling classes.   Instead of being the natural result
of principles called into action under slave institutions, it was only accomplished with difficulty
through the direct and forcible interposition of an
external authority.

So far as to ancient and modern precedents : they
are palpably inapplicable to the present case.   But
there are those who anticipate the growth of a liberal
policy in the South from the gradual operation of
economic causes in ultimately identifying the interests of planters with those of the general community.*   It will be worth while briefly to examine
the argument which is founded upon this view of

* See Appendix I.

the case. It is said that free labour (regarded from a purely economic point of view—moral considerations apart) being superior to slave labour, and this principle being exemplified by the whole industrial history of the Northern and Southern States—the former, though naturally less fertile, having far outstripped the latter in the race of material prosperity, —the truth must ultimately be recognised by the slaveholders themselves, and that so soon as this happens, they will be led by self interest to adopt a policy of emancipation. The case may indeed be put more strongly than this; for slavery has not merely thwarted the general prosperity of the South ; it may even be shown to have operated to the special detriment of the particular class for whose exclusive behoof it is maintained. For the slaveholders of the South are also its landed proprietors, and the uniform effect of slavery (as has been shown in a former part of this essay) has been, by confining cultivation to the rich soils, to prevent the growth of rent. So powerfully, indeed, has this cause operated, that it has been calculated, apparently upon good grounds,* that the mere difference in rent between the returns from lands of equal quality in the Free and Slave States would be more than sufficient to buy up the whole slave property of the South. By the abolition

* See Olmsted's *Seaboard Slave States,* pp. 170, 171. As much is admitted by Mr. De Bow.

of slavery in that country, therefore, not merely would the general prosperity of the inhabitants be promoted, but, by the rise of rent which would be the consequence of this measure, there would result to slaveholders a special gain—a gain which, it may reasonably be thought, would form a liberal compensation for any temporary inconvenience they might suffer from the change. Considerations so obvious, it is argued, must in the end have their effect on the minds of the ruling class in the South, and must lead them before long to abolish a system which is fraught with such baleful effects to the country and to themselves.

To the soundness of this reasoning, so far as it proves the beneficial results which would follow from the abolition of slavery, I do not think that any valid objection can be offered. It appears to me as demonstrable as any proposition in Euclid, that, extending our view over some generations, slavery has acted injuriously on every class and every interest in the South, and that its continued maintenance is absolutely incompatible with the full development of the resources of the country. Nevertheless it would, I conceive, be infinitely precarious from this position to infer that slaveholders will ever be induced voluntarily to abolish slavery. The slaveholders of the South are perfectly aware of the superior prosperity of the Free States : it is with them a

subject of bitter mortification and envy ; but, with the most conclusive evidence before their eyes, they persist in attributing this to every cause but the right one.* Supposing, however, that they are in the end convinced, by such arguments as I have referred to, of the injurious effects of their system, and that they are satisfied that the immediate loss from the abolition of slavery would be more than made good to their descendants in the future increase in the value of their land, still I apprehend that they would be as far as ever from being won over to a policy of abolition. For, whatever be the future advantages which may be expected from the change, it is vain to deny that the transition from slavery to freedom could not be effected without great inconvenience, loss, and doubtless in many cases, ruin, to the present race of slaveholders. The accumulated results of two hundred years of tyranny, cruelty, and disregard of the first of human rights are not thus easily evaded. A sacrifice there would need to be.†
And it is vain to expect that slaveholders, of whose system selfishness is the fundamental prin-

---

* De Bow's *Industrial Resources*, passim.

† The West Indian experiment, I conceive, proves this as conclusively as it proves that the ultimate and permanent results of emancipation are beneficial to the whole country in the highest degree.

ciple, and whose profits are purchased, not merely
at the cost of misery to a whole race of living men,
but at the cost of the future prosperity of their own
descendants, whose interests in the soil their spend-
thrift system anticipates—it is vain to expect that
they of all men should voluntarily devote themselves
for the good of their country. So long, therefore,
as slaveholders have at their disposal an unlimited
extent of fertile soil suited to slave products, it is,
I think, vain to hope that the question of slavery will
ever find its solution in economic motives.* But, in
truth, it is idle to argue this question on purely
economic grounds. It is not simply as a productive instrument that slavery is valued by its supporters. It is far rather for its social and political
results—as the means of upholding a form of society
in which slaveholders are the sole depositaries of
social prestige and political power, as the "corner
stone" of an edifice of which they are the builders—
that the system is prized. Abolish slavery, and you
introduce a new order of things, in which the ascendancy of the men who now rule in the South would
be at an end.† An immigration of new men would

* See APPENDIX J.

† "And, in this matter, let me add that about which I may speak
with the confidence of one who is familiar with the subject by a
lifetime of experience and observation. The relations subsisting in
America between the Africans and the inhabitants of European

set in rapidly from various quarters. The planters and their adherents would soon be placed in a hopeless minority in their old dominions. New interests would take root and grow; new social ideas would germinate; new political combinations would be formed; and the power and hopes of the party which has long swayed the politics of the Union, and which now seeks to break loose from that Union in order to secure a free career for the accomplishment of bolder designs, would be gone for ever. It is this which constitutes the real strength of slavery in the Southern States, and which precludes even the momentary admission by the dominant party there of any proposition which has abolition for its object.

And in view of this aspect of North American

blood can never be materially changed by the consent of the latter : which consent would be essential to ' *a gradual* ' enfranchisement of the slaves. Slavery, under the circumstances there existing, can only be eradicated by violence, sudden and overwhelming ! The first step taken by her enemies looking to emancipation, would arouse the entire South to an energetic and a bloody resistance, such as the world to this day has never witnessed ! Let no one be deceived in regard to the results which would follow swiftly upon the heels of such a movement ! The four millions of Africans, who are now inhabitants of the South, can only be emancipated and left upon the soil by the extermination or the entire subjection of eight millions of whites !"—*The South Vindicated*, p. 128. This is the frank declaration of a Southern writer in a work published by a London house, and addressed to English readers. If, after this, Englishmen persist in cherishing the delusion of gradual emancipation as the result of a triumph of the South, they have only themselves to blame.

slavery, we may see how perfectly futile, how absolutely childish, is ،the suggestion, that the Slave
party should be bought over by the Federal government through the offer of a liberal compensation,
after the precedent of Great Britain dealing with her
West Indian possessions.   Putting aside the magnitude of the sum, which, at the price of slaves which
recently prevailed, would certainly not be less
than £300,000,000 sterling, and the impossibility of
raising it in the present state of American credit, who
that knows anything of the aims of the Southern
party can suppose that the proposal, if made, would
not be rejected with scorn ?*   The suggestion supposes that men who have long held paramount
influence over the North American continent, and
who are probably now meditating plans of annexation and conquest, would at once abandon their
position as the chiefs of an independent confederacy,
and forego their ambitious schemes, for what?—for

---

* I am speaking, of course, of the reception which the proposition
would meet with while the Slave party were yet triumphant.   What
it might be induced to accept if thoroughly beaten by the North, is
another question which it is not necessary here to discuss.

Since these observations were written, the news of Mr. Lincoln's
project of emancipation has arrived.   It will be seen that the condition stated in the last sentence—the subjugation of the South—
is precisely the circumstance which gives to that scheme the least
chance of success.   Mr. Lincoln knew too well the men with whom
he had to deal to think of making such an offer till he was, or
thought himself, in a position to enforce it (April, 1862).

a sum of money which, if well invested, might perhaps enable them and their descendants to vegetate in peaceful obscurity !

But there is yet another influence to be taken account of in arguing this question. Slavery has not merely determined the general form and character of the social and political economy of the Southern States, it has entered into the soul of the people, and has generated a code of ethics and a type of Christianity adapted to its peculiar requirements.

At the epoch of the revolution, as has been already intimated, slavery was regarded by all the eminent men who took part in that movement as essentially an evil—an evil which might indeed be palliated as having come down to that generation from an earlier and less enlightened age, and which, having intwined itself with the institutions of the country, required to be delicately dealt with—but still an evil, indefensible on moral and religious grounds, and which ought not to be permanently endured.* The Convention of 1774 unanimously declared that "the abolition of domestic slavery was the greatest object of their desire." The Convention of 1787, while legislating for the continuance of slavery, resolved to exclude from the constitution the word "slave," lest it should be

---

* Hildreth's History of the United States, vol. iii. pp. 391–393.

thought that the American nation gave any sanction to "the idea that there could be property in
man." Washington, a native of the South and a
slaveholder, declared it to be among his first wishes
to see slavery abolished by law, and in his will
provided for the emancipation of his slaves. Jefferson, also a native of the South and a slaveholder,
framed a plan of abolition, and declared that in the
presence of slavery " he trembled for his country
when he reflected that God was just ;" that in the
event of a rising of slaves, " the Almighty had no
attribute which could take side with slaveowners
in such a contest." The other leading statesmen of
that time, Franklin, Madison, Hamilton, Patrick
Henry, the Randolphs, Munroe, whether from the
North or from the South, whether agreeing or not
in their views on the practical mode of dealing with
the institution, alike concurred in reprobating at
least the principle of slavery.

But it seems impossible that a whole people should
live permanently in contemplation of a system which
does violence to its moral instincts. One of two
results will happen. Either its moral instincts will
lead it to reform the institution which offends them,
or those instincts will be perverted, and become
authorities for what in their unsophisticated condition they condemned. The latter alternative is that
which has happened in the Southern States. Slavery

is no longer regarded there as a barbarous institution, to be palliated with whispering humbleness as an inheritance from a ruder age ; but rather as a system admirable for its intrinsic excellence, worthy to be upheld and propagated, the last and completest result of time.* The right of the white man to hold the negro in permanent thraldom, to compel him to work for his profit, to keep him in enforced ignorance, to sell him, to flog him, and, if need be, to kill him, to separate him at pleasure from his wife and children, to transport him for no crime to a remote region where he is in a few years worked to death—this is now propounded as a grand discovery in ethical and political science, made for the first time by the enlightened leaders of the Southern Confederation, and recommended by that philanthropic body to all civilized nations for their adop-

* Thirty years ago it was contended in the *Quarterly Review*, (Sept. 1832), " that there was not the slightest moral turpitude in holding slaves *under existing circumstances* in the South." But this qualified vindication is far from representing the present moral attitude of Southern writers in reference to the institution. On this subject, the reader is referred to a *Memoir on Slavery* by Chancellor Harper, prepared and read before the Society for the Advancement of Learning of South Carolina ; also to *Negro Slavery in the South* in a series of letters by Governor Hammond to Thomas Clarkson; and lastly to *The Philosophy of Secession* by Hon. L. W. Spratt. The two former will be found in De Bow's *Industrial Resources :* the last I have given in an Appendix. The religious aspect of the question will be found treated in an essay by the Rev. F. A. Ross, D.D. entitled " *Slavery ordained of God.*" Lippincott and Co. Philadelphia, 1857.

tion. This Confederation, which is the opprobrium of the age, puts itself forward as a model for its imitation, and calmly awaits the tardy applause of mankind. " The ideas entertained at the time of the formation of the old Constitution," says the Vice-president of the Southern Confederacy, " were that the enslavement of the African race was in violation of the laws of nature ; that it was wrong in principle, socially, morally, and politically. *Our new government is founded on exactly opposite ideas;* its foundations are laid, its corner-stone rests, upon the great truth that the negro is not equal to the white man ; that slavery—subordination to the superior race—is his natural and moral condition. *This our Government is the first in the history of the world based upon this great physical, philosophical, and moral truth.* . . . It is upon this our social fabric is firmly planted, and I cannot permit myself to doubt the ultimate success and full recognition of this principle throughout the civilized and enlightened world. . . . This stone which was rejected by the first builders 'is become the chief stone of the corner in our new edifice."* Opinion in the South has long passed beyond the stage at which slavery needs to be defended by argument. The subject is now never touched but in a strain such as the freedom conquered at Mara-

* Speech of Mr. A. H. Stephens, Vice-president of the Southern Confederacy, delivered March, 1861.

thon and Platæa inspired in the orators of Athens.
It is "the beneficent source and wholesome foundation of our civilization ;" an institution, "moral and
civilizing, useful at once to blacks and whites ;" "the
highest type of civilization yet exhibited by man."
"To suppress slavery would be to throw back civilization two hundred years." "It is not a moral
evil. It is the Lord's doing, and marvellous in our
eyes. . . . It is by divine appointment."

But slavery in the South is something more than
a moral and political principle : it has become a
fashionable taste, a social passion. The possession
of a slave in the South carries with it the same sort
of prestige as the possession of land in this country,
as the possession of a horse among the Arabs : it
brings the owner into connexion with the privileged
class ; it forms a presumption that he has attained
a certain social position. Slaves have thus in the
South acquired a factitious value, and are coveted
with an eagerness far beyond what the intrinsic
utility of their services would explain. A Chancellor of South Carolina describes slavery as in
accordance with "the proudest and most deeply
cherished feelings" of his countrymen—"feelings,
which others, if they will, may call prejudices." A
governor of Kansas declares that he "loves" the
institution, and that he votes for it because he
"loves" it. Nor are these sentiments confined to

the slaveholding minority.   The all-important circumstance is that they are shared equally by the
whole white population.   Far from reprobating a
system which has deprived them of the natural
means of rising in the scale of humanity, they fall
in with the prevailing modes of thought, and are
warm admirers, and, when need arises, effective
defenders, of an institution which has been their
curse.*   To be the owner of a slave is the chief
object of the poor white's ambition ; " *quot servos
pascit ?*" the one criterion by which he weighs the
worth of his envied superiors in the social scale.

And what is this system which is thus deeply
rooted in the interests, habits, ideas, and cherished
affections of the people of the Southern States ?—
which excites their ardent enthusiasm, which they
are now in arms to perpetuate and extend ?   We
have traced its principal economical and political
features : let us here glance briefly at some of its
moral aspects.   This system then is one under
which a whole race of men is deprived of all the
rights and privileges of rational creatures, and
consigned to a life of hopeless, unremitting toil,
in order that another race may live in idleness on

---

* " The ' white trash' of the South, though not themselves
owning slaves, have all the passions and prejudices of slaveholders
in their most exaggerated form . . . a formidable phalanx in
the democratic army of the South."—Stirling's *Letters from the
Slave States*, p. 86.

the fruits of its labours. It is a system under which, if we are to believe its admirers, the negroes are perfectly contented, but from which they are nevertheless constantly escaping in spite of the terrors of fugitive slave laws, of blood-hounds and man-hunters—a paradise, if you will, but a paradise from which its denizens escape to the Dismal Swamp.* Under this system a human being, convicted of no crime, may, in strict conformity with law, be flogged at the discretion of his fellow, and may even die under the lash without entailing

* "The Dismal Swamps are noted places of refuge for runaway negroes. They were formerly peopled in this way much more than at present; a systematic hunting of them with dogs and guns having been made by individuals who took it up as a business about ten years ago. Children were born, bréd, lived, and died here. Joseph Church told me he had seen skeletons, and had helped to bury bodies recently dead. There were people in the swamps still, he thought, that were the children of runaways, and who had been runaways themselves all their lives. What a life it must be; born outlaws; educated self-stealers; trained from infancy to be constantly in dread of the approach of a white man as a thing more fearful than wild-cats or serpents, or even starvation. . .

"I asked if they were ever shot. 'Oh, yes,' he said, 'when the hunters saw a runaway, if he tried to get from them, they would call out to him, that if he did not stop they would shoot, and if he did not, they would shoot, and sometimes kill him.'

"'*But some on 'em would rather be shot than took, sir,*' he added simply.

"A farmer living near the swamp confirmed this account, and said he knew of three or four being shot in one day.

"No particular breed of dogs is needed for hunting negroes:

any penalty on his murderer.*   Under this system
human beings may be, and within the last ten years
have been in several instances, burned alive.   All
property is for the negro contraband ; the acquisition of knowledge is for him a penal offence.   The
marriage tie receives no legal recognition, and no
practical respect.   Nay, it is worse than this.   Those
consequences, which in civilized communities form
the natural restraints on unlicensed desire, are
here converted into incentives ;   for the relation
between father and son is, in the presence of slavery,
less sacred than that between master and slave; and
the mulatto offspring of a white father is not a child
but a chattel : instead of entailing responsibilities it
brings to the author of its being so many dollars as
a price.†   Yes, I say that the laws of the Southern

blood-hounds, fox-hounds, bull-dogs, and curs were used, and one
white man told me how they were trained for it, as if it were a
common or notorious practice.   They are shut up when puppies,
and never allowed to see a negro except while training to catch
him.   A negro is made to run from them, and they are encouraged
to follow him until he gets into a tree, when meat is given them.
Afterwards they learn to follow any particular negro by scent, and
then a shoe or a piece of clothing is taken off a negro, and they
learn to find by scent whom it belongs to, and to *tree* him."—
Olmsted's *Seaboard Slave States,* pp. 159–61.

  * See APPENDIX K.

  † Let us hear upon this subject the testimony of a Virginian
woman.   "It is," she says, " one great evil hanging over the Southern Slave States, destroying domestic happiness, and the peace of
thousands.   It is summed up in the single word—*amalgamation.*

States permit fathers to enslave and sell their children, and that there are fathers in the Southern States who freely avail themselves of this law. To prove that this is so we have no lack of direct testimony ; but in truth the case is not one which stands in need of testimony. The crime is proclaimed by nature herself in language which cannot be silenced. There it stands revealed in the crowds of mulattoes, quadroons, and octoroons—many of them scarcely distinguishable in colour from Europeans—who now form so large a proportion of the whole enslaved population of the South. From what source has this European blood flowed into servile veins? From whence, but from the white caste in the South ?—from the men who commit their own flesh and blood to the charge of the brutal overseer* or

Neither is it to be found only in the lower order of the white population. It pervades the entire society. Its followers are to be found among all ranks, occupations and professions. The white mothers and daughters of the South have suffered under it for years —have seen their dearest affections trampled upon—their hopes of domestic happiness destroyed, and their future lives embittered, even to agony, by those who should be all in all to them, as husbands, sons, and brothers. I cannot," she adds, " use too strong language in reference to this subject, for I know that it will meet with a heart-felt response from every Southern woman."—Olmsted's *Seaboard Slave States*, p. 601.

* As to the character of these men, on which perhaps more than on any other circumstance the happiness of the negro population is immediately dependent, see Russell's *North America*, pp. 258-259, and Olmsted's *Seaboard Slave States*, p. 486.

to the more brutal trader in human flesh.* This is an aspect of the case which I would gladly have passed by ; but, in the present state of opinion, the facts are too serious to be blinked ; and before the people of this country, which has achieved its best renown in ridding its own lands of this curse, be committed to the countenance and support of a power, the final cause of whose existence is to extend this very evil, it is important that we should clearly understand what it is we are called upon to sustain.

This, then, is the system which we have seen gaining an ever-increasing hold on Southern sentiment. The progress of events, far from conducing to its gradual mitigation and ultimate extinction, has tended distinctly in the opposite direction—to the aggravation of its worst evils and the consolidation of its strength. The extension of the area subject to the Slave Power and the increase in the slave population have augmented at once the

---

* "There is not," said a Louisianian planter to Mr. Olmsted, "a likely-looking black girl in this state, that is not the paramour of a white man. There is not an old plantation in which the grand-children of the owner are not whipped in the field by his overseer. I cannot bear that the blood of the ———— should run in the veins of slaves." "The practice," he said, "was not occasional, or general, it was universal."—Olmsted's *Seaboard Slave States*, p. 602. And for this aspect of Slavery in Brazil, see *Revue des Deux Mondes*, 15 Juillet, 1862, pp. 395-396.

inducements for retaining the institution and the difficulty of getting rid of it; while the ideas of successive generations, bred up in its presence and under the influence of the interests to which it has given birth, have provided for it in the minds of the people a moral support. The result is, that the position of the slave in the Southern States at the present time, so far as it depends upon the will and power of his masters, is in all respects more hopeless than it has ever been in any former age, or in any other quarter of the world. A Fugitive Slave law, which throws into shade the former atrocities of slavery, has been enacted, and, until the recent disturbances, was strictly enforced. The education of the negro is more than ever rigorously proscribed. Emancipation finds in the growth of fanatical pro-slavery opinion an obstacle more formidable even than in the laws. Propositions have been entertained by the legislatures in some states for reducing all free coloured persons to slavery by one wholesale enactment; in others these people have been banished from the state under pain of this fate. Everything in the laws, in the customs, in the education of the people, has been contrived with the single view of degrading the negro to the level of the brute, and blotting out from his mind the hope and even the idea of freedom.

The thoroughness—the absolute disregard of all

consequences with which this purpose has been pursued, is but little understood in this country.   History can supply no instance of a despotism more
complete and searching than that which for some
years past has prevailed in the Southern States.
Since the attempt of John Brown at Harper's Ferry
its oppression has reached a height which can only
be adequately described as a reign of terror.   It is
long since freedom of discussion on any question
connected with slavery would have been tolerated.
But it is not merely freedom of discussion which is
now prohibited.   The design seems to have been
formed of putting down freedom of thought, and of
banishing from the South every trace of dissentient
opinion.   A system of espionage has been organized.
The mail bags have in many states been freely
opened, and the postmasters of petty villages have
exercised a free discretion in giving or withholding
the documents entrusted to their care.   In the
more southern states vigilance committees have
been established *en permanence*.   Before these self-
constituted tribunals persons of unblemished reputation and inoffensive manners have been summoned,
and, on a few days' notice, for no other offence than
that of being known to entertain sentiments unfavourable to slavery, have been banished from the
state where they resided ; and this in direct violation of a specific provision of the Constitution of

the United States.* Clergymen, who have broken
no law, for merely discharging their duties according to their consciences have been arrested, thrown
into prison, and visited with ignominious punishment. Travellers, who have incautiously, in ignorance of the intensity of the popular feeling, ventured to give temperate expression to anti-slavery
opinions, have been seized by the mob, tarred and
feathered, ducked, flogged, and in some instances
hanged. Nay, so sensitively jealous has the feeling
of the South become, that the slightest link of connexion with a suspected locality—to have resided
in the North, to have sent one's children to a
Northern School—is sufficient to secure expulsion
from a slave state. An abolitionist in the ethics of
the South is the vilest of all human beings, and
every one is an abolitionist who does not reside in
a slave state and share to the full the prevailing
pro-slavery sentiment.† Such is the point which

* "The citizens of each state shall be entitled to all the privileges
and immunities of citizens in the several states."—Art. iv., sec. ii.

† "An abolitionist," says the *Southern Literary Messenger*, in a
recent article, "is a man who does not love slavery for its own sake
as a divine institution; who does not worship it as a corner-stone
of civil liberty; who does not adore it as the only possible social
condition on which a permanent Republican Government can be
created; and who does not, in his inmost soul, desire to see it
extended and perpetuated over the whole earth as a means of
human reformation second only in dignity, importance, and sacred-
ness, to the Christian religion."

civilization has reached under slave institutions. Such is the system, and such is the cost at which it is maintained.*

* *The Reign of Terror in the South,* &c. *passim;* also, *Reports of the American Anti-Slavery Society,* for the years 1857–'60.

It may readily be conceived that Southern intolerance did not relax as the great social schism approached its crisis. M. Cucheval-Clarigny gives the following vivid sketch of the measures by which unionist sentiment was overborne in the South:—" Chaque jour on voyait arriver, dans les états du centre ou de l'ouest, des gens qui avaient été dénoncés comme mal pensans, et qui avaient reçu, par lettre anonyme, l'invitation d'émigrer dans les vingt-quatre heures, sous peine de voir leur maison incendiée et de recevoir un coup de couteau. Les journaux de la Nouvelle-Orléans, qui combattaient la séparation, furent contraints l'un après l'autre de cesser leur publication ou de changer complètement de langage. Dans les villes un peu importantes du sud, des bandes armées parcouraient les rues, précédées d'un drapeau avec le palmier, et des menaces de mort étaient proférées devant les maisons des gens suspects d'attachement à l'Union. Quand une législature paraissait hésiter devant un vote belliqueux, on tenait des réunions publiques pour gourmander sa lenteur, et on lui adressait des objurgations. On ne parlait de rien moins en effet dans certains états que de faire voter des mesures d'exception, l'emprisonnement ou l'exile des suspects, et la confiscation de leurs biens."—*Annuaire des Deux Mondes,* 1860, *p.* 617.

CHAPTER VI.

INTERNAL POLICY OF SLAVE SOCIETIES.

In the foregoing chapters an attempt has been made
to analyze the system of society presented in the
Slave States, and to ascertain the direction in which,
under ordinary circumstances, and in the absence of
intervention from without, the development of such
a system proceeds; and the result of an examination, as well of the several elements of which the
whole society is composed as of their joint action,
has been to show that it is essentially retrograde in
its character, containing within it no germs from
which improvement can grow, and no forces competent to counteract those which press it downwards.
In the remaining portion of this essay I shall endeavour to exhibit the working of this system in the
politics of the Union; and as, in relation to the
people who compose it, the social system of the Slave
States has been seen to be retrograde, so, in relation
to other societies with which it may come into
contact, it will be found to be aggressive—to be
constantly urged by exigencies, which it cannot
control, to extend its territory, and by an ambition
not less inevitable to augment its power.

The aggressive character of a social system deriving its strength from slavery—that is to say of a Slave Power—proceeds primarily from the well-known economic fact, already more than once adverted to—the necessary limitation of slave culture to soils of more than average richness, combined with its tendency to exhaust them. It results from this that societies based upon slavery cannot, like those founded upon free industrial institutions, take root, grow, and flourish upon a limited area. To secure their vigour, their roots must be always spreading. A constant supply of fresh soils of high fertility becomes, therefore, an indispensable requisite for the permanent industrial success of such societies. This is a fundamental principle in their political economy, and one which, we shall find, exercises a powerful influence on the course of their general history. As the principle will hereafter be frequently referred to, it is important to observe that it is one about which no controversy can be said to exist, being as fully recognized by the upholders as by the opponents of slavery. "There is not a slaveholder," says Judge Warner of Georgia, " in this house or out of it, but who knows perfectly well that, whenever slavery is confined within certain specified limits, its future existence is doomed ; it is only a question of time as to its final destruction. You may take any single slaveholding county

in the Southern States, in which the great staples of
cotton and sugar are cultivated to any extent, and
confine the present slave population within the
limits of that county. Such is the rapid natural
increase of the slaves, and the rapid exhaustion of
the soil in the cultivation of those crops (which add
so much to the commercial wealth of the country),
that in a few years it would be impossible to support them within the limits of such county. Both
master and slave would be starved out ; and what
would be the practical effect in any one county, the
same result would happen to all the slaveholding
States. Slavery cannot be confined within certain
specified limits without producing the destruction of
both master and slave ; it requires fresh lands,
plenty of wood and water, not only for the comfort
and happiness of the slave, but for the benefit of the
owner."*

It is further important to observe that the internal organization of slave societies adapts them in a
peculiar manner for a career of constant expansion.
"In free communities property becomes fixed in
edifices, in machinery, and in improvements of the
soil. In slave communities there is scarcely any
property except slaves, and they are easily movable.
The freeman embellishes his home ; the slaveholder
finds nothing to bind him to soils which he has

* *Progress of Slavery*, p. 227.

exhausted. Freedom is enterprising, but not mi-
gratory as slavery is. It is not in the nature of
slavery to become attached to place. It is nomadic.
The slaveholder leaves his impoverished fields with
as little reluctance as the ancient Scythian abandoned cropped pastures for fresh ones, and slaves
are moved as readily as flocks and herds."*

Slavery thus requires for its success a constantly
expanding field. It is also to be noted that within
this field it is exclusive of all other industrial systems. It is true, indeed, that, as has been already
observed, there exists in certain districts through the
Slave States a considerable free population engaged
in regular industry; but this forms no real exception to the essential exclusiveness of slave societies.
These settlements of free farmers occur only where,
from some cause, slavery has disappeared from
tracts of country large enough to form the abode of

---

* *Progress of Slavery*, p. 8. The moral and social consequences of
this mode of life are well pointed out by Mr. De Bow:—"When a
spirit of emigration prevails in a country, those who are under its influence cease to feel themselves as individuals identified with the community in which they live; they husband all their resources for the
purpose of enabling them to remove and establish new homes; and
they will not enter into any schemes for the improvement of either
the moral or physical condition of the country which they have resolved to abandon. This influence extends far beyond the number
who actually remove, for very many continue to consider their removal
as probable, for many years together, who do not eventually emi-
grate; and thus their moral energies are paralyzed, and the country
is deprived of their usefulness."—*Industrial Resources*, vol. ii. p. 110.

distinct societies ; as in Western Virginia, where the exhaustion of the soil, under a long continued cultivation by slaves, compelled at one time an extensive emigration of planters ; or along the slopes of the Alleghanies, where the land is better suited to cereal crops than to cotton or tobacco ; or, again, in Texas, where the available slave force has not been sufficient to enable planters to appropriate the vast regions suddenly placed at their disposal. In these cases, no doubt, colonies of free peasants are to be found in the midst of the Slave States ; but there is here no real intermixture of the two forms of society. "The systems," says Mr. Spratt, "cannot mix." The free settlements remain in the Slave States as distinct communities*—oases of freedom in the vast desert of slavery—without bond of interest or sympathy to connect them with the surrounding population. Slave society is thus essentially exclusive of all other forms of social life.†
Now this characteristic of it is as well understood by

* See Olmsted's account of the German settlement in Texas.— *A Journey through Texas*, pp. 143–146, 176–178.

† This is not only instinctively felt by the Southerns, but maintained in theory. The following passage from the *Richmond Inquirer* is sufficiently explicit : "Two opposite and conflicting forms of society cannot, among civilized men, co-exist and endure. The one must give way and cease to exist ; the other become universal. If free society be unnatural, immoral, unchristian, it must fall, and give way to slave society, a social system old as the world, universal as man."

the free population of the Northern States, as is the
necessity to their system of a constantly expanding
area by the planters of the South ; and hence it has
happened that, whenever free and slave societies
have come into contact on the same field, a mutual
antagonism has sprung up between them.   Each
has endeavoured to outstrip the other in the career
of colonization, and, by first occupying the ground,
to keep the field open for its future expansion
against the encroachments of its rival.   " It has
thus," says Mr. Weston, " become a race whether the
negro from Texas and Arkansas, or the white
labourer from Kansas and the free West, shall first
reach New Mexico and the Gulf of California."

But it is less in the economic, than in the moral
and social, attributes of slave societies that we must
look for the motive principle of their aggressive
ambition.   That which the necessity for fresh soils
is to the political economy of such communities a
lust of power is to their morality.   The slaveholder
lives from infancy in an atmosphere of despotism.
He sees around him none but abject creatures, who,
under fearful penalties to be inflicted by himself,
are bound to do his slightest, his most unreasonable,
bidding.   " The commerce between master and slave,"
says a slaveowner, "is a perpetual exercise of the
most boisterous passions—the most unremitting despotism on the one hand, and degrading submission

on the other.   Our children see this, and learn to
imitate it. . . . The parent storms, the child looks
on, catches the lineaments of wrath, puts on the
same airs in the circle of smaller slaves, gives a loose
to the worst passions, and thus nursed, educated,
and daily exercised in tyranny, cannot but be
stamped with its odious peculiarities."*   "The first
notion," says Tocqueville, "which the citizen of the
Southern States acquires in life, is that he is born
to command, and the first habit which he contracts
is that of being obeyed without resistance."   The
despot mood is thus early impressed on the heart
of the slaveholder; and it bears fruit in his manners and life.   "The existence of a dominant class
necessarily leads to violence.   Trained up from
youth to the unrestrained exercise of will, the
superior race or class naturally becomes despotic,
overbearing, and impatient.   In their intercourse
with their inferiors this leads to unresisted oppression; but with their equals, armed with similar
power and fired by the same passions, it breaks out
into fierce strife. . . . In this country the relation
of master and slave produces the same effect on the
character of the dominant class as was formerly produced in Europe by that of lord and serf.   There is
the same imperious will, the same impatience of
restraint, the same proneness to anger and ferocious

* Jefferson's *Notes on Virginia*, p. 39.

strife. The passions which are developed in the intercourse with inferiors show themselves, though in a different form, in the intercourse with equals. Thus, by an inevitable retribution, wrong is made self-chastising, and the hand of the violent man is turned against himself.

" Duelling is not the only form of this national proneness to acts of violence ; rather it is the modified form which it assumes among fair and honourable men, who, even in their anger, disdain to take advantage of an adversary, and who have at least sufficient self-command to give a semblance of reason to their passion.   There are others, whose hasty impulses disdain even this slight self-restraint, who carry with them habitually the means of deadly injury, and use them on the slightest provocation. . . . The custom of carrying arms is at once a proof of proneness to violence, and a provocation to it.   This habit, I am informed, prevails very extensively in the South.   When coming down the Mississippi, a Colonel B——, to whom I had been introduced, pointing to a crowd of men of all ranks clustered round the cabin stove, said : ' Now, there is probably not a man in all that crowd who is not armed ; I myself have a pistol in my state-room.' "*

* Stirling's *Letters from the Slave States*, pp. 270, 272.

" When my work was over I walked out and sat in the shade with a gentleman whose talk turned upon the practices of the Mississippi duello.   Without the smallest animus, and in the most

Such are the private influences by which the slaveholder is moulded to an intense craving for power. And what scope do the institutions of the South provide for the satisfaction, on a large theatre, of the passion which they generate? In free societies the paths to eminence are various. Successful trade, the professions, science and literature, social reform, philanthropy, furnish employment for the redundant activity of the people, and open so many avenues to distinction. But for slaveholders these means of advancement do not exist, or exist in scanty measure. Commerce and manufactures are excluded by the necessities of the case. The professions, which are the result of much subdivision of employment where population is rich and dense, can have small place in a poor and thinly-peopled

natural way in the world, he told us tale after tale of blood, and recounted terrible tragedies enacted outside bars of hotels and in the public streets close beside us. The very air seemed to become purple as he spoke, the land around a veritable 'Aceldama.' There may, indeed, be security for property, but there is none for the life of its owner in difficulties, who may be shot by a stray bullet from a pistol as he walks up the street.

"I learned many valuable facts. I was warned, for example, against the impolicy of trusting to small-bored pistols or to pocket six-shooters in case of a close fight, because, suppose you hit your man mortally he may still run in upon you and rip you up with a bowie knife before he falls dead; whereas if you drive a good heavy bullet into him, or make a hole in him with a 'Derringer' ball, he gets faintish and drops at once.

"Many illustrations, too, were given of the value of practical

country.   Science and literature are left without
the principal inducements for their cultivation,
where there is no field for their most important
practical applications.   Social reform and philanthropy would be out of place in a country where
human chattels are the principal property.   Practically, but one career lies open to the Southern
desirous of advancement—agriculture carried on by
slaves.   To this, therefore, he turns.   In the management of his plantation, in the breeding, buying, and
selling of slaves, his life is passed.   Amid the moral
atmosphere which this mode of life engenders his
ideas and tastes are formed.   He has no notion of
ease, independence, happiness, where slavery is not
found.   Is it strange, then, that his ambition should
connect itself with the institution around which are

lessons of this sort.   One particularly struck me.   If a gentleman
with whom you are engaged in altercation moves his hand towards
his breeches pocket, or behind his back, you must smash him or
shoot him at once, for he is either going to draw his six-shooter, to
pull out a bowie knife, or to shoot you through the lining of his
pocket.   The latter practice is considered rather ungentlemanly, but
it has somewhat been more honoured lately in the observance than
in the breach.   In fact, the savage practice of walking about with
pistols, knives, and poniards, in bar-rooms and gambling saloons,
with passions ungoverned, because there is no law to punish the
deeds to which they lead, affords facilities for crime which an uncivilized condition of society leaves too often without punishment,
but which must be put down or the country in which it is tolerated
will become as barbarous as a jungle inhabited by wild beasts."—
My Diary, North and South.   By William Howard Russell.

entwined his domestic associations, which is identified with all his plans in life, and which offers him the sole chance of emerging from obscurity ?

But the aspirations of the slaveholder are not confined within the limits of his own community. He is also a citizen of the United States. In the former he naturally and easily takes the leading place ; but, as a member of the larger society in which he is called upon to act in combination with men who have been brought up under free institutions, the position which he is destined to fill is not so clearly indicated. It is plain, however, that he cannot become blended in the general mass of the population of the Union. His character, habits, and aims are not those of the Northern people, nor are theirs his. The Northern is a merchant, a manufacturer, a lawyer, a literary man, an artisan, a shopkeeper, a schoolmaster, a peasant farmer ; he is engaged in commercial speculation, or in promoting social or political reform ; perhaps he is a philanthropist, and includes slavery-abolition in his programme. Between such men and the slaveholder of the South there is no common basis for political action. There are no objects in promoting which he can combine with them in good faith and upon public grounds. There lies before him, therefore, but one alternative : he must stand by his fellows, and become powerful as the assertor and propagandist of slavery ; or fail-

ing this, he must submit to be of no account in the
politics of the Union.   Here then again the slaveholder is thrown back upon his peculiar system as the
sole means of satisfying the master passion of his life.
In the society of the Union, no less than in that of
the State, he finds that his single path to power lies
through the maintenance and extension of this institution.   Accordingly, to uphold it, to strengthen
it, to provide for its future growth and indefinite
expansion, becomes the dream of his life—the one
great object of his existence.   But this is not all :
this same institution, which is the beginning and
end of the slaveholder's being, places between him
and the citizens of free societies a broad and impassable gulf.   The system which is the foundation of
his present existence and future hopes is by them
denounced as sinful and inhuman ; and he is himself
held up to the reprobation of mankind.   The tongues
and hands of all freemen are instinctively raised
against him.   A consciousness is thus awakened in
the minds of the community of slaveholders that
they are a proscribed class, that their position is one
of antagonism to the whole civilized world ; and
the feeling binds them together in the fastest con-
cord.   Their pride is aroused ; and all the energy
of their nature is exerted to make good their position against those who would assail it.   In this
manner the instinct of self defence and the sentiment

of pride come to aid the passion of ambition, and all tend to fix in the minds of slaveholders the resolution to maintain at all hazards the keystone of their social order.   To establish their scheme of society on such broad and firm foundations that they may set at defiance the public opinion of free nations, and, in the last resort, resist the combined efforts of their physical power, becomes at length the settled purpose and clearly conceived design of the whole body.   To this they devote themselves with the zeal of fanatics, with the persistency and secrecy of conspirators.

The position of slaveholders thus naturally fosters the passion of ambition, and that passion inevitably connects itself with the maintenance and extension of slavery.   Whether this ambition would find means to assert itself in the politics of the United States might at one time have seemed more than doubtful.   From the very origin of the Republic there were causes in operation which threatened, if not vigorously encountered, to exclude the South from that influence which it aspired to attain.   The institutions of the Union are based, in a large degree, on the principle of representation in proportion to numbers.   But, as we saw on a former occasion, the social system of the Southern States is ill calculated to encourage the growth of population, while the institutions of the North peculiarly favour it.   On

the formation of the Federal Union the North and
the South started in this respect upon nearly equal
terms ;* and for a while—so long as slave trading
with Africa was permitted—this equality was approximately maintained.   But in 1808 the African
slave trade was abolished ; and the principal external source on which the South relied for recruiting its population was thus cut off.   On the other
hand, free emigration from Europe continued to
pour into the Northern States in a constantly
increasing stream ; while at the same time the
natural increase of the Northern people, under the
stimulus given to early marriages by the great
industrial prosperity of the country, was rapid beyond precedent.   From the influence of these causes,
the original equality in numbers between North and
South was soon converted into a decided preponderance of the North ; and the natural course of events
tended constantly to increase the disproportion.

This state of things, it was obvious, threatened
ultimately the political extinction of the South,
incapable as it was of taking part in politics except

* In 1790 the numbers were respectively as follows :—

Free States.			Slave States.		
Whites	...	1,900,976	Whites	...	1,271,488
Free Blacks	...	27,102	Free Blacks ...		32,354
Slaves	...	40,364	Slaves	...	657,533
Total	...	1,968,442	Total	...	1,961,375

as a distinct interest. At first view, indeed, it might seem as if this consummation was not merely ultimately inevitable, but imminent. In point of fact, however, the South, far from being reduced to political insignificance, has, throughout the whole period that has elapsed since the foundation of the government, maintained paramount sway in the councils of the Union.

This result, so contrary to what one might at first sight have anticipated, it is the fashion to attribute to superior capacity for politics among the Southern people ; and the theory certainly receives some countenance from the fact, that of the illustrious men who founded the republic some of the most eminent were furnished by the South. It is, however, quite unnecessary to resort to so improbable an hypothesis, as that political capacity is best nourished by institutions which tend to barbarize the whole life in order to understand the part taken by the South in the politics of the Union. The sufficient explanation is to be found in two circumstances—in the nature of the Federal Constitution, regarded in connexion with the singleness of aim and steadiness of purpose, which naturally characterize men whose interests and ideas are confined within the narrow range permitted by slave institutions.

The Federal Constitution, as is well known, was a compromise between two principles—the democratic

principle of representation in proportion to numbers,
and the federal principle of representation according
to states.   In the Lower House of Congress—the
House of Representatives—the former principle prevailed ; the several states of the Union sending
members to this assembly in proportion to the relative numbers of their population.   In the Senate—
the Upper House—on the other hand, representation
took place according to states—each state, without
regard to extent or population, being there represented by the same number of senators.   In the
election of the President these two principles were
combined, and the voting power of the several states
was determined by adding to the number of their
representatives in the Lower House the number of
their representatives in the Senate—that is to say,
by the proportion of members which each state
respectively sent to both Houses.   Such was the
general character of the scheme.*

In the arrangement, as thus stated, there would
seem to be nothing which was not calculated to give
to numbers, wealth, and intelligence, their due share
in the government of the country.   But in applying

* The means by which it has been sought to preserve the balance
between these two principles of the Constitution are thus briefly
and comprehensively stated in the *Federalist :*—" The Constitution
is, in strictness, neither a national nor a federal Constitution, but a
composition of both.   In its foundation it is federal, not national ;
in the sources from which the ordinary powers of the government

to the South the principles just described, a provision
was introduced which had the effect of very materially altering, as regards that portion of the Union,
the popular character of the Constitution. This was
the clause enacting what is known as the three-
fifths votes. The House of Representatives professed
to be based on the principle of representation in
proportion to population ; but, by virtue of this
clause, in reckoning population slaves were allowed
to count in the proportion of five slaves to three
free persons. Now, when we remember that the
slaves of the South number four millions in a population of which the total does not exceed twelve
millions, it is not difficult to perceive what must be
the effect of such an arrangement upon the balance
of forces under the Constitution. In the Presidential
election of 1856, the slave representation was nearly
equal to one-third of the whole Southern representation ; from which it appears that the influence of the
South in the general representation of the Union
was, in virtue of the three-fifths vote, nearly one-half
greater than it would have been had the popular principle of the Constitution been fairly carried out. But

are drawn, it is partly federal and partly national ; in the operation
of these powers it is national, not federal ; in the extent of them
again it is federal, not national ; and, finally, in the authoritative
mode of introducing amendments, it is neither wholly federal nor
wholly national."—Story *on the Constitution of the United States,*
vol. i., p. 199.

the influence of the South, as we formerly saw, merely means the influence of a few hundred thousand slaveholders ; the whole political power of the Slave States being in practice monopolized by this body. The case, therefore, stands thus : under the local institutions of the Slave States, the slaveholding interest—a mere fraction in the whole population— predominates in the South ; while, under this provision of the Federal Constitution, the South acquires an influence in the Union by one-half greater than legitimately belongs to it. It is true this would not enable the Southern States, while their aggregate population was inferior to that of the Northern, to command a majority in the Lower House by means of their own members. But we must remember that the South is a homogeneous body, having but one interest to promote and one policy to pursue ; while the interests and aims of the North are various, and its councils consequently divided. " The selfish, single-purposed party," says Mr. Senior,* " to which general politics are indifferent, which is ready to ally itself to Free-traders or to Protectionists, to Reformers or to Anti-reformers, to Puseyites or to Dissenters, becomes powerful by becoming unscrupulous. If Ireland had been an independent country, separated from England, the Ultra-Catholic party, whose only object is the domination of the

* *Slavery in the United States*, pp. 16, 17.

clergy and of the Pope, would have ruled her. This is the source of the influence of a similar party in France. The Clerical, or Jesuit, or Popish, or Ultramontane faction—whatever name we give to it—has almost always obtained its selfish objects, because those objects are all that it cares for. It supported the Restoration, its priests blessed the insurgents of February, 1848, and it now worships Louis Napoleon. The only condition which it makes is ecclesiastical and Popish supremacy, and that condition the governor for the time being of France usually accepts.

" Such a party is the Southern party in the United States." Its single aim has been the consolidation and extension of slavery ; and to the accomplish-ment of this end it has always been ready to sacri-fice all other interests in the country, and, if neces-sary, the integrity of the Union itself.   We may see, then, in what consists the vaunted aptitude for poli-tics exhibited by Southern men : it lies simply in the intense selfishness and utter absence of scruple with which they have persistently pushed their object.   They have acted steadily together—a course for which no political virtue was necessary where there was but a single interest to promote, and that interest their own.   They have contrived, by an un-scrupulous use of an immense patronage, to detach from the array of their opponents a section suffi-

ciently large to turn the scale of divisions in their
favour :—in other words, they have been successful
practitioners in the art of political jobbery.   Lastly,
they have worked on the apprehensions and the
patriotism of the country at large by the constantly
repeated threat which they have now proved themselves capable of putting in force—of dissolving the
Union.*

The actual inferiority in population of the Southern to the Northern States, even under the peculiar
advantage conferred by the three-fifths clause, rendered it necessary that the slaveholders should procure an ally among the Northern people ; and this
indispensable ally they found in the Democratic
party.   It has been frequently remarked upon with
surprise that, in seeking a political connexion, the

---

* " Figurez-vous sur un vaisseau un homme debout près de la
sainte-barbe, avec un mèche allumée ; il est seul, mais on lui obéit,
car, à la première désobéissance, il se fera sauter avec,tout l'équi-
page.   Voilà précisément ce qui se passait en Amérique depuis
qu'elle allait à la dérive.   La manœuvre était commandée par
l'homme qui tenait la mèche.   'A la première désobéissance, nous
nous quittons."   Tel a été de tout temps le langage des Etats du
Sud.   On les savait capables de tenir parole: aussi n'y avait-il plus
qu'un argument en Amérique, la scission.   'Révoquez le compro-
mis, sinon la scission ; modifiez la législation des Etats libres, sinon
la scission; courez avec nous les aventures, et entreprenez des con-
quêtes pour l'esclavage, sinon la scission; enfin, et par dessus tout,
ne vouz permettez jamais d'élire un président qui ne soit pas nôtre
candidat, sinon la scission.' "—*Un Grand Peuple qui se relève*, p. 37.

South—whose social and political system is intensely aristocratic—should have attached itself to that party in the Union in which the democratic principle has been carried to the greatest extreme. But the explanation is to be found in the circumstances of the case. The peculiarity of the industrial and social economy of the Southern States led them from the first to lean to the doctrine of state rights, as opposed to the pretensions of the central government; and the doctrine of state rights is a democratic doctrine. On this fundamental point, therefore, the principles of the Southern oligarchy and those of the Northern democracy were the same. But the alliance was not destitute of the cement of interest and feeling. The Democratic party had its principal seats in the great towns along the Northern seaboard; and between the capitalists of these towns and the planters of the South the commercial connexion had always been close. Capital is much needed under a slave system, and is at the same time scarce. In the Northern cities it was abundant. To the capitalists of the Northern cities, therefore, the planters in need of funds for carrying on their industry had recourse; and a large amount of democratic capital came thus to be invested on the security of slave property. A community of interest was in this way established. But there was also a community of sentiment; for the Northern

cities had formerly been the great emporia of the
African slave trade, and had never wholly abandoned the nefarious traffic ; and the tone of mind
engendered by constant familiarity with slavery in
its worst form naturally predisposed them to an
alliance with slaveholders.   Widely sundered, therefore, as were the Southern oligarchy and the Democratic party of the North in general political
principle, there was enough in common between
them to form the basis of a selfish bargain.   A
bargain, accordingly, was struck, of which the consideration on the one side was the command of the
Federal government for the extension of slavery
and, on the other, a share in the patronage of the
Union.   On these terms a coalition between these
two parties, so opposed in their general tendencies,
has, almost from the foundation of the republic,
been steadily maintained ; and in this way the
South—vastly inferior though it has been to its
competitor in wealth, population, and intelligence
—in all the conditions to which political power
attaches in well-ordered states—has, nevertheless,
contrived to exercise a leading influence upon the
policy of the Union.

These considerations will suffice to explain how
the South has been enabled, even when in a minority, to engage with success the representatives of
the North.   In the Lower House of Congress it has

been always of necessity in this position ; representation being here in proportion to population, in
which, even including slaves, the South is inferior
to its rival. But in the Upper House—the House
which under the Constitution enjoys the most important prerogatives and the highest influence—the
South has found itself at less disadvantage. In the
Senate, as has been already stated, representation
takes place according to states; each state returning
two members without regard either to the number
of its inhabitants or to the extent of its territory.
To maintain itself, therefore, on an equal footing
with the North in this assembly, the South had only
need to keep the number of slave states on an
equality with that of the free ; and this did not
seem to be beyond its power. For, the tendency of
slavery being to disperse population, a given number of people under a slave *régime* would naturally
cover a larger space of country, and consequently
would afford the materials for the creation of a
greater number of states, than the same number
under a *régime* of freedom. What, therefore, the
South required to secure its predominance in the
Senate, was a territory large enough for the creation
of new slave states as fast as the exigencies of its
politics might demand them. To keep open the
territory of the Union for this purpose has, in consequence, always been a capital object in the politics

of the South; and in this way a political has been added to the economic motive for extended territory. Two forces have thus been constantly urging on the Slave Power to territorial aggrandisement—the need for fresh soils, and the need for slave states. Of these the former—that which proceeds from its industrial requirements—is at once the most fundamental and the most imperative; but it has not been that which, in the actual history of the United States, has been most frequently called into play. In point of fact, the political motive has in a great measure superseded the economic. The desire to obtain fresh territory for the creation of slave states, with a view to influence in the Senate, has carried the South in its career of aggression far beyond the range which its mere industrial necessities would have prescribed. Accordingly, for nearly a quarter of a century—ever since the annexation of Texas—the territory at the disposal of the South has been very much greater than its available slave force has been able to cultivate; and its most urgent need has now become, not more virgin soils on which to employ its slaves, but more slaves for the cultivation of its virgin soils.* The important bear-

---

* " At another time the conversation turned upon the discussions as to the Missouri Compromise, and elicited the following quaint remark from the President, ' It used to amuse me some (*sic*) to find that the slaveholders wanted more territory because they had not room enough for their slaves, and yet they complained of not having

ing of this change on the views of the Slave Power will hereafter be pointed out : for the present, it is sufficient to call attention to the fact.

A principle of aggressive activity, in addition to that which is involved in the industrial necessities of slavery, has thus been called into operation by the conditions under which the Slave Power is placed in the Senate. But we should here be careful not to overrate the influence exercised on that Power by its position in the Federal Union. It would, I conceive, be an entire mistake to suppose that this desire for extended territory, which, under actual circumstances, has shown itself in the creation of slave states with a view to influence in the Senate, is in any such sense the fruit of the position of the South in the Federal Union as that we should be justified in concluding that, in the event of the severance of the Union, the South would cease to desire an extension of its territory on political grounds. Such a view would, in my opinion, imply an entire misconception of the real nature of the forces which have been at work. The lust of dominion, which is the ruling passion of the Slave Power, is not accidental but inherent—has its source, not in the constitution of the Senate, but in the fundamental institution of the Slave States ; and the lust

the slave trade, because they wanted more slaves for their room.'"— *Macmillan's Magazine*, May 1862, p. 24.

of dominion, existing in an embodied form in a new continent, cannot but find its issue in territorial aggrandisement.   This by no means depends upon speculative inference.   It admits of proof, as a matter of fact, that the projects of the South for extending its domain have never been more daring, and have never been pushed with greater energy, than during the last five years*—the very period in which the Southern leaders have been maturing their plans for seceding from the Union.   The Federal connexion may have facilitated the ambitious aims of the South while the Federal government was in its hands, but, far from being the source of its ambition, it is because it offers, under the changed conditions, impediments to the expanding views of the more aspiring minds of the South, that the attempt is now made to break loose from Federal ties.   Extended dominion is in truth the very purpose for which the South has engaged in the present struggle; and the thought which now sustains it through its fiery ordeal is (to borrow the words of the ablest advocate of the Southern cause) the prospect of "an empire in the future . . . extending from the home of Washington to the ancient palaces of Montezuma—uniting the proud old colonies of England with Spain's richest and most romantic

* See Reports of the American Anti-slavery Society for the years 1859 and 1860.

dominions—combining the productions of the great valley of the Mississippi with the mineral riches, the magical beauty, the volcanic grandeur of Mexico."* In plain terms, the stake for which the South now plays is Mexico and the intervening Territories. The position of the Slave Power in the Union has thus determined the mode, not supplied the principle, of its aggressive action. It has brought out into more distinct consciousness, and presented in a more definite shape, the connexion between the ruling passion of the Slave Power and the natural means for its gratification. But the passion and the means for its gratification were there independently of the political system of the United States; and the Slave Power, with a vast unoccupied or half-peopled territory around it, could not have failed under any circumstances, in the Union or out of it, to find in the appropriation of that territory its natural career.

* Spence's *American Union*, p. 286. Here for a moment the genius of the South is revealed in naked majesty. It is but for a moment. A few pages further on (p. 291) the scene changes, and the South is restored to its proper *rôle*. We have presented to us the aspect of a people spurning the idea of conquest, bounding its aspirations to the lowest requirement of free men—the demand for autonomy :—" Be our ignorance of the merits of this question ever so great, we behold a country of vast extent and large numbers earnestly desiring self-government. It threatens none, demands nothing, attacks no one, but wishes to rule itself, and desires to be ' let alone.' "

" Amphora cœpit
Institui ; currente rotâ cur urceus exit ?"

CHAPTER VII.

THE CAREER OF THE SLAVE POWER.

THE aggressive ambition of the Southern States has been traced in the last chapter to two principles— the economic necessities forced upon them by the character of their industrial system, and the growth of passions and habits, generated by the presence of slavery, which require for their satisfaction political predominance. In the present chapter I propose to show how these two principles have operated in the actual history of the United States.

At the time of the establishment of the Federal Union the position of slavery in North America was that of an exceptional and declining institution. Many circumstances conspired to produce this result. The war of independence had kindled among the people a spirit of liberty which was strongly antagonistic to compulsory bondage. In the leaders of the revolt this spirit burned with peculiar intensity ; and though many of them were natives of the South and slaveholders, they were almost to a man opposed to the system, and anxious for its abolition. From the Northern States, where slavery had originally been planted, it was rapidly disappearing. In

the unsettled territory then at the disposal of the
central government*—notwithstanding that this
territory had been ceded to it by a slave state—the
institution was by an ordinance of the central
government proscribed.   Economic causes were also
tending to its overthrow.   The crops which are
adapted to slave cultivation are, as we have seen,
few in number.   Those which at this time formed
the principal staples of the slave states of the Union
were rice, indigo, and tobacco.   The last was already produced in quantities more than sufficient
for the market; and in the two former India was
rapidly supplanting the United States.   Sugar was
not yet grown in the Union.   Cotton was still an
unimportant crop.   But it happened that about this
time several causes came into operation, which in
their effect completely reversed the direction of
events, drove back the tide of freedom, and gave to
slavery a new vitality and an enlarged career.   It
was now that the steam engine, having undergone
the improvements of Watt, was first applied on a
large scale to manufacturing industry.   Contempor-
aneously the inventions of Hargreaves, Arkwright,
and Crompton in cotton spinning had been made.

* That is to say the 'Territory' to the North-west of the Ohio—this
being all the territory which up to this time had been ceded to the
central government.—Hildreth's *History of the United States*, vol. 3,
p. 527.

But these inventions, momentous as they were, would have failed in great part of their effect, had they not been supplemented by another—the invention of the saw-gin by Whitney. Previously to this invention the only cotton grown in America, which was available for the general purposes of commerce, was that which was known as the Sea Island kind. This was long-fibred and only grew in a few favoured localities. The bulk of the cotton crop consisted of the short-fibred varieties, but the difficulty of separating the seed from the wool in this species of the plant by the methods then in use, was so great as to render it for the ordinary purposes of cotton manufacture of little value. It was to overcome this difficulty that Whitney addressed himself; and the success of his invention was so complete, that the whole American crop came at once into general demand. At the same time, while these causes were conducing to a great increase in the general consumption of cotton, a vast territory, eminently adapted for the cultivation as well of this as of most other slave products, came into the possession of the United States. The combined effect of all these occurrences was to give an extraordinary impulse to the cultivation of cotton, and cotton being pre-eminently a slave product, and moreover only suited to those districts of the United States where slavery was already established, this was followed by a corresponding extension of slavery. In a few years after Whitney's invention, the exports of cotton from the United States were decupled; by the year 1810, they had been multiplied more than a hundredfold, and, from being a product of small account, cotton rapidly rose to be the principal staple of the Southern States.

The early progress of the Southern planters, under the stimulus thus given to their enterprise, attracted little observation. To the west of the original slave states—Virginia, the Carolinas, and Georgia—lay extensive districts still unsettled, well suited for cultivation by slave labour, and from which it was not in the power of the government of the United States to exclude it. Kentucky, which had been an integral portion of Virginia, had been slave-holding from its original settlement, and subsequently retained slavery in the exercise of its right to legislate for its domestic concerns. Tennessee, Alabama, and Mississippi were formed out of Territory which had been ceded to the central government by North Carolina and Georgia, but on the express condition that it should be reserved for slave settlement.* Over these regions, therefore, the planters could carry their institution without encountering any obstacle. But in 1804 an immense range of country was gained to the United

---

* Hildreth's *History of the United States*, vol. iii. chap. xlviii.

States by purchase from France, with respect to which the authority of Congress was entirely unrestrained, and which, including some of the richest portions of the valley of the Mississippi from its junction with the Missouri to its mouth, offered equal attractions to settlers from both divisions of the Union.   This was the Territory of Louisiana, out of which the States of Louisiana, Arkansas, Missouri, and Kansas have since been formed ; and it was here that the rival pretensions of the two systems of freedom and slavery first came into collision.

Over the Territory thus acquired the authority of Congress was, as I have just intimated, actually uncontrolled.   It, in fact, stood, in its relations to the central government, on precisely the same footing with that large tract known as the North-Western Territory, which had at an earlier period, by cession from Virginia, come into possession of the United States, and for the government of which provision had been made by the celebrated ordinance of 1787.   This ordinance had been enacted by Congress while yet constituted under the Articles of Confederation, and it has been questioned whether, in issuing it *while so constituted*, Congress did not exceed its proper powers.*   The question is, how-

* *The Federalist, No.* 38.   See Story on *The Constitution of the United States,* vol. i. p. 184.

ever, curious rather than important; for in framing
the Constitution of the United States an article was
introduced to provide for this very case. By this
article it was enacted that "Congress should have
power to dispose of, and make all needful rules and
regulations respecting, the Territory or other property belonging to the United States." In the absence, therefore, of special conditions restraining
this power, the competency of Congress, *under the
Constitution*, to legislate for the Territories was placed
by this article beyond dispute ; and in point of fact
Congress has on more than one occasion exercised the
authority thus conferred in the prohibition of slavery.* There was, consequently, no legal barrier to
applying to the new acquisition obtained from France
the same rule which had by the ordinance of 1787
been applied to the North-Western Territory. But
there were practical difficulties in the way. Slaves
already existed in considerable numbers, in some portions of the Territory of Louisiana ; and when the occasion arose for providing for the government of the
remainder, it happened that the attention of the
North was fully occupied with its foreign relations;
for this was the time when those negotiations with
England were in progress which resulted in the war of

---

* For example, in Indiana and Illinois, while yet under 'territorial'
government, several attempts were made to establish slavery; but
Congress always steadily refused its assent. See Kent's *Commenta-
ries*, vol. 1, p. 422.

1812. These circumstances were favourable to the advances of the Slave Power. From the basis of operations supplied by the French slave colony at the mouth of the Mississippi the planters rapidly carried their institution along the western bank of that river. By degrees they reached the district which now forms the State of Missouri, and by the year 1818 had acquired there so firm a footing as to be enabled to claim for it admission into the Union as a slave state.

The admission of Missouri to the Union forms for many reasons an epoch in the grand struggle between free and slave labour in North America. It was on this occasion that both parties appear first to have become sensible of the inherent antagonism of their respective positions, and to have put forth their whole strength in mutual opposition. The contest was carried on with extraordinary violence, and was terminated by a compromise, which was long considered in the light of a national compact irrevocably binding on the combatants on both sides. The occasion being of this importance, it is desirable that we should appreciate with as much precision as possible the stake which was at issue, and the motives which animated the contending parties.

And here, though at the risk of wearying the reader, it may be well once more to repeat that the aggressive character of the Slave Power has been traced to two principles—the one economic, proceeding from the necessity to slavery of a constant supply of fresh soils ; the other political, having its roots in that passion for power which the position of slaveholders—as a dominant race, isolated from their equals, and shut out from the pursuits which distribute the energies of free communities into various channels—inevitably engenders. Again, it has been seen that this latter principle, under the Constitution of the United States, exerts itself chiefly in the effort to increase Southern representation in the Senate through the creation of new slave states. Lastly, it has appeared that the system of society which slavery produces is in its nature an exclusive system—its presence acting as a cause of repulsion towards free societies—and that, consequently, when these two forms of society come into contact on the same territory, an inevitable antagonism springs up between them, an antagonism which displays itself in the efforts which they make to outstrip each other in a race of colonization, each side endeavouring by prior occupation of the soil to exclude its rival and keep open for itself a field for future growth.

These being the principles which governed the conflicting interests, we shall find that the stake which was at issue in the Missouri controversy was well calculated to call them actively into play.

The position of Missouri is one of the most commanding in the central portion of North America. Possessing great agricultural and mineral resources, it is watered by two of the noblest rivers in the continent—the Mississippi and the Missouri. It is in the direct line of movement westward from the Free States. If established as a free state, it would become a centre of colonization for the North, from which free labour would pour along the valleys of the Mississippi, the Missouri, and the Arkansas, and thence to Northern Texas. On the other hand, if occupied by slave institutions, it would cut off the natural expansion of the Free States, and turn the stream of free emigration in the direction of the north-west—to less fertile and less genial regions. But the political consequences depending upon the settlement of this question were not less momentous than the industrial and social. When the proposal for the admission of Missouri was first brought before Congress, the Free and the Slave States were exactly equal in number. The admission of Missouri as a slave state would just turn the scale in favour of the South, and, by consequence, give it a superiority in the Senate—a superiority, which, in conjuction with the advantages it possessed in the Lower House in virtue of its capacity for combined action, could scarcely fail to render it the paramount power in the Union. The success of the South, moreover, in this instance, owing to the commanding geographical position of Missouri, would open for it the path to future conquests ; for, by diverting the stream of Northern emigration to the north-west, it would secure for the future use of the Slave Power the vast reach of fertile territory lying between that state and Texas—an area which comprised some of the richest and best watered lands within the domain of the Republic. The terms, therefore, on which Missouri should be admitted to the Union became a question of prime importance, in connexion with the present and future interests of slave and free institutions on the continent of North America.

Accordingly, no sooner was the proposition made for the admission of Missouri to the Union, than the North rose energetically against the demand, and a violent political contest ensued. It lasted for nearly three years, and was terminated by the celebrated Compromise which has become a landmark in American history. Under this settlement Missouri was received into the Union as a slave state, on the condition that in future slavery should not be carried north of the parallel 36° 30' of north latitude. In all essential respects this was a victory for the slaveholders. They obtained all that they then desired

—the most commanding position in central America, a path to future conquests, a recognized footing in the Territory of the Union; and in return for this they gave but a naked promise, to be fulfilled at a future time, and which could be revoked as easily as it was given. Their triumph was slightly qualified by the admission about the same time of Maine as a free state, but it was sufficiently complete, and it entailed all the consequences which might have been, and which were, foreseen to be involved in it. From the passing of the Missouri Compromise down to the Presidential election of 1860 the predominance of the Slave Power in the politics of the Union has suffered no effectual check.

The episode of the Seminole war—the next prominent scene in which the Slave Power figured—though sufficiently costly and humilating to the United States, need not detain us here at any length. It was little more than a protracted slave-hunt, carried on with circumstances of more than usual cruelty, by means of the forces of the Union, against the Indians of Florida to whom a multitude of slaves had escaped. In this war Oceola, the celebrated Indian chief, was treacherously captured by two American generals, while "holding a talk" with them. In this war also the soldiers of the Union allowed themselves to be disgraced by co-operating with bloodhounds, imported for the purpose from

Cuba, in hunting down the Indians. The general who commanded the Union forces in this ignoble service, and who is said to have lent his sanction to these atrocities, was General Zachary Taylor, afterwards rewarded for his zeal in the cause of the Slave Power by elevation to the Presidency. The war lasted seven years, cost the country, it is estimated, 40,000,000 dollars, and resulted in the capture of a few hundred slaves.

If the Seminole war led to no important results, it was far otherwise with the annexation of Texas. This transaction has long passed into a byeword for unprovoked and unscrupulous plunder of a weak by a strong power. The designs of its authors have always been notorious. Still, as affording a typical example of a mode of aggression which has since been frequently employed, and is probably not yet obsolete, it may be well to recall some of its leading incidents at the present time.

Texas, as all the world knows, was before its annexation to the Union a province of Mexico— a country at peace with the Union, and anxious to cultivate with it friendly relations. Mexico, however, was a weak state, still fresh from the throes of revolution. The district in question was one of great fertility, possessing in this respect, as well as in its climate and river communications, remarkable advantages for slave settlement: it was,

moreover, but very thinly peopled, and was separated
by an immense distance from the seat of government. So early as 1821, while Spanish authority
was still maintained in Mexico, three hundred families from Louisiana were permitted to settle in this
tempting region, under the express condition that
they should submit to the laws of the country. By
this means a footing was obtained in the district.
The original immigrants were in time followed by
others, who like their predecessors undertook to
conform to the laws of Mexico ; and for some years
the proceedings of the new settlers were conducted
with proper respect for the authority of the state in
which they had taken up their abode. But this
aspect of affairs did not long continue. As the
colony increased in numbers and wealth, it became
evident to the slaveowners of the neighbouring
states that they had a "natural right" to the
territory. It offered an admirable field for slave
cultivation ; it was in their immediate proximity ;
of all claimants they were the strongest and "smart-
est :" in short, they wanted the country, and felt
themselves able to take it ; and they resolved it
should be theirs. "Manifest destiny" beckoned them
forward, and they prepared, with reverent submission to the decrees of Providence, to fulfil their
fate.*

* "Texas," says the pious De Bow, "which in an evil hour we

The agency by which the annexationists proceeded to give effect to their natural right was land speculation. Grants of extensive districts were corruptly obtained from local bodies which had no competency to make them ; these were made the basis for a creation of scrip, which was thrown in large quantities upon the markets of the United States. To give an idea of the scale on which these transactions were carried on, one grant, obtained from the legislature of Coahuila, conveyed in perpetuity to American citizens, in direct violation of the laws of Mexico, no less than four hundred square leagues of the public land—an area as large as Lancashire—for a consideration of 20,000 dollars ! In addition to transactions of this kind, a manufacture of titles purely fictitious was freely carried on. By this means great numbers of the people in the United States became the possessors of nominal titles to land in Texas—titles, which, being of course unrecognized by the central authority in Mexico, could only be substantiated by setting aside that authority. " Texan independence could alone legalize the mighty frauds of the land speculators. Texas must be wrested from the country to which she owed allegiance, that her soil might pass into the hands of cheating and cheated foreigners."

sacrificed to Spain, was watched over by a benignant Providence, and brought back with its gallant populace to its republican brotherhood across the Sabine."—*Industrial Resources, &c.* vol. i. p. 417.

But the motive of rapacity was reinforced by a stronger one. Mexico from the moment of her independence had shown a creditable determination to uphold the most essential of human rights. By a law, passed shortly after her severance from Spain, slavery was abolished in her dominions, and prohibited for all future time. Such a law was far from being in keeping with the views of the new settlers. Accordingly, they proceeded to evade it by various artifices. The most usual expedient was that of introducing slaves into the country under the guise of apprentices, the term of whose service commonly extended to ninety-nine years. On the point, however, of maintaining freedom of labour in their dominions, the Mexican authorities were in earnest, and the move of the settlers was met by a decree of the legislatures of Coahuila and Texas, annulling all indentures of labour for a longer period than ten years, and providing for the freedom of children born during apprenticeship. But slaveholders were not to be so baffled. " The settled invincible purpose of Mexico to exclude slavery from her limits created as strong a purpose to annihilate her authority. The project of dismembering a neighbouring republic that slaveholders and slaves might overspread a region which had been consecrated to a free population, was discussed in the newspapers as coolly as if it were a matter of

obvious right and unquestioned humanity."* The
plot having been carried to this point, the consummation of the plunder was easy. A conspiracy was
hatched ; a rebellion organized ; filibusters were
introduced from the border states ; and a population which at the commencement of the outbreak
did not number twenty thousand persons, asserted
its independence, was recognized by the Federal
Government, and, in the face of the strenuous opposition of the Northern States, with little delay annexed to the Union.†

The annexation of Texas was too successful a
stroke of policy not to be regarded as a precedent.
It was accordingly followed by the Mexican war
of 1846, which resulted in an easy victory over
an unequal antagonist. By the treaty concluded
between the United States and Mexico in 1848, the

* Channing's Works, *Letter on Texas.*

† "The measure of annexation was carried upon a stipulated
division of it between free and slave labour, and could have been
carried in no other way. The line of division, the parallel of thirty-
six degrees thirty minutes, is set down in the act of annexation.
Texas, north of that line, has since been made national territory, at
a cost of ten millions of dollars, and appears now on the map as a
part of New Mexico and of the Indian Territory behind Arkansas ;
but the obligation of good faith, that it shall be free from slavery,
still attaches to it unimpaired. The obligation is only twelve years
old, but is already forgotten ; and if it is enforced at all, it must be
by free emigration, as the obligation of 1820 recently has been in
the case of Kansas."—*Progress of Slavery,* pp. 103, 104.

immense range of country, extending from Texas
to the Pacific in one direction, and from the present
frontier of Mexico to the territory of Oregon in the
other, and including the magnificent prize of California, was added to the domain of the Republic.
The disposal of this opulent spoil became at once a
subject of overwhelming interest, and for two years
the Union was shaken by the contests which it produced. The point on which the immediate interest
centred was California. Was it to be a free or a
slave state ? The Southern party which had forced
on the war had no other intention than to appropriate this, its richest fruit ; but the discovery of
gold in the alluvial sands of the Sacramento, just
at the time when the annexation was accomplished,
had attracted thither from the North a large preponderance of free settlers, and these pronounced
loudly for free institutions. The question was
settled, as so many similar questions had been
settled, by a compromise. The Slave party con-
sented to waive its claim, but not without stipu-
lating for a concession in return. The admission of
California as a free state was purchased by the
Fugitive Slave Law.* The price was a shameful

---

* To which the opponents of slavery contrived to add a bill for
the exclusion of the slave-market from the District of Columbia.
The same series of measures also included bills for the settlement
of the Territories of Utah and New Mexico.

one ; yet it seems certain that this transaction forms
an exception to the ordinary course of dealing between the Slave Power and its opponents, and that
in the event the balance of advantage lay largely
with the Free States. The Fugitive Slave Law
has been for the Slave Power a questionable gain.
Amongst its first fruits was *Uncle Tom's Cabin.* On
the other hand, the acquisition of California has
been a solid advantage for the free party. A free
state has thus been established in the rear of the
Slave Power, a centre henceforward for free immigration, and probably destined at no distant time
to play an important part in the struggle between
the rival principles. Thus, by the accident of a gold
discovery, the well laid plans of the Slave party
were frustrated, and a war which was undertaken
by slaveholders in the interest of slavery has
eventuated in a serious blow to their power.

The differences arising out of the conquests made
in the Mexican war having been adjusted by the
compromises of 1850, the Slave Power was again
at liberty to look around it and to meditate
new acquisitions. The Territory which had fallen
to slavery under the Missouri Compromise had
now been appropriated; Florida had also been
acquired ; Texas had been annexed ; New Mexico
lay open, but for the present it was too distant for
settlement, and the numerous tribes of Indians

which inhabited it made it an undesirable abode for slaveholders, whose experience in Florida naturally rendered them averse to such neighbours. But the territory of Kansas and Nebraska was comparatively close at hand, and was inviting from its fertility and salubrity. On political grounds, moreover, there was need that the Slave Power should bestir itself. The occasion was not unlike that which had preceded the admission of Missouri to the Union. From the passing of the Missouri Compromise down to the year 1850 the balance between the Free and Slave States had been fairly preserved. The North had during that time acquired Michigan, Iowa, and Wisconsin; the South, Arkansas, Florida, and Texas; the natural expansion of the one section had been steadily counterpoised by the factitious annexations of the other. But the admission of California as a free state had disturbed this equilibrium. To restore it there was need of a new slave state; and where could this be more conveniently placed than in the rich contiguous Territory of Kansas?

But to the realization of this scheme there was an obstacle in the way. The Territory of Kansas was part of the great tract obtained by purchase from France in 1804, and being north of the line traced by the Missouri Compromise, was therefore by the terms of that measure withdrawn from the field of slave settlement.   Now, the Missouri Compromise was something more than an ordinary legislative act.   It was a compact between two great opposing interests, in virtue of which one of those interests obtained at the time valuable consideration on the condition of abstaining from certain pretensions in the future.   It was, moreover, eminently a slaveholders' measure. " It was first brought forward by a slaveholder—vindicated by slaveholders in debate—finally sanctioned by slaveholding votes—also upheld at the time by the essential approbation of a slaveholding President, James Munroe, and his cabinet, of whom a majority were slaveholders, including Mr. Calhoun himself."*   The measure was thus binding on the Slave Party by every consideration of honour and good faith.   But honour and good faith have always proved frail bonds in restraining the ambition of the Slave Power.   The Missouri Compromise had served its end.   Under it the most commanding central position in the continent had been secured.   Under it Arkansas had been added to the slave domain. There was nothing more to be gained by maintaining it.   The plea of unconstitutionality, therefore,— " like the plea of usury after the borrowed money has been enjoyed"—was set up.   In passing the Missouri Compromise Congress was said to have exceeded its competence.   It was not for it to " legis-

* Mr. Sumner's Speech.

late" freedom or slavery into the Territories. This
was a question to be determined by the inhabitants
of those Territories, whose right it was to "regulate
their domestic institutions in their own way." Accordingly, in 1854, a bill known as the Kansas and
Nebraska Bill was introduced by Mr. Douglas, a
Northern democrat and an aspirant to the Presi-
dence. By this bill the Missouri Compromise was
abrogated, and in its place a principle was established, popularly known as that of "squatter sovereignty," by which it was resolved that the future
settlement of the Territories should be determined.
The principle is thus described in the words of the
act :—" It being the true intent and meaning of this
act not to legislate slavery into any state or territory,
nor to exclude it therefrom, but to leave the people
thereof perfectly free to form and regulate their
domestic institutions in their own way, subject only
to the Constitution of the United States." By this
plausible measure—plausible because it appeared to
extend to the settlement of the question of slavery
the democratic principle which was acknowledged
as the basis of the general government—the inconvenient restraints of the Missouri Compromise were
got rid of, and the ground was cleared for the operations of the Slave Power.

Meanwhile, however, the North, aroused by the
discussions which had taken place to a sense of the

importance of the crisis, was preparing to try issues with its opponent on the ground which it had chosen. On the 30th of May, 1854, the territory of Kansas was by Act of Congress thrown open to settlers; and at once from all quarters of the Free States crowds of emigrants flocked to the debatable land. The work of settlement was pushed with character- istic ardour. The land was rapidly cleared; culti- vation was commenced; the foundations of towns were marked out: the whole country glowed with the bustle of colonizing activity. In a few months the free settlers had acquired a decided preponder- ance over their rivals in the new territory; and all things seemed to promise—the will of the inhabi- tants being the arbiter of the question—that Kansas would ere long be peaceably enrolled in the Union as a Free State. But the Slave Power had other resources in store. It could not, and probably did not, hope to triumph on a fair field in a coloniza- tion struggle with the North. In all the quali- fications requisite for such a struggle the North was immeasurably its superior. It had at its disposal a vastly larger population, and this population, energetic, intelligent, and enterprising, was in all essential respects far better adapted to the work in hand than any which the South could bring against it. But it was not by fair means that the South hoped to attain its object. Kansas adjoined Missouri. In Missouri, as in all the Slave States, there was a "mean white" population—a population utterly unfit for the work of colonization, but well qualified and well disposed to take part in any expedition which promised rapine and blood. It was on the services of this people that the Slave Power relied for the success of its scheme. It could not out-colonize the freesoilers from the North, but it could, it was hoped, make the territory too hot to hold them, and ultimately, being left master of the field, it might occupy it at leisure. This, however, was not its only resource. In the government at Washington it had a sure ally, which, though af-fecting to disapprove, could be depended upon to connive at, and when necessary to sustain, its law-less proceedings. Resting upon these supports, the Slave Power took its measures. It was necessary, in the first place, that a staff of functionaries should be appointed for the Kansas territory. Of these the nomination lay with the President, and needed to be confirmed by the Senate. But the President was the nominee of the South, and in the Senate the South was all-powerful. There was, therefore, no difficulty in securing officials on whom the South could thoroughly rely. Meantime preparations were made for active operations. Bands of border ruf-fians were mustered on the Missouri frontier, and held in leash to be let slip at the decisive moment.

That moment at length arrived. On the 29th of November, 1854, the infant Territory was to elect a delegate to appear and speak in its behalf in the national Congress. On that day the myrmidons of slavery, led by experienced filibusters from the South, rushed upon the scene, seized by force upon the ballot-boxes, and crushed all free action among the inhabitants. On the 30th of March following the Territorial legislature was to be chosen. The invasion was repeated on a larger scale and with a more complete organization. Armed violence was now reduced to system. Again and again were these raids renewed with circumstances of ever-increasing atrocity, turning the Constitution into a mockery—a pliant instrument in the hands of a reckless faction. Under these auspices the elections were held. The result was the return, by a population of whom the great majority were freesoilers, of a pro-slavery delegate, the erection of a pro-slavery legislature, and the promulgation of a pro-slavery constitution.

Some of the provisions of this strange instrument deserve to be recorded. Taking the laws of their own state as their model, the invaders, in the first place, re-enacted in the gross the code of Missouri. But more stringent measures than the Missourian code contained were required to meet the present emergency. Accordingly, all persons holding anti-

slavery opinions were by a single stroke disfranchised.   On the other hand—the object being to
rule the territory through the armed rabble of
Missouri—it was enacted that every one might vote,
whether resident or not, who, holding opinions
favourable to slavery, should pay one dollar on the
day of election, and swear to uphold the Fugitive
Slave Law and the Nebraska Bill.   The ideas which
the Slave Power entertained on the subject of freedom of the press may be gathered from one enactment, which provided that the advocacy of anti-
slavery opinions should be treated as felony, and
punished with imprisonment and hard labour; while
its notions of lenity are illustrated by its mode of
dealing with the offence of facilitating the escape of
slaves.   Against this—of all crimes in the ethics
of the Slave Power the most heinous—and against
other modes of attacking slave property, the penalty
of death was denounced no less than forty-eight
different times.

Such was the mild and liberal spirit of the Leavenworth Constitution.   Once promulgated, it became
necessary to carry it into effect; and the means
adopted for this purpose were in keeping with all
which had gone before.   The country was given
over to be dealt with by the invaders at their
pleasure.*   Gangs of these armed ruffians, making

* General statements fail to convey any idea of the atrocities

no pretence of being settlers, having no other means of support than pillage, patrolled the country, "preserving," so it was phrased in Congress, "law and order." The Federal functionaries, meanwhile, looked on in silence, contenting themselves with ratifying the Constitution which had been

which were committed. The following anecdote is told by Mr. Thomas K. Gladstone—an Englishman who visited Kansas during the time of the disturbances—in his work entitled *Kansas; or, Squatter Life and Border Warfare in the Far West :*—

"Individual instances of barbarity continued to occur almost daily. In one instance, a man, belonging to General Atchinson's camp, made a bet of six dollars against a pair of boots that he would go and return with an Abolitionist's scalp within two hours. He went forth on horseback. Before he had gone two miles from Leavenworth on the road to Lawrence, he met a Mr. Hops, driving a buggy. Mr. Hops was a gentleman of high respectability, who had come home with his wife, a few days previously, to join her brother, the Rev. Mr. Nute of Boston, who had for some time been labouring as a minister in Lawrence. The ruffian asked Mr. Hops where he came from. He replied he was last from Lawrence. Enough! The ruffian drew his revolver, and shot him through the head. As the body fell from the chaise, he dismounted, took his knife, scalped his victim, and then returned to Leavenworth, where, having won his boots, he paraded the streets with the bleeding scalp of the murdered man stuck upon a pole. This was on the 19th of August. Eight days later, when the widow, who had been left at Lawrence sick, was brought down by the Rev. Mr. Nute, in the hope of recovering the body of her murdered husband, the whole party, consisting of about twenty persons in five waggons, was seized, robbed of all they had, and placed in confinement. One was shot the next day for attempting to escape. The widow and one or two others were allowed to depart by steamer, but penniless. A German incautiously condemning the outrage was shot; and another saved his life only by precipitate flight."

passed; while the Federal troops, by abstaining from all interference with the apostles of " order," and, when necessary, by overawing the disaffected, proved useful allies of the movement.

By such means the Slave Power succeeded in establishing itself in Kansas; but its reign was brief.

The following letter from John Brown I extract from *The Life and Letters of Captain John Brown*, edited by Richard D. Webb, pp. 118–120 :—

" Trading Post, Kansas, Jan., 1859.

" Gentlemen,—You will greatly oblige an humble friend by allow-- ing the use of your columns while I briefly state two parallels in my poor way.

" Not one year ago, eleven quiet citizens of this neighbourhood, viz. William Robertson, William Colpetzer, Amos Hall, Austin Hall, John Campbell, Asa Snyder, Thomas Stilwell, William Hairgrove, Asa Hairgrove, Patrick Ross, and B. L. Reed, were gathered up from their work and their homes by an armed force under one Hamilton, and, without trial or opportunity to speak in their own defence, were formed into line, and, all but one, shot— five killed and five wounded. One fell unharmed, pretending to be dead. All were left for dead. The only crime charged against them was that of being free-state men. Now, I enquire, what action has ever, since the occurrence in May last, been taken by either the President of the United States, the governor of Missouri, the governor of Kansas, or any of their tools, or by any pro-slavery or administration man, to ferret out and punish the perpetrators of this crime?

" Now for the other parallel. On Sunday, December 19, a negro man named Jim came over to the Osage settlement from Missouri and stated that he, together with his wife, two children, and another negro man, was to be sold within a day or two, and begged for help to get away. On Monday [the following] night, two small com- panies were made up to go to Missouri and liberate the five slaves,

The atrocities it had committed roused a spirit for which the South was not prepared. The settlers, finding themselves betrayed by the government which should have protected them, rose in arms. The injuries to which they had been exposed only fixed them in the resolution to defend the country

together with other slaves. One of these companies I assumed to direct. We proceeded to the place, surrounded the buildings, liberated the slaves, and also took certain property supposed to belong to the estate. We, however, learned before leaving, that a portion of the articles we had taken belonged to a man living on the plantation as a tenant, who was supposed to have no interest in the estate. We promptly returned to him all we had taken.

" We then went to another plantation, where we found five more slaves, took some property and two white men. We moved all slowly away into the territory for some distance, and then sent the white men back, telling them to follow us as soon as they chose to do so. The other company freed one female slave, took some property, and, as I am informed, killed one white man (the master), who fought against the liberation.

" Now for a comparison. Eleven persons are forcibly restored to their natural and inalienable rights, with but one man killed, and all " hell is stirred from beneath." It is currently reported that the governor of Missouri has made a requisition upon the governor of Kansas for the delivery of all such as were concerned in the last named ' dreadful outrage.' The marshal of Kansas is said to be collecting a posse of Missouri [not Kansas] men at West Point in Missouri, a little town about ten miles distant, to ' enforce the laws.' All pro-slavery, conservative-free-state, and dough-face men and administration tools are filled with holy horror.

" Consider the two cases, and the action of the administration party.

" Respectfully yours,

" JOHN BROWN."

which was rightly theirs; and the story of their wrongs, being carried to the North, excited there a feeling which brought flocking to their assistance crowds of freemen. The efforts of the Slave party though violent, were fitful; those of the Free settlers were resolute and sustained. After a desultory civil war, the former was utterly defeated, the pro-slavery constitution was overthrown, and a free legislature and free institutions were established.

Such was the result of the experiment of "squatter sovereignty" in the Territories. After a long career of success, the South had at length been forced to give way, and to abandon a design which it had deliberately formed. But the defeat in Kansas was not an ordinary reverse. It could be attributed neither to remissness nor to fortune. The South had brought into action all its available strength, and the contest had been fought under conditions which it had itself prescribed. It had selected its own ground; it had taken its opponents by surprise; it had not hesitated to employ every means, legal and illegal, in the prosecution of its end; in all its measures it had been powerfully sustained by the central government; and yet, with all these advantages, it had been utterly defeated. The experiment was absolutely decisive; and it was henceforth certain that, with the resources at present at the disposal of the two parties, slaveholders were no match in the work of colonization for the freemen of the North.

This was a serious result for a community for which territorial expansion was a necessity of prosperous existence. But the crisis assumed a still graver aspect from the movements of political parties to which the events in Kansas led. These events brought home to the Northern people with irresistible force the real aims and character of the power to whose domination it had submitted. It was not simply that the South in Kansas sought to extend the area of slavery—this was a familiar fact; it was that in prosecuting this object it had shown itself prepared to perpetrate any atrocity, any perfidy; it was that, in promoting its ambitious schemes, it had turned with utter unscrupulousness those powers of government, with which it had been entrusted for the general good, to the purpose of crushing the liberties and taking away the lives of those who dared to thwart it. A feeling of profound indignation, mingled with alarm, pervaded the people of the Free States. It was felt that the time had come when all who were not content to yield themselves up to the tender mercies of this unscrupulous and wicked Power should take measures for their safety. A strong reaction set in, and the earliest fruit of the reaction was the formation of the Republican party.

The policy of this party was first given to the world by a manifesto issued in the summer of 1856. The Republican party, it was declared, had no purpose to interfere with slavery in the states where it was already established. Within those limits it had been recognized by the Constitution, and to transcend constitutional bounds was no part of the Republican programme. But it was denied that the authority of Congress, or of any other power in the Union, so long as the present Constitution was maintained, could give legal existence to slavery in any Territory of the United States. The fundamental principle of the party was thus the non-extension of slavery. Taking its stand on this ground, it invited the co-operation of all who were opposed to the dominion of the Slave Power, asking them to lay aside past political differences and divisions, and by one grand effort to rescue the country from the rule of the common foe.*

This was in the summer of 1856. In the autumn of the same year the Presidential election gave occasion for the first trial of strength between the new party and its opponents. The contest occurred within a few months from the time when the first idea of a party on the basis indicated had been formed, and before its leaders had had time to

* See the Republican platform adopted at Philadelphia, June 18, 1856.

complete its organization. As might have been expected, it was defeated, but under circumstances which inspired the strongest hope of ultimate victory. " The Republicans," said the central association at Washington, addressing the country after the event of the election, " wherever able to present clearly to the public the real issues of the canvass— slavery restriction, or slavery extension—have carried the people with them by unprecedented majorities, almost breaking up in some States the organization of their adversaries. . . . . . Under circumstances so adverse, they have triumphed in eleven, if not twelve of the Free States, pre-eminent for enterprise and general intelligence, and containing one half of the whole population of the country. . . . . " We know," continued this body, " the ambition, the necessities, the schemes of the Slave Power. The policy of extension, aggrandisement, and universal empire is the law of its being, not an accident—is settled, not fluctuating. Covert or open, moderate or extreme, according to circumstances, it never changes in spirit or aim. . . . . The true course of the Republican party is to organize promptly, boldly, and honestly upon their own principles, and, avoiding coalitions with other parties, appeal directly to the masses of all parties to ignore all organizations and issues which would divert the public mind from the one danger that now threatens the honour and interests of the country, and the stability of the Union."

The long ascendancy of the Slave Power in the Union was thus at length seriously threatened, and on its ascendancy depended its existence as a Power. The leaders of the South were not slow to appreciate the critical nature of their position. With a boldness and practical sense characteristic of men long and successfully conversant with the affairs of government, they looked the danger in the face, and, perceiving that the emergency was one in which ordinary expedients would be unavailing, they resolved upon a policy of " Thorough," and, without hesitation or compunction, advanced straight to their object.

The real cause of the defeat of the South in the Kansas struggle it was not difficult to discover. It lay in the want of a population adapted to the purpose in hand—slavery colonization. The South had conquered the ground, but, owing to the insufficiency of its slave force, it had been unable to hold it, and the result was its defeat. The remedy, therefore, was plain. It would be necessary to increase the slave force of the South in such a manner as to put it on a par in point of disposable population with its Northern rival, and, meantime, pending the accomplishment of this result, to find means to maintain a footing in the Territories in

spite of the legislation of the freesoilers.   Such was
the problem proposed to the South.   Nothing short
of this would enable the Slave Power to keep open
the Territories for its future expansion, and to
retain its hold on the Federal Government.   Nothing short of this would give it predominance in
the Union.   There was need, therefore, of " Thorough."   It resolved to give effect to this policy
in all its fulness, or, failing this, to dissolve the
Union.

With a view to the first point—the augmentation
of the supply of slave labour—the obvious, and the
only adequate, expedient was the re-opening of the
African slave trade.   That trade had been prohibited by an act of Congress in 1808, and the prohibition had, up to the present time, been acquiesced
in by all parties.   But, like every other enactment
which stood in the way of the freest development of
slavery, this prohibition was now discovered to be
' unconstitutional.'   Congress had, it seemed, exceeded its proper powers in passing the act.   It was,
accordingly, determined that an agitation should
forthwith be set on foot for its repeal.

The idea of re-opening the African slave trade,
like most of those ideas which have been born of
pro-slavery fanaticism, had its origin in South Carolina.   It was first seriously mooted in 1853 ;* but

* " I was the single advocate of the slave trade in 1853: it is

so rapid was the growth of public sentiment in
its favour that within two years the subject was
taken up by several grand juries and recommended
by them to the consideration of the state legislature.   In 1856 the seizure of a slaver led to some
resolutions being brought forward in Congress, of
which the object was to embarrass the government
in the execution of the law ; and, in the discussions
which then took place, Southern members did not
shrink from expressing opinions, not only against the
constitutionality of the Federal prohibition, but in
favour of the morality of the trade.*   The public
mind was thus ripe for the announcement of the
new policy when Governor Adams of South Carolina,
in his address on opening the session of 1857,
brought the matter formally before the legislature
of his state.   The obnoxious prohibition was denounced in vehement terms.   It was the fruit of " a
diseased sentimentality," of a "canting philanthropy."
It was, moreover, a violation of the Constitution,

now the question of the time."—The Hon. L. W. Spratt of South
Carolina.

* For example, Mr. Dowdell of Alabama thus expressed himself :—"I will take this occasion to say, without discussing the expediency of re-opening the slave trade, a matter which properly
belongs to the sovereign states whose industrial policy is to be
affected by it, that the laws are highly offensive in defining that to
be piracy upon the high seas which is not robbery, and in attaching
the death penalty to an act which in itself is not necessarily
immoral."—Almanack, p. 32.

and it interfered with the essential interests of the South. By the closing of the African slave trade the equilibrium between North and South had been destroyed, and this equilibrium could only be restored in one way—by the re-opening of that trade. Let this once be accomplished—let the South have free access to the only labour market which is suited to her wants—and she has no rival whom she need fear.

The key-note having been struck, the burden of the strain was taken up by other speakers, and the usual machinery of agitation was put in motion through the South. The Southern press freely discussed the scheme.* It was brought before the

* The Charleston *Standard*, complaining that the position of the South had hitherto been too much one of defence and apology, adds, "To the end of changing our attitude in the contest, and of planting our standard right in the very faces of our adversaries, we propose, as a leading principle of Southern policy, to re-open and legitimate the slave trade." And then it proceeds, in a series of articles, to argue at length the rightfulness and expediency of this measure, expanding and elaborately enforcing the following propositions, viz. :—"That equality of states is necessary to equality of power in the Senate of the Union; that equality of population is necessary to equality of power in the House of Representatives ; that we cannot expand our labour into the Territories without decreasing it in the States, and what is gained upon the frontier is lost at the centres of the institution; that pauper white labour will not come into competition with our slaves, and, if it did, that it would not increase the integrity and strength of slavery, and that, therefore, to the equality of influence in the Federal legislature, there is a necessity for the slave trade."

annual conventions for the consideration of Southern affairs, and received the energetic support of the leaders of the extreme Southern Party.*   At one of these conventions held at Vicksburg, Mississippi, in May, 1859, a vote in favour of the re-opening of the trade was passed by a large majority ; and this was followed up by the formation of an " African Labour Supply Association," of which Mr. De Bow, the editor of the leading Southern review, was the president.   In Alabama, a " League of United Southerners " issued a manifesto in which the Federal

* Mr. Yancey has denied this in a letter to the *Daily News* and declared that he " does not know two public men in the South, of any note, who ever" advocated the restoration of the trade, and that "the people there are and have been almost unanimously opposed to it." It is unnecessary to re-open a question which has been disposed of, and I therefore refer the reader, who wishes to ascertain the authenticity of Mr. Yancey's statement, to the *Daily News* of the 27th and 28th January, 1862. One or two specimens, however, may be given of the views of Southern politicians upon this subject. The Hon. L. W. Spratt of South Carolina, in a speech at Savannah, in favour of the African slave trade, thus expressed himself :—" The first reason for its revival is, it will give political power to the South. Imported slaves will increase our representation in the national legislature. More slaves will give us more states ; and it is, therefore, within the power of the rude untutored savages we bring from Africa to restore to the South the influence she had lost by the suppression of the trade. We want only that kind of population which will extend and secure our peculiar institutions, and there is no other source but Africa."

Mr. A. H. Stephens, the present Vice-president of the Southern Confederation, has thus pointedly put the argument for the opening of the trade :—" We can divide Texas into five slave states, and get

prohibition of the foreign slave trade is denounced as an unworthy concession to the demands of Northern fanaticism, and which insists on "the necessity of sustaining slavery, not only where its existence is put directly in issue, but where it is remotely concerned." In Arkansas and Louisiana the subject was brought before the state legislatures. A motion brought forward in the Senate of the former state, condemnatory of the agitation for the revival of the African slave trade, was defeated by a majority of twenty-two. In the latter a bill em-

Chihuahua, Sonora, &c. if we have the slave population, and it is plain that *unless the number of African stock be increased*, we have not the population, and might as well abandon the race with our brethren of the North in the colonization of the Territories . . . slave states cannot be made without Africans. I am not telling you to do it, but it is a serious question concerning our political and domestic policy; and it is useless to wage war about abstract rights, or to quarrel and accuse each other of unsoundness, unless we get more Africans. . . . Negro slavery is but in its infancy."

And Mr. Jefferson Davis, while declaring his disapprobation of opening the trade in Mississippi, earnestly disclaimed "any coincidence of opinion with those who prate of the inhumanity and sinfulness of the trade. The interest of Mississippi, not of the African," he said, "dictates my conclusion. Her arm is, no doubt, strengthened by the presence of a *due proportion* of the servile caste, but it might be paralyzed by such an influx as would probably follow if the gates of the African slave-market were thrown open. . . . This conclusion, in relation to Mississippi, is based upon my view of her *present condition, not upon any general theory. It is not supposed to be applicable to Texas, to New Mexico, or to any future acquisitions to be made south of the Rio Grande.*"

bodying the views of the advocates of the trade was passed successfully through the Lower House, and only by a narrow majority lost in the Senate. In Georgia the executive committee of an agricultural society offered " a premium of twenty-five dollars for the best specimen of a live African imported, within the last twelve months, to be exhibited at the next meeting of the society." Nor was the principle of competition confined to the show-yard. Southern notions would have been shocked if so solemn a work had missed the benediction of the church. Accordingly, it was proposed in the *True Southern*, a Mississippi paper, to stimulate the zeal of the pulpit by founding a prize for the best sermon in favour of free trade in human flesh.

Meanwhile those who were immediately interested in the question had taken the law into their own hands, and the trade in slaves with Africa was actually commenced. Throughout the years 1859 and 1860 fleets of slavers arrived at Southern ports, and, with little interference from the Federal Government,* succeeded in landing their

* " Not, however, it is satisfactory to learn, without interruption from the English cruisers. A correspondent of the New York *Journal of Commerce*, writing from the coast of Africa, mentions the capture of no less than twenty-two vessels as having been effected by English cruisers in the summer and autumn of 1857. "All but one were American, and the larger number belonged to New York."

cargoes.* The traffic was carried on with scarcely an attempt at concealment. Announcements of the arrival of cargoes of Africans, and advertisements of their sale, appeared openly in the Southern papers ; † and depôts of newly imported "savages" were established in the principal towns of the South. " I have had ample evidences of the fact," said Mr. Underwood, a gentleman of known respectability, in a letter to the New York *Tribune,* " that the re-opening of the African slave trade is already a thing commenced, and the traffic is brisk and rapidly increasing. *In fact, the most vital question of the day is, not the opening of the trade, but its suppression.* The arrival of cargoes of negroes, fresh from Africa, in our Southern ports is an event of frequent occurrence." ‡

One-half of the policy of "Thorough" was thus fairly inaugurated. But the process of augmenting a population is slow ; and, even on the supposition that the Federal prohibition of the external slave trade were removed, some years would elapse before

* See APPENDIX L.

† For example, the *Richmond* (Texas) *Reporter* of the 14th of May, 1859, contained this advertisement :—

" FOR SALE : Four hundred likely AFRICAN NEGROES, lately " landed upon the coast of Texas. Said negroes will be sold upon " the most reasonable terms. For further information, inquire of " C. K. C., Houston, or L. R. G., Galveston."

‡ Annual Reports of the American Anti-Slavery Society, 1857–8, 1858–59, 1859–60.

the South could hope to renew, with any prospect of success, the colonization struggle with the freesoilers. During the interval the movements of the North must by some means be held in check; the Territories must be kept open.   It was necessary, therefore, to devise a principle of policy on which the party could act together with a view to this end : and for this purpose the South, according to its custom in similar emergencies, had recourse to the Constitution of the United States.   True, the whole tenor of the Constitution ran in an opposite direction.   But the leaders of the party did not despair.   Though they might not find their favourite principle, *totidem verbis*, in the Constitution, nor yet, perhaps, *totidem syllabis*, " they dared engage," like the book-learned brother in a like difficulty, " they should make it out *tertio modo*, or *totidem literis*."*

It was beyond question that the Constitution had recognized the right of property in human beings. This could not be denied, and this was a sufficient basis for the policy of the South.   The recognition, it is true, was partial and local, so admittedly so, that, even under the rule of the Slave party, the whole course of law and government had proceeded upon this assumption.   The latest enactment, for example, bearing upon the question was the Kansas and Nebraska bill.   This measure had been brought

* *Tale of a Tub.*

forward by a Democratic member acting in concert with the whole South, and had been carried against a vehement Northern opposition.   Yet even this measure did not assume an equality between slavery and freedom under the Constitution ; for, while it left it open to the inhabitants of a Territory to pro-hibit slave labour therein, it permitted no corre-sponding prohibition to be directed against free labour ; while it refused to recognize property in slaves under certain circumstances, and left such property unprotected by law, it contemplated no occasion on which other kinds of property should not receive recognition and protection.   The very expression " peculiar institution" showed the light in which slavery was popularly regarded.   But the Slave party had now resolved neither to see nor to admit any of these qualifying considerations.   It took its stand on the principle that the Constitution recognized the right of property in man ; and, refusing to acknowledge anything which did not harmonize with this, it reasoned with ruthless con-sistency to the conclusion that Congress, which was the organ of the Constitution, was bound to protect this property in whatever part of the Union it might be found.   The doctrine of "squatter sovereignty," which left it open to the inhabitants of a district to decide for or against slavery—albeit a doctrine fabricated to order, with a view to meet the special

exigencies of the Slave Power—was therefore denounced as no less unconstitutional than the Missouri
Compromise, as no less dangerous than the Wilmot
Proviso.   It was not for the people of a Territory to
say what property was to be protected, and what to
be left without protection ; but it was for Congress,
to which it belonged to give effect to the Constitution over the whole Union, to protect all property
without distinction, whatever might be its nature,
and in whatever part of the Union it might be
placed—whether consisting of human or of other
chattels, whether existing in the States or in the
Territories, in the Slave States or in the Free.

Such was the daring doctrine* advanced by the
leaders of the South in the critical position of their
affairs at which they had now arrived.   To make
good their ground, they had need of two things;
first, a judicial decision by the highest Federal authority in their favour; and secondly, a government
at Washington prepared to supply the necessary administrative machinery for giving full effect to this
decision.   The Supreme Court of the United States
is the tribunal of ultimate appeal in constitutional
questions.   This court had for a long series of years

* " Reconnaître qu'une constitution, dont les rédacteurs n'ont pas
osé écrire le mot esclave, consacre et garantit le droit de l'esclavage
à se propager et à s'étendre, c'eût été mentir à la vérité, au bon sens
et à l'honneur."—M. Cucheval-Clarigny in the *Annuaire des Deux
Mondes.*

been composed of the most eminent lawyers of the
Republic, and had maintained a high character for
learning and wisdom, as well as for the spirit of
enlightened impartiality with which it discharged
its high functions. But this court was now destined
to suffer from the same causes which had affected
injuriously so many other institutions of the Union.
The judges of the Federal courts were appointed by
the President and approved by the Senate. In the
Senate the Slave party was predominant, and it had
hitherto been able to nominate the President. It
had, therefore, the appointments to the national
judicatory in its own hands ; and for some years
—foreseeing that in the controversies which were
pending it would be of importance to have the
judicial bench on its side—it had been silently shaping to its purpose this great organ of the nation's
power. With such success had the process been
carried on, that in 1855, although the North had
always furnished by far the greatest share of legal
talent and learning to the bar of the Union, out
of the nine judges who constituted the Supreme
Court of the United States, five were Southern men
and slaveholders, and the rest, though not natives of
the South, were known to be in their sympathies
strongly Southern. The tribunal of ultimate appeal
in the Union was thus brought to a condition which
commended it to the confidence of the " thorough "

politicians,* and before the court so constituted a
case was submitted for judgment, involving the principle which it was desired to establish. This was
the celebrated Dred Scott case. The facts of it are
sufficiently simple. A slave of the name of Dred
Scott had been carried by his master from Missouri,
his native state, first to Illinois, a free state, and
subsequently to the United States territory north of
Missouri, which, under the Missouri Compromise,
was free territory. On being brought back to Missouri, the slave claimed his freedom on the ground
that his removal by his master to a free state and
territory had emancipated him ; and that, once free,

---

* The following, which occurs in the judgment of Chief Justice
Taney in the Dred Scott case, will give the reader an idea of the
spirit with which the court was animated. The question before
the court was whether coloured persons are legally citizens of the
United States. Chancellor Kent had laid it down in his Commen-
taries, that " it is certain that the Constitution and statute law of
New York speak of men of colour as being citizens ;" and that " if
a slave be born in the United States, and lawfully discharged from
bondage, or if a black man be born free in the United States, he
becomes thenceforth a citizen." But Chief Justice Taney contended
that coloured persons were incapable of enjoying this privilege.
" Such persons," he said, " had been regarded as unfit to associate
with the white race, either in social or political relations, and so far
inferior that they had no rights which the white man was bound
to respect, and that *the negro might justly and lawfully be reduced to
slavery for his benefit ; that this opinion was, at that time, fixed and
universal in the civilized portion of the white race, and was regarded
as an axiom in morals as well as politics, which no one thought of
disputing, or supposed to be open to dispute.*"

he could not be enslaved by being brought again into a slave state. This demand was strictly in accordance with the prevailing course of decisions over the whole South up to that time ; and was thus, in conformity with precedent, conceded by the state court of Missouri, before which it was in the first instance brought. But the defendant appealed against this decision, and the case came on under a writ of error first before the Supreme Court of the State, and ultimately, having in the interval passed through one of the circuit Federal courts, before the Supreme Court of the Union. The result was the reversal by a majority of the Supreme Court of the judgment of the court below. In announcing the decision, Chief Justice Taney, who delivered judgment, laid down two principles which went the full length of the views of the Slave party. He declared, first, that in contemplation of law there was no difference between a slave and any other kind of property; and secondly, that all American citizens might settle with their property in any part of the Union in which they pleased.

Such was the momentous decision in the Dred Scott case. Its effect was to reverse the fundamental assumption upon which up to that time society in the Union had been based ; and, whereas formerly freedom had been regarded as the rule and slavery the exception, to make slavery in future the

rule of the Constitution. According to the law, as
expounded by the Chief Justice of the Supreme
Court, it was now competent to a slaveholder to
carry his slaves not merely into any portion of the
Territories, but, if it pleased him, into any of the
Free States, to establish himself with his slave reti-
nue in Ohio or Massachusetts, in Pennsylvania or
New York, and to hold his slaves in bondage there,
the regulations of Congress or the laws of the particular state to the contrary notwithstanding. The
Union, if this doctrine were to be accepted, was
henceforth a single slaveholding domain, in every
part of which property in human beings was equally
sacred. So sweeping were the consequences involved in the Dred Scott decision. Reading that
decision in the light of subsequent events, we cannot but admire the sagacious foresight of Tocqueville :—" The President who exercises a limited
power may err without causing great mischief in
the state. Congress may decide amiss without destroying the Union, because the electoral body in
which Congress originates may cause it to retract
its decision by changing its members. But if the
Supreme Court is ever composed of imprudent men
or bad citizens, the Union may be plunged into
anarchy or civil war."

The Slave Power had thus accomplished its first
object. The Constitution had been turned against

itself, and, by an ingenious application of the " *toti-dem literis* " principle of interpretation, the right to extend slavery over the whole area of the Union was declared by the highest tribunal in the Republic to be good in constitutional law. But it was further necessary to give practical effect to this decision ; and this could only be accomplished through a government at Washington favourable to the principle it embodied. It was therefore resolved that, in the approaching Presidential election, the party of the South should be reconstructed on the basis of this principle in its application to the Territories ; (for it was thought prudent for the present to abstain from extending the new doctrine to the Free States). This policy was, however, in the last degree hazardous. The South had hitherto carried its measures through an alliance with the Democratic party of the North ; but this party was now led by Mr. Douglas, and Mr. Douglas was the author of the Kansas and Nebraska bill, the repeal of which was for the moment the main object of the South. Mr. Douglas was, therefore, plainly told that he must recant his former principles—principles which, at the cost of much loss of credit among his Northern friends, he had devised expressly for the benefit of the Slave Power—and that he must make up his mind to uphold slavery in the Territories in spite of anti-slavery decisions by the "squatter sovereignty," or forfeit the support of the South. Now this was a length to which Mr. Douglas and the section which he led—highly as they prized the Southern alliance, and indulgently and perhaps approvingly as they regarded the institution of slavery—were not prepared to go.* Mr. Douglas was, therefore, cast aside. The combined phalanx which had so long ruled the Union was broken in two, and the Slave Power stood alone. This position of affairs could only lead to one result—that which actually occurred—the triumph by a large majority of the

* Yet every point was strained to meet the views of the South. The distinction between the programmes of the two sections as they were ultimately amended, is so fine that it may easily escape the inattentive reader. The essence of the demand of the extreme (Breckenridge) section was contained in the second of the amendments made in the Cincinnati platform; which was to the effect " That it is the duty of the Federal government, *in all its departments,* to protect when necessary the right of persons and property in the Territories, and wherever else its constitutional authority extends"; while the Douglas party embodied in its amendments the principle of the Dred Scott decision. Theoretically, the positions were identical, but practically they involved an important difference. The Douglas programme, although acknowledging the right of slave property to protection in the Territories, gave to the slaveholders no other guarantee than a resort to the ordinary tribunals; whereas the assertion in the Breckenridge programme of the duty of the Federal government, " in all its departments, to protect" slavery, was understood to imply the necessity of drawing up a black code for use in the Territories. " There must," says the *Richmond Enquirer,* " be positive legislation. A civil and criminal code for the protection of slave property in the Territories ought to be provided."

Republican party. The South having thus failed to make good the one alternative of its 'thorough' policy, at once accepted the other ; and the dissolution of the Union was proclaimed.

Such has been the career of aggression pursued by the Slave Power in North America for the last fifty years. It forms, as it seems to me, one of the most striking and alarming episodes in modern history, and furnishes a remarkable example of what a small body of men may effect against the most vital interests of human society, when, thoroughly understanding their position and its requirements, they devote themselves deliberately, resolutely, and unscrupulously to the accomplishment of their ends. It has indeed been contended that "the action of the South on this subject [the extension of slavery], though in appearance aggressive, has in reality been in self-defense, as a means of maintaining its political status against the growth of the North."* And in one sense this is true, though by no means in the sense in which the author of this argument would have us believe it. What is suggested is, that the political ascendancy of the South has been necessary to prevent its being sacrificed to the selfish ends of the Northern majority ; and that it has been with a view to this object—security against Northern rapacity—and not at all on its own account, that

* Spence's *American Union*, p. 107.

the extension of slavery has been sought. The policy of slavery extension by the South is thus represented as but a means to an end—that end being the legitimate development of its own resources. Such is the theory. One more strikingly at variance with the most conspicuous facts of the case it would perhaps be difficult to imagine. The extention of slavery sought as a means to an end! and that end free trade, fiscal equality, and the internal development of the Southern States! Why, if these were the real objects of the South, where was the need, and what was the meaning, of secession? They were all secured to it by the Cincinnati platform ; they had all been advocated by Mr. Douglas. Why then reject the Democratic manifesto and the Democratic candidate, and break with the Democratic party—if this was all that was sought? Were state rights threatened by the Cincinnati platform? Was Mr. Douglas a protectionist? Yet if the South had not broken with this party—a party whose motto was state rights and free trade, a party which regarded slavery with something more than indulgence—the Democratic organization might never have been shaken, and the South might still have been in possession of the Federal Government. "But why discuss on probable evidence notorious facts? The world knows what the question between the North and South has been for many years, and

still is. Slavery alone was thought of, alone talked
of. Slavery was battled for and against, on the
floor of Congress and in the plains of Kansas ; on
the slavery question exclusively was the party constituted which now rules the United States ; on
slavery Fremont was rejected, on slavery Lincoln
was elected ; the South separated on slavery, and
proclaimed slavery as the one cause of separation."*

But, though not true in the sense suggested by
the English champions of the Southern cause, there
is a sense in which it is strictly true that the aggressions of the Slave Power have been defensive movements. This is indeed the essence of the case which
I have endeavoured to establish. For I have endeavoured to show that, while the economic necessities of the South require a constant extension of the
area of its dominion, and while its moral necessities
require no less urgently a field for its political
ambition, it is yet, from the peculiarity of its social
structure, incapable of amalgamating with societies
of a different type, and has no objects which it can
pursue with them in common ; and that, consequently, it can only attain its ends at their expense.
It must advance ; it cannot mix with free societies ;
and, where these meet it in the same field, it must
push them from its path. In this sense it must be
allowed that the aggressive movements of the South

* Mr. Mill in *Fraser's Magazine* for February, 1862.

have been but efforts prompted by the instincts of
self-defence ; but whether the fact, when thus understood, is likely to help the argument of those who
employ it, it is for them to consider.   It is suggested, indeed, that this necessity of aggression
rises from the relative inferiority of the South in
wealth and numbers—that its encroachments are
but " means of maintaining its political status
against the growth of the North."   But in all
political aggregates particular members or groups
of members must be inferior to other members or
groups, or to the rest combined, and if this were
a reason for political separation, there could be
no such thing as political union.   The Southern
States are not more inferior in wealth and numbers
to the Northern than is Ireland to Great Britain,
or Scotland to England and Ireland ; yet neither
Ireland nor Scotland is compelled in self-defence
to pursue towards the more powerful section of the
unity to which they severally belong a policy of
aggression.   Why should it be different with the
Southern States of the Union ?   Let the champions
of the South address themselves to this problem,
and if they can solve it without being brought at
last to slavery as the ultimate cause of all other
dissensions—the one incompatibility in the case—
they will show more ingenuity than they have ever
yet displayed.   I venture to suggest that solution

which has been foreshadowed by Tocqueville, and which is at once the most obvious and the most profound. The South has been compelled to pursue a policy of aggression towards the North, not because it is less rich or less populous, but because it is different, and all the differences which divide North and South have originated in slavery—in an institution which prevents the growth of interests, ideas, and aims in which free societies can share, and which can prosper only by perpetually encroaching on their sphere.*

* Some explanation, perhaps, is needed why in the foregoing sketch no mention has been made of one of the most signal and devoted acts of heroism in modern times—the attempt of John Brown to open a guerilla warfare against slavery in Virginia. The omission has been made designedly. The enterprise, however worthy of being recorded, having yet originated exclusively in the noble heart of the man who conducted it, and having been carried into operation without the connivance of any considerable party in the United States, could not properly be included in a sketch of which the object was to trace the working of those parties. The effort stood apart from the combination of agencies which were working towards the same end ; yet it would not be correct to say that it was without influence on the cause which it was designed to serve. Its connexion with the history of the movement appears to have been this. The alarm which the attempt created in the South had the effect of strengthening the influence of the extreme party there, and of transferring the conduct of affairs in the Slave States from such men as Hammond and Hunter, Wise and Clingham, to such men as Jefferson Davis, Stephens, and Yancey—from the representatives of the Border to those of the Cotton States. (See *Annuaire des Deux Mondes*, 1860, pp. 553–555.) It

can scarcely be doubted that this hastened the split in the Democratic party, and thereby the triumph of the Republicans.   In this manner the enterprise of John Brown conduced directly to the present crisis, and, through this, we may now with some confidence assert, to the downfall of the great crime against which he had sworn undying enmity.   The reflection will be welcome to those who would deplore that an act of such serene self-devotion should be performed in vain.

> "Actions of the just
> Smell sweet in death, and blossom in the dust."

The reader who desires to see a faithful and spirited sketch of this worthy representative of the sturdy virtue of the Pilgrim Fathers is referred to the *Life and Letters of Captain John Brown*, edited by Richard D. Webb.   London: Smith, Elder, and Co. 1861.

CHAPTER VIII.

THE DESIGNS OF THE SLAVE POWER.

WE have traced in the foregoing chapter the career of the Slave Power. In the present it is proposed to consider its probable designs. This, indeed, might well seem to be a superfluous inquiry ; since, if we have correctly appreciated the past history of that Power, and the motives which have carried it to its present perilous attempt, we shall not easily err as to the objects which it would pursue in the event of that attempt being successful. Combinations of men do not in a moment change their character and aims ; of all combinations aristocracies are the most persistent in their plans ; and of all aristocracies an aristocracy of slaveholders is that the range of whose ideas is most limited, and whose career, therefore, is least susceptible of sudden deviation from the path which it has long followed.

Nevertheless, it will not be expedient to take for granted what would seem to be in such little need of proof ; for there are those who tell us that this party, whose whole history has been a record of successful aggression and of pretensions rising with each success, has engaged in this last grand effort from motives the reverse of those which have hitherto notoriously inspired it; and who would have us believe that the Slave Power, which in the space of half a century has pushed its boundary from the foot of the Alleghanies to the borders of New Mexico, and which, from the position of an exceptional principle claiming a local toleration, has reached the audacity of aspiring to embrace the whole commonwealth in its domain—that this Power has suddenly changed its nature, and, in now seeking to secede from the Union, aims at nothing more than simple independence—the privilege of being allowed to work out its own destiny in its own way.

This assumption, indeed, however paradoxical to those who are familiar with the exploits of the Southern party, underlies most of the speculation which has been current in this country upon the probable consequences of a severance of the Union, and is that which has procured for the cause of secession the degree of countenance which it has enjoyed. It will therefore be desirable to consider how far the basis of the assumption is warranted—how far the altered position of the South—supposing it to make good its ground in the present struggle—is calculated to affect the character which it has hitherto sustained, and to convert an unscrupu-

lous and ambitious faction into the moderate rulers
of an inoffensive state.

And here we must advert to principles already
established. We have seen the causes which have
made the Slave Power what it is : in its new position which of these causes will cease to operate ?
Slavery is to remain the " corner stone" of the republic more firmly set than ever. The economic
and moral attributes of the South will therefore
continue to be such as slavery must make them.
Cultivation will be carried on according to the old
methods : the old process of exhaustion must, therefore, go on; and thus the necessity for fresh soils will
be not less urgent under the new *régime* than under
the old. The stigma which slavery casts on industry will still remain: there will, therefore, still be an
idle and vagabond class of "mean whites ;" and, since
cultivation must still be contracted to the narrow
area which is rich enough to support slave labour,
there will, as now, be the wilderness to shelter them.
There they must continue to drag out existence,
lawless, restless, incapable of improvement, eager as
ever for filibustering raids on peaceful neighbours.
Lastly, the moral incidents of slavery must remain
such as we have traced them. The lust of power
will still be generated by the associations and habits
of domestic tyranny, and the ambition of slaveholders will still connect itself with that which is

the foundation of their social life, and offers to them their only means of emerging from obscurity. In a word, all those fundamental influences springing from the deepest roots of slave society, which have concurred to mould the character and determine the career of the Slave Power while in connexion with the Union, will, after that connexion has been dissolved, continue to operate with unabated energy.

Nor does this adequately represent the case. While the same motives to ambition will remain, the appetite for power will be still further stimulated by the exigencies of its new position. Connected with the North, the Slave Power was sustained by the prestige of a great confederation. Through the medium of its government it was brought into harmonious relations with free countries ; under the ægis of its protection it enjoyed almost complete immunity from foreign criticism. It so happened, too, that, during the chief period of its connexion with the Union, the South contrived to hold the reins of government in its own hands, and was thus enabled in the prosecution of its designs to wield a power far greater than its own, and to compass ends which, in the absence of such support, could not have failed to call up in other countries effectual opposition. But, separated from the North it will neither command the same resources nor enjoy among foreign powers the same consideration.

Its position will be one of absolute isolation from
the whole civilized world : it will be compelled to
encounter without mitigation the concentrated reprobation of all free society.   " It were madness
now," says one of the ablest of Southern writers, " to
blink the question.   We are entering at last upon a
daring innovation upon the social constitutions of
the world.   We are erecting a nationality upon a
union of races, where other nations have but one.
We cannot dodge the issue ; we cannot disguise the
issue ; we cannot safely change our front in the face
of a vigilant adversary.   Every attempt to do so,
every refusal to assist ourselves, every intellectual
or political evasion, is a point against us.   We may
postpone the crisis by disguises, but the Slave Republic must forego its nature and its destiny, or it
must meet the issue." *   Such a position will only be
permanently tenable on one condition—that of
vastly augmented power.   The South will not be
slow to discover this ; and thus, by more powerful
inducements than it has yet experienced, the Slave

* Spratt's *Philosophy of Secession* (APPENDIX).   In an article in
De Bow's *Industrial Resources,* the writer, advocating sheep farming as a means of employing the poor whites of the South, remarks,
" This would enlarge the capacity of the country to sustain its increasing population, and keep within its limits a physical and moral
power necessary for the preservation of the peculiar institutions of
the South—*a policy that should never be lost sight of by the slaveholder."*—vol. ii. p. 112.

Power will be precipitated upon a new career of aggression.

These considerations apply to every conceivable hypothesis as to the terms on which the independence of the Southern Confederacy may be accomplished. But, in order to bring out more distinctly the views which are likely to govern this body as an independent power, it will be convenient to consider the case on three distinct suppositions.

We may suppose, first, that the independence of the Slave Republic is recognized on the terms of permanently limiting its area to those portions of the South which are already definitely settled under slavery.

Or, secondly, we may suppose its independence to be recognized on the condition of its being restricted for the present to the above limits, but with liberty of colonising, and, after colonization, of annexing the unsettled districts on equal terms with the North —the question of free or slave institutions being left to be determined by some principle analogous to " squatter sovereignty."

Thirdly, we may suppose an equal division of the unsettled portions of the public domain between the contending parties, the South taking that portion which lies westward of its own boundary, including the Indian Territory and New Mexico.

Taking the first of these suppositions—the recog-

nition of the independence of the South on the terms
of being permanently confined within the limits of
country already settled under slavery—this would
involve a considerable curtailment of the present
area of the Slave States. Extensive districts included
in this area cannot in any correct sense be said to be
settled at all ; and others are settled under freedom.
The latter observation applies to large portions of
Virginia, Kentucky, and Missouri, which would,
therefore, on the hypothesis we are at present considering, pass to the side of the North ; the former
applies to Texas, and, in a considerable degree, to Arkansas.   Thus, Texas, comprising an area of 274,356
square miles—an area greatly larger than that of
France—contained in 1850 but 58,161 slaves ; and
Arkansas, extending over 52,198 square miles—an
area larger than that of England—contained but
47,100 slaves.* Districts in which the slaves are not
more numerous than this—albeit they may have
been enrolled as slave states to meet the political
exigencies of the Slave Power—cannot be said to
have been yet appropriated by slavery.   The task of

* Between 1850 and 1860, these numbers had largely increased.
According to the census of the latter year they were for

   Texas ... ... 182,566 slaves.
   Arkansas ... ... 111,115 ,,

Even, as thus augmented, however, the slave population over the
whole area was considerably under the proportion of one slave on
an average to the square mile, leaving the argument in the text

their colonization is yet to be performed ; and on the supposition, therefore, that the Slave Power were restricted within the country which it has really settled, these districts with the others would pass from its grasp. Now, what future would lie before the Slave Power in the event of its being shut up within these limits? It seems to me we can have little difficulty in forecasting its destiny. If there be any truth in the best established conclusions, independence upon such terms could only be the prelude to an early overthrow of the present social and political fabric of the South. Once confine the operations of slavery to the tracts which it already occupies, and the ultimate extinction of the system becomes as certain as the ultimate surrender of the garrison of a beleaguered town which is absolutely cut off from relief. Emancipation would be gradually but surely forced upon slaveholders by irresistible causes ; and scope would at length be given for the resuscitation of society upon wholesome principles. Each year would bring, on the one hand, an increase of the slave population, and on the other—as the soil de-

substantially unaffected. But since 1860 another change has occurred. From the most recent accounts, it seems certain that already a complete break up of the slave system has occurred in those quarters. Vast numbers of slaves have escaped ; and of those who remain, many are working as freemen at wages. So far as Texas and Arkansas are concerned, the problem of abolishing slavery has already well nigh solved itself.

teriorated under the thriftless methods of slave culture—a diminished area of land suitable for its employment; and the process would continue till, in the words of Judge Warner, "both master and slave would be starved out." The process of decay would commence in the older states. There would be a fall in the price of slaves : breeding would no longer be profitable; and thus the single prop which has for fifty years supported slavery in those states would be at once withdrawn.* For a time the working states might not be losers, and might even be gainers by the change. The price of labour might fall more rapidly than their lands would deteriorate. But it would be for a time only. The decreasing productiveness of the slave's exertions would at length reach the point at which the returns from them would not equal the cost of his support, and then the progress towards the catastrophe would be rapid. The fate of the older states would overtake every portion of the slave domain ; and the whole body of slaveholders would be compelled to face the fearful problem of doing justice to four million victims of their own and their ancestors' wrong. It is not to be supposed, however, that the solution would be

* " If the Mississippi had formed the boundary of slavery on the west, perhaps Maryland and Virginia might have been free long before now, and Kentucky and Tennessee, in their turn, would soon have been forced to abandon the institution."—*Russell's North America*, p. 299.

postponed to the last moment.   So soon as the end
came distinctly into view, provision would doubtless
be made to meet the inevitable change ; and the
gradualness of the process would allow time for the
action of palliative influences.   Such, it seems to
me, would be the result of independence on the terms
involved in the first hypothesis.   In such terms,
however, we may be well assured, the Southern
leaders, fully understanding as they do their own
case, would only acquiesce after complete subjugation.

But, secondly, we may assume, as the condition of
Southern independence, that the unsettled portions
of the public domain (including under this expression, besides the Territories technically so called,
the greater part of Arkansas and nearly the whole
of Texas) should be open for slave colonization,
while a like liberty should be accorded for free
settlement ; and we have now to consider what
would be the effect of its position, as thus determined,
on the fortunes of the Slave Power.   Now I think it
is plain that, in view of the competition which such
a determination of the question would inevitably
engender, the necessity would at once be forced
upon the South of maintaining a footing in the
unsettled districts at whatever cost.   The attractions
offered by the fertile soils and fine river systems of
Texas and Arkansas could not fail to draw from the

North, on the one hand, and from California, on the other, crowds of free settlers, who would quickly establish themselves upon the most eligible sites. If the South did not proceed with equal energy, it would find itself forestalled at every point. A cordon of free states would in no long time be drawn around its border, barring its advance towards the rich lands of Mexico, and throwing it back upon its exhausted fields. Is it likely that the Slave Power would quietly contemplate this consummation,— that it would look forward to what Mr. Spence aptly calls " the painful process of strangulation," without making an effort to break the bands which were gradually but surely closing around it? The supposition is incredible. Freedom and slavery would therefore once more renew their race in the colonization of the Territories. And on what grounds could the South hope for success in such a contest? The mortifying lesson taught in Kansas has not been forgotten. The South knows well that a renewal of the contest under conditions which then brought signal defeat must inevitably lead to a like result. But the conditions of the new trial of strength would, in one respect at least, be far less favourable for the Southern cause than those which proved disastrous in Kansas. The Slave Power would no longer find an accomplice enthroned at Washington. What happened in Kansas, therefore, would of necessity be repeated in Texas and New Mexico; the South would be out-colonized by its rival, and the goal would appear in no distant view. There would be but one escape from this fate—such a rapid increase of its disposable slave population as would supply the defect from which it suffered in its former attempts; and this increase could only be accomplished in one way—by a revival of the African slave trade. The revival of this trade would, accordingly, in the event we are considering, become a vital question for the South. Whether the measure would really prove effectual for the purpose designed is a question which I do not think we have sufficient data to resolve; but that such would be the case is undoubtedly the opinion of the Southern leaders. "We can divide Texas into five slave states," says the Vice-president of the Southern Confederation, "and get Chihuahua and Sonora, if we have the slave population; but unless the number of the African stock be increased we have not the population, and might as well abandon the race with our brethren of the North in the colonization of the Territories. Slave states cannot be made without Africans." "Take off," says Mr. Gaulden of Georgia, "the ruthless restrictions which cut off the supply of slaves from foreign lands . . take off the restrictions against the African slave trade, and we should then want no protection, and I would be willing to let you have

as much squatter sovereignty as you wish. Give us
an equal chance, and I tell you the institution of
slavery will take care of itself." From all this it
seems to follow—assuming a separation on the terms
of an open field for free and slave colonization over
the still unsettled districts—that the only chance of
permanently establishing the Southern Republic on
that "corner stone" which its builders have chosen,
would lie in re-opening the African slave trade, and
rapidly increasing the supply of slaves; and that
the Southern leaders would, in the contingency supposed, at once adopt this expedient I cannot for a
moment doubt. As we have seen in a former chapter, the trade had actually been commenced on an
extensive scale before the breaking out of the civil
war; and, with vastly more urgent reasons for reviving it, while there would be entire freedom from
the restraints of Federal legislation, it is difficult to
believe that there would be any hesitation about re-
curring to the same course.

But there is yet another condition under which
the independence of the South may be regarded.
We may suppose that the Union is dissolved on the
terms of an equal division of the unsettled districts
between the contending parties. This arrangement
would probably satisfy the utmost aspirations of the
Southern party. It would probably also—so far as
any distinct ideas on the subject exist—fall in with

the conception of an independent South which for the most part rises before those who in this country take the Southern side, including, it may be observed, some whose sincerity in disclaiming all sympathy with slavery it is impossible to doubt.   It becomes, therefore, of importance that the consequences involved in this mode of establishing Southern independence be carefully examined.

The argument by which the support of the Southern cause, understood as I have just stated it, is reconciled with the avowal of anti-slavery opinions, is one with the basis of which the reader is now familiar.   It is this, that under the proposed arrangement the limits of slavery would be fixed ; and that, this point being attained, the downfall of the system would in due time follow.   " The Southern Confederacy, hemmed in between two free and jealous neighbours [the Northern States and Mexico], will henceforth see its boundaries, and comprehend and accommodate itself to its future conditions of national existence.   The moment slavery is confined definitively within its present limits, according to the best opinions, its character becomes modified and its doom is sealed, though the execution of the sentence may seem to be relegated to a very distant day."*

This theory, it will be remarked, involves a sus-

* *North British Review* for February, 1862, p. 269.

picious paradox. It supposes that the most complete success which the South can hope for in the present war would effectually defeat the precise object for which the South has engaged in war. It supposes that Englishmen know more of the real necessities of slavery than the men whose lives have been spent in working the system, and who have now staked them on an attempt to establish it upon firm foundations. Before accepting so improbable a doctrine, it will be worth considering whether there may not be more to be said for the wisdom of Mr. Jefferson Davis and his friends, than those would have us think who in this country favour their cause.

It seems difficult to believe that those who speculate on the prospects of slavery in the manner of the writer from whom I have quoted, have attended to the geographical conditions under which, in the case supposed, the institution would be placed. The South is described as " hemmed in " between Mexico and the North. The expression implies ideas of magnitude truly American ; for the Power thus "hemmed in " would be master of a space as large as all Europe west of the Vistula, and would have at its disposal a region, still unsettled and available for slave colonization, little less extensive than the whole area of the present Slave States.* Under an

* That is to say, the whole of those of them which are actually settled under slavery—a description which would exclude nearly

arrangement which professes to provide for the extinction of slavery a new field would be thus secured
for its extension, equal to that which now employs
4,000,000 slaves.

But it will perhaps be said that, whatever might
be the immediate effects of Southern independence
established upon these terms, still, the bounds of
slavery being absolutely fixed, provision would be
made for its ultimate extinction.   Those opponents
of slavery who find comfort in this view of the case
must possess more far-reaching sympathies than I
can pretend to.   It may be worth their while, however, to consider whether even their longanimity
may not in the end be balked of its reward.   For,
ere the time would arrive when the Slave Power,
having occupied the vast regions thus secured for it,
would begin to feel the restraints of its spacious
prison, at least a quarter of a century would have
elapsed, and at least two million slaves would be
added to the present number.   With this increase
in the area of its dominion, and in the number of
its slave population, and with the time thus allowed
it for consolidating its strength, and maturing its

the whole of Texas, Florida, and Arkansas.   See ante, p. 232,
note.   "Texas," says Mr. Weston, "may easily furnish room for
millions of slaves, and at this rate a long period must elapse before
it is filled up ; and in the mean time where is the slave population
which is to overrun Sonora, Lower California, and finally the whole
of Mexico ?"

plans, it cannot be doubted that the power of the
South would have become indefinitely more formidable than it has ever yet shown itself. And as
little, I think, can it be doubted that its audacity
would have grown with its strength ; for it would
now, by actual trial, have proved its prowess against
the only antagonist whom it has really to dread,
and it would enter on its career of independence
amid all the *éclat* of victory. In the mood of
mind produced by the contemplation of its achievements and the sense of its supremacy, is it likely that
the South would be content to bridle its ambition,—
much less to accept a lot, acquiescence in which
would be tantamount to signing its own doom ?

It will be said that the Slave Power, severed from
the Union, would find itself on all sides surrounded
by watchful and jealous neighbours, whose office it
would be to counteract its intrigues and to hold its
ambition in check ; and that, in discharging this
office, the free communities of America would be
sustained by the moral, and, if need were, by the
physical, support of the Great Powers of Europe. It
cannot be denied that there is much weight in this
consideration ; yet its importance may easily be
over-rated. The Northern States, once shut out
from Mexico and Central America by the vast range
of territory which, under this determination of the
quarrel, would be alienated from their confederacy,

would have little object in staying the progress of
the South in that direction.   It is, moreover, important to observe that one of the most popular
projects among all sections of the Northern people,
for some years past, has been the providing of railway communication between the Atlantic and the
Pacific States*—a project which, so soon as the re-
establishment of peace shall allow time for the prosecution of industrial schemes, will doubtless be
resumed.†   Now, this idea once carried into effect,
the chief reason with the Northern people for
desiring influence in the Gulf of Mexico would be
removed.   Again, it is not impossible that, before
the time should arrive when intervention might
be required, the position of affairs among the Northern States might be considerably altered.   Although
I am quite unable to see the ground for the appre-
hension now so prevalent, and apparently so influential, in the North, that, a severance of the Union
once effected, the process of disintegration would go
forward till society should be reduced to its primary

* On this point at least the Republican and Democratic parties
are at one.   See their respective platforms.

† Since the above was written a bill for a Pacific Railway was
passed through Congress.   The passing of this measure of provident
industry in the midst of the turmoil of civil war recals the confidence
of the Roman senators in the destiny of the republic, evinced by
the sale at undiminished prices of the land on which Hannibal's
army was encamped.

elements; still I think it cannot be doubted that the example would be contagious; and thus it is no violent supposition, that, as in course of time a difference of external conditions among several groups of the Northern States resulted in the growth of different interests and different modes of regarding political questions, the present would be followed by future secessions, until, in the end, several communities should take the place of the existing Confederation. Now it is obvious to reflect that, were such an order of political relations once established, the Northern States would find, in the clashing interests and mutual jealousies developed among themselves, more tempting matter for diplomatic activity than in counteracting the designs of Southern ambition in a part of the world from which their connexion, alike commercial and political, had been almost wholly cut off.

And still less is European intervention to be relied upon. The Powers of Europe have doubtless strong reasons that Central America should be held by hands which they can trust; and they would naturally be disposed to offer obstacles to the progress of a Slave Power. But Europe is far removed from the scene of Mexican intrigue; and an European war, or even a serious complication in European politics, might easily relax their vigilance. Taking into consideration all the circumstances of the case

—the period which would elapse before the new lands could be occupied, a period during which the Slave Power would have time to organize its forces and to study the weakness of its opponents—the chances that in the interval disunion in the North, or complications of policy in Europe, would produce contingencies favourable to its designs—the persistency of aristocracies in pushing schemes on which they have once entered—the eminent examples of this quality which the South has already furnished—the passion, amounting to fanaticism, with which it has long cherished this particular scheme—above all, the absolute necessity under which it would in the end find itself of extending its domain—who, I say, with all these circumstances in view, can feel assured that, once established on the broad basis of an empire reaching from the Potomac to the Rio Grande, the Slave Power would not hold out a serious menace of realizing the vast projects of its ambition; and that the world might not one day be appalled by the spectacle of a great slaveholding confederacy erecting itself in Central America, encircling the Gulf of Mexico, absorbing the West Indies, and finally including under its sway the whole tropical region of the New World ?*

* " Vers le milieu de l'année 1859, il se forma dans les états qui cultivent le coton, et spécialement dans la Louisiane et le Mississipi, une association mystérieuse, dont les statutes étaient couverts d'un

If there be any force in these speculations, it will be seen that Mr. Jefferson Davis and his associates were not so widely mistaken in the selection of their means as has been commonly supposed, and that they may contemplate with considerable compla-

secret inviolable, et dont les membres s'intitulaient les *chevaliers du cercle d'or*. Ces chevaliers appartenaient exclusivement aux classes aisées ; ils avaient une organisation toute militaire et devaient être pourvus d'armes. Les progrès rapides de cette association attirèrent quelque attention ; mais comme Walker parcourait à ce moment le sud, et commençait les préparatifs de l'expédition dans laquelle il devait perdre la vie, on crut qu'il se méditait un nouveau coup de main contre le Nicaragua ou contre quelqu'une des provinces du Mexique, que l'objet de l'association était de recueillir de l'argent et de recruter des hommes pour le compte du célèbre flibustier. D'autres pensèrent que le succès qui avait couronné les tentatives faites pour introduire des nègres d'Afrique par les bouches du Mississipi avait donné naissance à de vastes opérations de traite. Comme il s'agissait, dans les deux cas, de violer les lois et de déjouer la surveillance des autorités fédérales, le mystère dont s'entourait l'association s'expliquait tout naturellement. Les projets des chevaliers étaient beaucoup plus ambitieux cependant : ils tendaient à détacher de la confédération les états qui cultivent le coton pour en former une république nouvelle dont l'esclavage serait l'institution fondamentale, et qui puiserait dans le rétablissement de la traite les élémens d'une rapide prospérité. Dès que sa force d'expansion ne serait plus arrêtée par la cherté de la main-d'œuvre, la nouvelle république ne pouvait manquer d'absorber en quelques années le Mexique, le Nicaragua et la Bolivie ; elle acquerrait de gré ou de force toutes les Antilles, et fonderait au centre du continent américain l'état le plus riche et le plus puissant du monde. Le *cercle d'or*, c'étaient donc les pays et les îles qui forment autour du golfe du Mexique une ceinture d'une incomparable fécondité."—*Annuaire des Deux Mondes*, 1860, p. 602.

cency the "euthanasia" which has been predicted for their favourite institution.*   That the establishment of Southern independence upon equal terms will "modify the character" of slavery, I am far from denying.   But it is important to determine in what direction the modification will take place; and, in connexion with this subject, I shall revert to a topic to which I have already more than once referred, but the importance of which deserves a somewhat fuller consideration than has yet been given to it—I mean the possibility of a revival of the African slave trade.

The audacity of this conception and its incongruity with the prevailing modes of thought in Europe, and especially in England, have on this side of the Atlantic caused general incredulity as to the fact that such a project has been really entertained. It seems almost too monstrous that a party claiming admission as an equal member into the community of Christian nations, should deliberately conceive the plan of reviving in the full light of modern civilization a scandal which has long lain under its ban.   It is not then strange that the disclaimers by

* " This euthanasia of slavery [the consummation of Southern independence, as conceived by the writer] we admit to be slow and distant; but we solemnly believe it to be both safe and certain. And, at least, it *is* an euthanasia—a natural and not a violent death." —*North British Review* for February, 1862, p. 272.

Southern agents of any intention on the part of the
South to revive the trade have, for the most part, obtained an easy acceptance in Europe.   But those
who are thus easily satisfied can scarcely have attended to the prevailing tendencies of Southern politics, or be aware of the steps which, previous to the
outbreak of the civil war, had been actually taken in
this direction by the party now dominant in the
South.   Of the strong interest of the Slave Power in
the revival of the trade, in the event of its independence being established on any terms which give it a
chance of maintaining itself in the Territories, there
cannot I think be a doubt.   It has been already
shown that, on one supposition, the question would
become absolutely vital.   It would be only a choice
between the re-opening of the trade and acquiescence
in a condition of things which would be tantamount
to early extinction.   On the hypothesis last considered, there would not, indeed, be the same vital
necessity for the measure ; nevertheless, the temptation to it would be strong.   The labour force
of the South has long been unequal to the requirements of the planters.   Of this the steady
rise in the price of slaves during half a century is
a sufficient proof.   But, with the whole Southern
Territory secured for exclusive slave settlement, the
insufficiency of the home supply to meet the necessities of the case would be more manifest than ever.

With the advance in price breeding would no doubt be stimulated in the older states ; but the process of augmentation by natural increase would be slow, while, on the other hand, the high price of labour would greatly curtail the profits of cultivation. Under these circumstances, it is difficult to believe that the planters of the South would long tolerate an impediment which stood between them and the realization of vast schemes of aggrandisement,* more especially when the maintenance of the obstacle could only be justified on grounds of morality which the whole South would reject with disdain. The continued prohibition of the trade would be denounced as an unworthy subserviency to the fanaticism of foreign governments—as (to quote language which has already been employed in this cause) " branding every slaveholder in the land with the mark of guilt and dishonour."† Slaveholders would be called upon as before, but in tones rendered more authoritative by the increased prestige which the cause of slavery would have acquired,

* "The extension of negro slavery over Mexico and Central America, which fires the imaginations and rounds the periods of Southern orators, will be found, when subjected to the logic of figures, to be impossible, on the basis of the actual negro population of the United States. It can only be made possible by the revival of the African slave trade."—*Progress of Slavery*, p. 172.

† Mr. John Forsyth, late minister to Mexico, in the Mobile *Register*.

to remove " the degrading stigma " from " their most essential political institution," and, as the means at once of filling their pockets and clearing their fame, to repeal a law jarring alike with their moral and material susceptibilities. As opposed to these motives, two counter-considerations only can be assigned—the provision in the Montgomery Constitution,* prohibiting the African slave trade, and the interests of the breeding states in maintaining the monopoly of the Southern markets. Let us endeavour to appreciate the probable efficacy of these restraining causes.

With regard to the former—the constitutional prohibition against the trade—those who attach the slightest importance to this as a security for the future conduct of the politicians who enacted it, must either be unacquainted with their past history, or must suppose that there is something in an act of wanton rebellion so restorative to the moral faculties as to convert in a moment a band of actual conspirators and life-long intriguers into trustworthy statesmen. The men who drew up this Montgomery Constitution are the men, or the political descendants and associates of the men, who passed

* The Confederate Constitution was passed provisionally on 8th February, 1861, at Montgomery, Alabama. On the 11th March, 1861, the Constitution thus passed was, with some modifications, adopted as the permanent Constitution of the Confederate States.

and repealed the Missouri Compromise, who accepted and repudiated the Nebraska Bill. These were regarded by the Free States in the light of national compacts ; and they were compacts by which the Southern party—the authors of this Montgomery Constitution—obtained for the time what they desired. The reader of the previous chapter is aware in what manner these compacts were observed. In the case of the Missouri Compromise the bargain was adhered to till the Southern party had appropriated its advantages ; in the case of the Nebraska Bill, till the measure was proved unequal to the task that was required of it. In both cases solemn engagements were set aside the moment they became inconvenient. What is there in the circumstances under which the Montgomery Constitution has been adopted to warrant the supposition that it will be regarded as more sacred than the Missouri Compromise, or than the Nebraska Bill—to lead us to expect that any provision it contains will be adhered to one moment longer than it suits the convenience of the men who have framed it ? The provisional constitution was, in the first instance, passed in secret session. Subsequently, when brought forward in its present form for adoption, the proceedings were open, and among the few debates which occurred, one took place on the clause prohibiting the foreign slave trade. It is instructive to observe the grounds on which the prohibition was attacked and defended. On the one side, it was asked, if such legislation was not incompatible with a constitution which broadly proclaimed the perpetuity and inviolability of slavery. If the legitimacy of the institution was so incontestable that Congress was to be excluded from the power of ever decreeing its abolition,* did it not follow that every means of recruiting the system was equally legitimate? Why should it be permitted to purchase slaves in Virginia, and forbidden to purchase them in Africa? The anomaly was the less justifiable as the foreign slave trade confers on the imported negro an advantage to which there is nothing corresponding in the case of the domestic slave trade—it introduces him to Christianity and civilization. Against these arguments of the opponents of the clause, its defenders had nothing better to advance than considerations of temporary expediency. The young republic was not yet sufficiently established to expose itself to the double danger arising from the wounded susceptibilities of European powers, who had made the abolition of the slave trade a point of honour, and from the alienated sympathies of the slave-breeders of Virginia, Kentucky, and Maryland, who would be naturally apprehensive of foreign competition. At this time,

---

* "No law denying or impairing the right of property in negro slaves shall be passed."—*Confederate Constitution*, Art. I. sec. ix. 4

it will be remembered, the Border slave states
had not yet declared themselves on the question
of secession ; and it was a condition absolutely
vital to the success of the movement that at least
the principal of these states should join the revolution.   Without this the whole scheme must inevitably have collapsed.   It is, therefore, not strange
that the arguments of expediency prevailed.   The
clause prohibiting the African slave trade was passed,
and the task of providing for the enforcement of this
prohibition was remitted to Congress.*   And now let
us observe how the Confederate Congress performed
the task confided to it.   Under the Federal constitution slave trading with foreign countries is piracy,
and is punished capitally.   The Confederate Congress attenuated the capital crime to a misdemeanor,
against which it directed a proportional penalty—
confiscation of the vessel taken *flagrante delicto!*
The chance of capture, to be effected by agents
sympathizing with the crime, and, in the rare case
where the stolen chattels are actually found in the
thief's possession, to be followed by confiscation
of the vessel—this was the penalty by which it was
proposed—shall we say in irony ?—to balance the

* " The importations of negroes of the African race from any
foreign country other than the slaveholding states or territories of
the United States of America is hereby forbidden ; and Congress is
required to pass such laws as shall effectually prevent the same."—
Confederate Constitution, Art. I. sec. ix. 1.

temptations of a most lucrative traffic! But the
bitter jest did not end here : there is a further feature in the case which bears still more unmistakably
the brand of slave legislation. It was necessary to
provide for the disposal of the negroes who should
be found on the captured slavers. Under the Federal
law they are transferred to Liberia at the expense of
the Federal government. How did the Confederate
Congress propose to deal with them ? It introduced a
clause into its bill which directed that they should be
taken to the nearest port and sold for the benefit of
the state! This was the compensation provided by
these beneficent legislators for the victims of the inhuman cupidity of their countrymen. It is thus that
a Slave Republic legislates against the slave trade ;
and it is to the good faith of the men who are the
authors of this notable law that Englishmen are
asked to trust as a security against the revival of a
trade to which their strongest feelings and interests
draw them on.* But such a law, as it could have

* "It is absurd to say that a step like this has been taken merely
to conciliate European opinion. . . . It is simply dishonest to
pretend, in the face of such evidence, that the South contemplates,
now or hereafter, the revival of the traffic which she has so peremp-
torily and irrevocably abolished. Common fairness should impel
the most bitter enemies of the Confederate States to admit that, for
whatever reason, the dominant party in the Slave States desires, by
every means in its power, to render the future re-opening of the
African slave trade impossible."—*Saturday Review.*

deceived no one, must have frustrated the ends for which it was designed. The President, therefore, more prudent than his councillors, met it with his veto, communicating his reasons for this step to Congress in secret session. The question has since been indefinitely adjourned.*

The prohibition of the foreign slave trade in the Montgomery Constitution thus stands at present a mere abstract proposition, unaccompanied with any provision for its practical enforcement. Even thus, however, it has not failed to give offence to the more uncompromising spirits in the South ; and already the demand for its repeal has been raised in no faltering tones. " For God's sake," says the *Southern Confederacy*, a Florida paper, " and the sake of consistency, do not let us form a Union for the express purpose of maintaining and propagating African slavery, and then, as the Southern Congress have done, confess our error by enacting a constitutional provision abolishing the African slave trade. The opening of the trade is a mere question of expediency, to be determined by legislative enactment hereafter, but not by constitutional provision." " Why adopt this measure?" says Mr. Spratt in a letter addressed to one of the members of the Montgomery Convention, "Is it that Virginia and the other Border states require it ? . . . They have

* *Annuaire des Deux Mondes* (1861), pp. 585-586.

no right to ask that their slaves or any other products should be protected to an unnatural value in the markets of the West. If they persist in regarding the negro but as a thing of trade—a thing which they are too good to use, but only can produce for others' uses—and join the Confederacy, as Pennsylvania or Massachusetts might do, not to support the structure, but to profit by it, it were as well they should not join, and we can find no interest in such association. . . . Is it that foreign nations will require it ? As a matter of taste they might perhaps. There is a mode upon the subject of human rights at present, and England, France, and other states that are leaders of the mode, might be pleased to see the South comply with the standard of requirement, and, provided only no serious inconvenience or injury resulted, would be pleased to see the South suppress not only the slave trade but slavery itself. But will our failure to do so make any greater difference in our relations with those states ? Men may assume it if they will, but it argues a pitiable want of intelligence and independence, an abject want of political spirit, to suppose it. . . They will submit to any terms of intercourse with the Slave Republic in consideration of its markets and its products. An increase of slaves will increase the market and supply. They will pocket their philanthropy and profits together. And so

solicitude as to the feeling of foreign states upon
this subject is gratuitous : and so it is that our
suppression of the slave trade is warranted by no
necessity to respect the sentiment of foreign states."
While such language is openly employed through the
South by its most energetic politicians, we may judge
of the value of an anti-slave-trade clause, unprovided
with any means for its enforcement, in a revolutionary constitution.

But it will perhaps be thought that, although
constitutional restraints may be weak, the interests
of the Border states, which have been strong enough
to procure the prohibition, may be trusted to secure
its being permanently maintained.   That the Border
states have this interest in a pecuniary sense is
indeed abundantly evident.   But the point to be
considered is this :—will the pecuniary interest of
the Border states be allowed permanently to prevail
against, not merely the equal pecuniary interests of
other states in the opposite policy, but against the
requirements, in the largest sense, of the whole Slave
Republic ?   A consideration of the course pursued
under analogous circumstances on former occasions
will show the extreme improbability of such a supposition.

There is perhaps nothing more remarkable in the
past career of the Slave Power than the unanimity
with which the whole body of slaveholders have

concurred in supporting a given policy, so soon as it
was clearly understood that the public interests of
slavery prescribed its adoption ; yet with the line of
policy which, in view of this necessity, has been
actually followed, the interests of the Slave States
have been far from being equally identified.   The
slave-breeding states of Virginia and Kentucky had
a very distinct and palpable advantage in opening
new ground for slave cultivation across the Mississippi.   They thereby created a new market for their
slaves, and directly enhanced the value of their
principal property.   But the slave-working States of
Alabama and Mississippi, which were buyers, not
sellers, of slaves, which were producers, not consumers, of cotton, had a precisely opposite interest as
regards this enterprise.   The effect of the policy of
territorial extension, in relation to them, was to raise
the price of slaves—the productive instrument which
they employed ; and, on the other hand, to reduce
the price of cotton—the commodity in which they
dealt.   It at once increased their outlay and diminished their returns.   Yet this did not prevent the
whole body of Slave States from working steadily
together in promoting that policy which the maintenance of the Slave Power, as a political system,
demanded.   A still more striking instance of the
readiness to sacrifice particular interests to the political ascendancy of the body is furnished by the

conduct of the South in its dealings with Cuba. The annexation of this island has long been, as all the world knows, a darling project of Southern ambition. The bearing of the acquisition on the general interests of the South is very obvious. It would add to its domain a district of incomparable fertility. It would give it a commanding position in the Gulf of Mexico. It would increase its political weight in the Union. But there is one state in the South which could not fail to be injured in a pecuniary sense by the acquisition. The principal industry of the State of Louisiana is the same as that of Cuba—the cultivation of sugar. But the soils of Louisiana are far inferior to those of Cuba— so much so that the sugar planters of that State are only able to hold their ground against the competition of their Cuban rivals by the assistance of a high protective duty. Now the immediate consequence of the annexation of Cuba to the South would be the abolition of the protection which the planters of Louisiana now enjoy—an event which could not fail to be followed by the disappearance, in great part, of the artificial production which it sustains. Nevertheless, Louisiana has formed no exception to the general eagerness of the South to appropriate Cuba : so far from this, it has curiously enough happened that the man who has been most prominent among the piratical party who have advocated this step is

Mr. Slidell,* the senator in Congress for the State of Louisiana. The sympathies which bind slaveholders together have thus always proved more powerful than the particular interests which would sunder them ; and whatever course the necessities of slavery, as a system, have prescribed, that the whole array of slaveholders, with a disregard for private ends, which, in a good cause, would be the highest virtue, has never hesitated to pursue.

The precedents, therefore, afforded by the past history of the South would lead us to expect that, so soon as the expediency of the African slave trade, in promoting the political interests of the Slave Power, became clear, the private advantage of particular states would be waived in deference to the requirements of the whole Confederacy. But, though this should not be so—though the Border states, when the trial came, should prove deficient in that public spirit which the working states in similar circumstances have never failed to exhibit—it is still quite inconceivable that what the public interests required should be permanently postponed to an opposition resting on such a basis. The men who now guide the councils of the Confederacy, from the moment of their accession to power to

---

* This was the gentleman selected by Southern tact to recommend the cause of the South to Europe.

the present time, have never shrunk from any act essential to their ends : such men, having carried their party triumphantly through a bloody civil war, would hardly allow themselves to be baffled by the selfish obstinacy of a few of their number. Indeed already the particular expedient to which, in the event of protracted obstinacy, recourse might be had, has been hinted at in no obscure terms. Mr. De Bow has advocated the re-opening of the African slave trade upon the distinct ground that it is necessary to extend the basis of slavery by bringing slaves within the reach of a larger number than, at their present price, are able to purchase them. By this means, he argues, increased stability would be given to the institution in proportion as the numbers interested in maintaining it should be increased. Of the soundness of this policy from the stand-point of the Slave Power there can, I think, be no question ; and for the means of carrying it out in the last resort the extreme party could be at no loss. Let the reader observe the purpose to which this argument might be turned in the event of a schism between the breeding and the working states on the point in question. It is well known that the possession of a slave is the great object of the poor white's ambition, and the most effectual means of gratifying this ambition would be to make slaves cheap. To rally, then, to the cause of free trade in slaves this numerous class would be, indeed, an easy task. Nothing more would be needed than to appeal to their most obvious interest, to give play to their most cherished passion.* Everywhere—in Virginia and Kentucky no less than in the States of the extreme South—the opening of the African slave trade would be hailed with enthusiasm by the great bulk of the people; and thus, whenever convenience demanded it, the resistance of an interested section might be overborne by the almost universal voice of the rest of the community.

To sum up the results of this part of the discussion :—on every hypothesis of Southern independence, save that which would be equivalent to the early extinction of the Slave Power, the re-opening of the African slave trade would be recommended to the South by almost irresistible inducements— in one contingency by considerations which appeal

---

* "Of one thing there can be no doubt—a slave state cannot long exist without a slave trade. The poor whites who have won the fight will demand their share of the spoils. The land for tilth is abundant, and all that is wanted to give them fortunes is a supply of slaves. They will have that in spite of their masters, unless a stronger power than the Slave States prevents the accomplishment of their wishes."—*Russell's Diary.*

"Les petits blancs . . . leur unique rêve était de voir le prix des nègres tomber assez bas pour leur permettre de devenir propriétaires d'un ou deux esclaves. Toute révolution qui promettait de conduire à ce résultat était assureé de leur appui."—*Annuaire des Deux Mondes* (1861), p. 583.

to interests that are vital. The only restraints upon
its action would be a clause in the Constitution and
the private interests of a limited section. The anti-
slave-trade clause, avowedly introduced from considerations of temporary expediency of which the
urgency daily diminishes, unaccompanied by any
provisions for its enforcement, and already set at
defiance by public opinion, would not improbably,
in the event of the ends of the Confederacy being
made good, be formally repealed, but would, we
may confidently assume, at all events be practically disregarded. As to the private interests
of the breeding states, they would undoubtedly
present a real obstacle to the revival of the trade ;
but we have seen that, in the history of the
South, private interests have always yielded to the
demands of public policy, and they would probably
do so in this case. Should, however, the monopolists
of the 'old dominion' prove refractory, the leaders of
the extreme party would have the remedy in their
own hands. The protest of a narrow minority
would be wholly powerless to stem the tide of
popular feeling which they have it in their power at
any moment to evoke.

CHAPTER IX.

GENERAL CONCLUSIONS.

WHAT is the duty of European nations towards North America in the present crisis of its history? I answer—to observe a strict neutrality between the contending parties, giving their moral support to that settlement of the question which is most in accordance with the general interest of the world. What ground is there for European interference in the quarrel? In the present aspect of affairs absolutely none—none, that is to say, which would not equally justify interference in every war which ever occurred. I say in the present aspect of affairs, for in a different aspect of affairs I can well imagine that a different course would be justifiable, and might even become a duty. Supposing free society in North America in danger of being overborne by the Slave Power, would not the threatened predominance in the new world of a confederacy resting on slavery as its corner stone, and proclaiming the propagandism of slavery as its mission, be an occasion for the interference of civilized nations? If there be reason that civilized nations should combine to resist the aggressions of Russia—a country containing the germs of a vigorous and progressive civilization—would there be none for opposing the establishment of " a barbarous and barbarizing Power "—a Power of whose existence slavery is the final cause ?   But that contingency is happily not now probable ; and in the present position of the American contest there is not even a plausible pretext for intervention.   It is unhappily true that our trade is suffering, that much distress prevails in our manufacturing districts, and that we are threatened with even more serious consequences than have yet been felt.*   But is this a plausible pretext for interfering in a foreign war ?   How can a great war be carried on without disturbing the commerce of the world ?   For what purpose are blockades instituted and permitted ?   To say that, because we are injuriously affected by a blockade we will not recognize it, is simply to say that we do not choose to be bound by laws longer than it suits our convenience—is to throw away even the pretence of justice.†   But interference in the present case would be not merely

* This was written in April, 1862.

† How little the real sufferers by the American civil war are liable to this reproach has recently been shown in a signal manner at a meeting of operatives in the Free Trade Hall, Manchester.   The address of cordial sympathy and encouragement to Mr. Lincoln in his anti-slavery policy adopted on that occasion is the answer of the working men of England to the profligate solicitations of the *Times* —an answer which history will make known, though the journal which it rebukes affects to ignore it by excluding it from its

immoral, it would be futile—nay, if the relief of distress be really the object of those who urge it, it would, we can scarce doubt, aggravate a hundred-fold the evils it was intended to cure. For, supposing the blockade of the Southern ports to be raised, to what purpose would be this result if the war continued ? It would, doubtless, carry comfort to the Slave Confederacy; it might possibly bring a few hundred thousand bales of cotton to Europe; but, in the present condition of the South, with Northern armies encamped on its soil, it would not cause cotton to be grown, and still less would it open Northern markets to our manufactures. A fleet may raise a blockade, but it cannot compel a people to buy goods who do not want them. Intervention in America would, therefore, fail to restore trade to its normal channels ; and it is admittedly to a disturbance in the normal channels of trade far more than to scarcity of any single commodity—to a cessation of Northern demand far more than to an interruption of Southern supply—that the dis-

columns. Every shred of pretext has thus been torn away from the party here, which, with new-born regard for the working man, has sought to draw England from her international obligations in order to support a cause, whose very name is a loathing and affront to every true workman. It should never be forgotten that, in their hour of sorest trial, the working men of England have shown themselves more alive to the claims of political morality than a large section of those who arrogate for themselves the exclusive possession of the qualities which fit for political power.

tress now experienced in England is due.* Now the cessation of Northern demand will continue as long as the war continues; so that the effect of intervention on manufacturing distress would depend on its effect on the duration of the war. And what would be this effect? On such a subject it would be absurd to speak with confidence; but there is one historical parallel which comes so close to the present case that we should do well to ponder it. In 1792 an armed intervention of European Powers took place in France. The allied sovereigns were not less confident of their ability to impose conditions on the French people, than are those who now urge intervention in America of the ability of France and England to settle the affairs of that continent. But we know how the intervention of 1792 ended. The spirit of democracy, allying itself with the spirit of patriotism, kindled in the people of France an energy which not merely drove back the invaders from their soil, but which carried the invaded people as conquerors over the length and breadth of continental Europe. Such was the effect of a policy of intervention in the affairs of a great European nation. What reason have we to expect a different result from a similar policy pursued in America? Has democracy in America shown less energy than in Europe? Is its organization less

* See the *Economist*, 26th April, 1862.

effective ?   Is the spirit of its patriotism less powerful ?   Are the resources which it commands for war
less extensive ?   Or will the adversaries of democracy fight it with greater advantage across the
reach of the Atlantic ?   I am assuming that an
intervention, if attempted, would be resolutely carried out : that a mere interference by our navies
would only exacerbate and prolong the quarrel is
so obvious as to disentitle such a proposition to a
moment's serious regard.   The duty of neutrality is,
therefore, in the present case as plainly marked out
by the dictates of selfish policy as by the maxims of
morality and law.   While intervention would fail
to alleviate the evils under which we suffer, it would
almost certainly add to those evils the calamity of
a great war—a war which would bequeath to the
posterity of the combatants a legacy of mutual
hatred, destined to embitter their relations for centuries to come.

    But the duty of neutrality is not incompatible
with the rendering of moral support.   We may be
required to abstain from giving effect to our convictions by force, but we can never be justly required
to abstain from advancing them by moral means.
Nay, so long as the conflict between good and evil
lasts, the obligation to sustain the right cause by
sympathy and counsel is one from which we cannot
relieve ourselves.   It becomes, therefore, of extreme

importance to consider what is that settlement of
the American contest which deserves the moral
support of Europe.

There are two modes of terminating the present
war, either of which must, it seems to me, be almost
equally deprecated by every friend of freedom and
of the American people :—such a triumph of the
Southern party as would give to it the command of
the unsettled districts to the south and west ; and
such a reconstruction of the Union as would restore
slavery to its former footing in the Republic.   It is,
I think, difficult to say which of these results would
be the more extensively disastrous.   The one would
establish, amid all the *éclat* of victory, a slave empire, commanding the resources of half a continent,
fired with an ardent ambition, and cherishing vast
designs of aggression and conquest.   The other
would once more commit a moral and freedom-
loving people—the main hope of civilization in the
New World—to complicity with the damning guilt
of slavery.   The Union, restored on the principle of
restricting slavery, would not indeed be the same
Union as that in which the Slave Power was predominant.   But fortune is capricious in politics as
in war.   A few years might bring a change in the
position of parties ; and a revolution of the wheel
might once again commit the central government
to the propagandists of slavery.   Even should this

worst result not happen, the corrupting influence of the alliance would remain ; the continued connivance at the perpetration of a great wrong would again force the Republic into degrading compliances, and the progress of political degeneracy, arrested for a moment by the shock of violent reaction, would proceed as before. Between the evils of such a termination of the contest and the absolute triumph of the Slave power, it would, perhaps, not be easy to decide.

A year ago either of these results, almost equally to be deplored, seemed almost equally probable. The Northern people, taken by surprise, its leaders unaccustomed to power, its arsenals in the hands of its enemies, with traitors in its public offices, divided into parties holding discordant views and recommending different courses, unanimous only in one strong wish—a desire at all events to uphold the Union—seemed for a time prepared to make almost any concession which promised to secure this end. On the other hand, no vacillation marked the South. With the directness of men who, fixed in their ends, have little scruple in their choice of means, its leaders were urgent to precipitate the catastrophe. Their skilfully contrived treason had secured for them the principal forts and almost the whole military stores of the Republic. The most experienced officers in the United States' army were their trusted agents, and were rapidly passing over to their side. Elated by success and confident in their resources, it seemed, at the outset of the contest, that they had all but accomplished their daring scheme—that little remained for them but to seize upon Washington,* and dictate from the capitol the terms of separation.

Such was the position of affairs when the contest opened. A year has passed, and contingencies which then appeared imminent seem no longer within the range of possible events. In presence of the searching test which real danger applies to political theories, and amid the enthusiasm kindled by war, the political education of the North has

---

* "M. Lincoln, en prenant possession du pouvoir, avait trouvé le gouvernement complétement désorganisé. Les pionniers des prairies, malgré leurs incessantes réclamations, étaient sans protection et sans lois. Le trésor était à bout de ressources ; les dépenses de l'exercice courant dépassaient de beaucoup les recettes, et les détournemens commis par M. Floyd, ministre de la guerre sous M. Buchanan, avaient achevé de mettre à sec les caisses publiques. Le ministre de la marine n'avait trouvé disponible qu'un seul bâtiment de guerre, le Powhattan, qui revenait d'une croisière de trois années dans les mers de Chine, dont la mise en réparation avait été ordonnée, et qu'il fallut réarmer immédiatement. L'armée était éparpillée aux extrémités du territoire fédéral, et c'était à grand'peine que le général Scott avait pu réunir quelques compagnies pour la protection de Washington. Les arsenaux du nord étaient vides, et M. Floyd se faisait un mérite auprès de ses compatriotes d'en avoir fait enlever toutes les armes, pendant les derniers mois de son administration, pour les accumuler dans les arsenaux du sud, où elles étaient tombées au pouvoir des confédérés."— *Annuaire des Deux Mondes*, 1861, p. 603.

made rapid progress. The true source of disaffection to the Union, so long concealed by the arts of temporizing politicians, has been laid bare, and is no longer doubted. The impossibility of bringing free and slave societies into harmonious co-operation under the same political system begins to be understood. The absolute necessity of, at all hazards, breaking the strength of the Slave Power, as the first step towards re-establishing political society in North America, is rapidly becoming the accepted creed. Meanwhile, the advance of the Northern armies in the field has kept pace with that of opinion in the public assemblies, and, by an almost unbroken series of fruitful victories, the military superiority of the North seems now to be definitively established.* In this aspect of affairs—with anti-slavery opinions making rapid way in the North, and Northern armies steadily advancing on the Southern States—the reconstruction of the Union, with slavery retained on its former footing, and still more the complete triumph of the Slave Power, may, it seems to me, be fairly dismissed from our consideration. Nay, I think, the actual state of facts, taken in connexion with the resources of the contending parties, warrants us in going a step further, and holding that, in the absence of foreign intervention, the South must in the end succumb to its opponent. If

* Written in April, 1862.

this be so, what remains to be decided is this : on
what terms shall the submission of the South be
made ?—shall it return to the Union to be ruled by
the North, or secede under conditions to be prescribed by its conqueror? Assuming these to be the
practical issues involved in the struggle at the stage
to which it has now attained, I shall proceed to consider to what determination of it the moral support
of Europe should be given.

It seems impossible to doubt that, at the present
time, the prevailing purpose of the Northern people
aims at no less than a complete reconstruction of
the Union in its original proportions. The project
admits of being regarded under several aspects :—
how far is it justifiable ?—how far is it practicable ?
—how far is it expedient ? On each of these points
some remarks suggest themselves.

The forcible imposition on some millions of human
beings of a form of government at variance with
their wishes, is an act which undoubtedly demands
special grounds for its justification. Whether the
South be regarded as a portion of the same nation
with the North, or as a distinct people, it seems, on
either view of the case, impossible that an attempt
to subjugate, for the purpose of ruling, it, can be
reconciled with the maxims of political morality
which we regard in this country as applicable to the
ordinary practice of civilized nations. If, then,

these maxims admit of no exception, this branch of the argument is resolved, and the justification of the present views of the North must be given up. But, writing in a nation which holds in subjection under despotic rule two hundred millions of another race, it is scarcely necessary to say that maxims which condemn, without regard to circumstances, the imposition on a people of a foreign and despotic yoke are no portion of the moral code of this country. The people of India may or may not desire to be governed by Great Britain; but assuredly the wishes of the people of India are not the grounds on which an English statesman would justify Great Britain in holding that country in subjection. It follows, then, that it is consistent with political morality, as conceived in this country, that in certain cases the principles of constitutional government and those of non-intervention should be set aside, and that a government should compel a portion of its subjects, or a people should intervene to compel another people, to accept a form of government at variance with the wishes of those on whom it is imposed.*

* "There are few questions which more require to be taken in hand by ethical and political philosophers, with a view to establish some rule or criterion whereby the justifiableness of intervening in the affairs of other countries, and (what is sometimes fully as questionable) the justifiableness of refraining from intervention, may be brought to a definite and rational test. Whoever attempts this will be led to recognize more than one fundamental distinction, not

Now, if it be admitted that circumstances can in any case create an exception to the ordinary rules of political and international practice regarded as binding upon civilized nations, we need have little hesitation in asserting that the present case is exceptional.

What is the fact with which we have to deal ? A few hundred thousand slaveholders break loose from the political system with which they were connected, and erect a confederacy on the avowed basis of slavery. From the past history of these men, and from the condition of society presented in the country

yet by any means familiar to the public mind, and in general quite lost sight of by those who write in strains of indignant morality on the subject. There is a great difference (for example) between the case in which the nations concerned are of the same, or something like the same, degree of civilization, and that in which one of the parties to the situation is of a high, and the other of a very low, grade of social improvement. To suppose that the same international customs, and the same rules of international morality, can obtain between one civilized nation and another, and between civilized nations and barbarians, is a grave error, and one which no statesman can fall into, however it may be with those who, from a safe and unresponsible position, criticize statesmen. Among many reasons why the same rules cannot be applicable to situations so different, the two following are among the most important. In the first place, the rules of ordinary international morality imply reciprocity. But barbarians will not reciprocate. They cannot be depended on for observing any rules. Their minds are not capable of so great an effort, nor their will sufficiently under the influence of distant motives. In the next place, nations which are still barbarous have not got beyond the period during which it is likely to be

which they govern, we have the clearest proofs as to what this scheme involves. We know that it involves the maintenance of a social system at once retrograde and aggressive—retrograde towards those on whom it is imposed, and aggressive towards the communities with which it comes into contact. We know that it involves the design of extending the power of this confederation, and, with its power, the worst form of human servitude which mankind has ever seen, over the fairest portions of the New World. We know that in all probability—with a probability approaching to certainty—it involves an

for their benefit that they should be conquered and held in subjection by foreigners. Independence and nationality, so essential to the due growth and development of a people further advanced in improvement, are generally impediments to theirs. The sacred duties which civilized nations owe to the independence and nationality of each other, are not binding towards those to whom nationality and independence are either a certain evil, or at best a questionable good. The Romans were not the most clean-handed of conquerors, yet would it have been better for Gaul and Spain, Numidia and Dacia, never to have formed part of the Roman Empire? To characterize any conduct whatever towards a barbarous people as a violation of the law of nations, only shows that he who so speaks has never considered the subject. A violation of great principles of morality it may easily be; but barbarians have no rights as a *nation* except a right to such treatment as may, at the earliest possible period, fit them for becoming one. The only moral laws for the relation between a civilized and a barbarous government, are the universal rules of morality between man and man."— *A Few Words on Non-Intervention*, by J. S. Mill. *Fraser's Magazine*, December, 1859.

attempt to revive a great scandal, the African slave trade—a scandal which all Christian nations have agreed to stigmatize, and which Great Britain in particular has for half a century devoted her best influence, and a vast outlay of treasure, to suppress. We know that this body aims at political independence, not for that lawful purpose which makes political independence the first of national rights— the purpose of working out a people's proper destiny —but for a purpose which makes it the greatest of national crimes—the purpose of riveting dependence upon another race—the purpose of extending and consolidating a barbarous tyranny.   Now, these being the ends for which the Southern Confederacy seeks to establish itself, is its subjugation by the North justifiable ?   I hold that the right is as clear as the right to put down murder or piracy. As a nation, we, in common with civilized Europe, have proscribed as piracy the African slave trade. In the opinion of competent judges the inter-state slave trade in the South involves enormities as great as any that have been enacted on the coast of Guinea or in the middle passage ;* and it is certain that the

* " I affirm that there exists in the United States a slave trade, not less odious or demoralizing, nay, I do in my conscience believe, more odious and more demoralizing than that which is carried on between Africa and Brazil. North Carolina and Virginia are to Louisiana and Alabama what Congo is to Rio Janeiro. . . God forbid that I should extenuate the horrors of the slave trade in any

purpose for which the Confederacy is established—
the appropriation of the Territories for slave cultivation—cannot be carried into effect without giving
a powerful impulse certainly to one, and probably
to both, of those crimes.   Unless, therefore, we are
prepared to retreat from the position which, as a
nation, we have deliberately taken up and consistently held for half a century, we cannot deny that
the overthrow of the Southern Confederacy would
be a public benefit ; and, even though we should
question the perfect purity of the motives of those

form ! But I do think this its worst form.   Bad enough is it that
civilized men should sail to an uncivilized quarter of the world
where slavery exists, should there buy wretched barbarians, and
should carry them away to labour in a distant land : bad enough !
But that a civilized man, a baptized man, a man proud of being a
citizen of a free state, a man frequenting a Christian church, should
breed slaves for exportation, and, if the whole horrible truth must
be told, should even beget slaves for exportation, should see children, sometimes his own children, gambolling around him from
infancy, should watch their growth, should become familiar with
their faces, and should then sell them for four or five hundred
dollars a head, and send them to lead in a remote country a life
which is a lingering death, a life about which the best thing that
can be said is that it is sure to be short; this does, I own, excite
a horror exceeding even the horror excited by that slave trade
which is the curse of the African coast.   And mark : I am not
speaking of any rare case, of any instance of eccentric depravity.   I
am speaking of a trade as regular as the trade in pigs between
Dublin and Liverpool, or as the trade in coals between the Tyne
and the Thames."—Lord Macaulay's *Speech on the Sugar Duties.*

who undertake it, the act itself must be acknowledged as a service to the civilized world.

That the overthrow of the Southern Confederacy
is justifiable—so far as the duties of the North to
that community are concerned—appears to me,
therefore, as clear as any doctrine in the code of
political ethics. But, being justifiable, is it practicable ? Into the general merits of this branch of
the argument it would not become me to enter ;
but, without pretending to pronounce an opinion on
the ability of the North to subdue the revolted states,
it may be permitted me to advert to some considerations bearing upon this part of the case which do
not appear to have received from those who have
undertaken to discuss it that degree of attention to
which their importance would seem to entitle them.

The argument of those who deny the ability of
the North to effect its purpose of reconstructing
the Union rests, for the most part, on historical analogies, and, more particularly, on the successful resistance made by the ancestors of the present belligerents to the authority of Great Britain. Now a brief
consideration will show that the present case differs
from all previous examples of successful revolt in
some important respects, and we shall find that, in
every instance in which the analogy fails, the difference points in the same direction—it indicates
greater facility of conquest in the present struggle.

In the parallel furnished by the revolutionary war of the last century it is an obvious point of difference that Great Britain, in that case, carried on the contest under the enormous disadvantage of being separated from her enemy by an intervening ocean—a disadvantage of such magnitude as, in the opinion of Tocqueville, to detract indefinitely from the prowess of the victors—whereas now the North stands close to its foe. Such a difference is almost enough to deprive of all force arguments drawn from the analogy of the two cases ; yet the circumstance has been scarcely adverted to by those who have most strenuously pressed the analogy. But, passing by a point which is peculiar to the comparison with the war of independence, there are others in which the present is distinguished from all previous examples of insurrectionary success.

And, first, while the South is in the present war liable to an absolute interruption of its external trade, it is of all countries which ever existed the least capable of encountering such a crisis. I say the South is liable to an absolute interruption of its external trade, for, notwithstanding the exploits of the *Merrimac*, it is quite inconceivable—having regard to the mercantile marine and the mechanical resources of the contending parties—that the North should not be able in the long run to maintain a

permanent superiority at sea. It may, therefore, be
assumed that the new Confederacy will be absolutely
cut off from commercial intercourse with foreign
nations ; and, this being so, it is obvious further to
remark that of all communities in the world it is
the one least prepared to meet such an emergency—
the least capable of supplying its own wants. To
feel convinced of this we have but to recall its
industrial system—a system composed of slaves
brutalized by ignorance and tyranny, accustomed
to perform a few routine operations, and utterly
inefficient if taken from their ordinary tasks. It is
true, indeed, the crisis has compelled a certain deviation from the old routine ; the cultivation of corn
has already in some places been substituted for that
of cotton. But it cannot be doubted that the change
has been effected at a great loss of industrial power,
and, however slaves may be turned from one kind
of agricultural pursuit to another, beyond the range
of agriculture they must be absolutely useless. The
plantation slave of the South can never be converted
into a skilled artisan ; consequently, all those commodities for the supply of which the South has been
accustomed to rely on the industrial skill of foreign
countries it must now be content to dispense with
altogether. Now amongst such commodities are
many which are absolutely essential for the conduct
of war. The consideration, therefore, is one which

touches a vital point in the ability of the South to maintain a prolonged resistence. Hitherto, by its plunder of the military stores of the United States while its leaders were in possession of the government, and by the fruits of its early victories, it has been enabled to maintain itself ; but, as its present supplies become exhausted and cease to be replenished by successes in the field, it is not easy to see how this necessity can be met.

Another circumstance which has been almost wholly overlooked in this argument, is the change which railways may effect in the facilities for aggressive warfare. In none of those cases in which a war of independence has been maintained with success against the superior forces of an invader has this resource been available. This consideration applies directly to a point on which great stress has been laid by the partisans of the South—the difficulties offered to conquest by mere vastness of extent. There can, I suppose, be no doubt that this circumstance gives a great advantage to the party which is on the defensive ; but a country traversed by railways is, for practical purposes, reduced to a tenth of its real size. That the novel conditions thus imported into military tactics have not been overlooked by the commanders on either side is fully proved by the nature of their plans, which have been conceived chiefly with a view to utilizing

this new arm of warfare.   Thus the expeditions to
Hatteras, to Roanoke Island, and to Port Royal,
appear now to have been dictated by a consideration
of the command conferred by these positions over
the railways which connect the Carolinas with Virginia on the one hand, and with Georgia on the
other.   Again, the importance of Nashville, as a
strategical point, consists in its being the central
terminus of three grand lines, proceeding respectively from Washington, from Richmond, and from
Charleston to the West ; and the possession of
Corinth was rendered important by an analogous
reason.   Railways have thus introduced a new
element into warfare of sufficient importance to
modify the whole plan of a campaign ; and railways
apply directly to overcoming the impediment of
distance—the circumstance which has been urged
as the most insuperable obstacle to the conquest of
the South.*

* "This is the first great war, if we except the Italian campaign,
in which railways, on any large scale, have figured in warlike operations.   How greatly they may modify the ordinary canons of
strategy it is yet impossible to tell.   Already many movements have
taken place, and positions been occupied and abandoned, which,
except upon the supposition of the new element introduced by
railways, would have been utterly irreconcilable with the old principles of securing the base and protecting the flanks of an army.
Where there is a railway, troops may be moved through a hundred
miles in the time required to march over twenty.   And, *vice versâ*,
twenty miles to be marched over may chance to neutralize the benefits

Again, in no war of independence which has been successfully waged has the invaded nation included among its inhabitants a multitude, one-third of its whole number, who were either positively hostile, or at least absolutely indifferent to the cause. Such a multitude exists in the midst of the Southern population ; and by this hostile and indifferent multitude the whole productive industry of the country is carried on. Now, as the Federal armies advance into the Southern States, what will be the behaviour of the negro population ? They will probably do as they have done hithertó : they will fly to the Federal lines ; and though they should not rise in insurrection, they will at least cease to work. Now, when the negroes cease to work, how is the South to maintain an army ? The " white trash " may be made to fight, but they will

of a hundred miles of rail. But not only is a new and indefinite element introduced into the calculations of military distances by the unequal means of locomotion available at different points, but in America the vastness itself of the different lines of railway gives rise to a distinct and special class of problems. It is easy to destroy twenty miles of railway and even a hundred. A hundred miles were lately destroyed by the Confederates. But it would be very difficult to destroy several thousand. Moreover, the extent of the country must always make it doubtful at what point it becomes expedient to destroy so useful an auxiliary until it is found too late to do so. It follows, we think, pretty conclusively, the cardinal maxim in any American war involving large tracts of country must be to take possession of the railroads."—*National Review*, April, 1862, p. 496.

scarcely be made to work—at all events they will be
unable to do both. It would seem, therefore, that,
so soon as the South is once thoroughly penetrated
by the Northern armies, a collapse of its productive
system is inevitable.

These are some of the circumstances in which the
present contest in America differs from those successful wars of defence with which it is usual to
compare it. I am far from intending to say that
the considerations which have been adduced prove
the possibility of accomplishing the object which the
North has now in view; but they seem to me to
show that the facilities for that purpose are greater
than is commonly supposed, and they at least suggest caution against building hasty conclusions upon
inapplicable precedents.

But, thirdly, assuming the reconstruction of the
Union to be practicable, is it expedient?   And here
we are met at once by the consideration—how is the
conquered South to be governed?   I can see but
one way in which this can be effected—by the overthrow of representative institutions in the Southern
States, and the substitution of a centralized despotism wielded by the Federal government.   I cannot
imagine that there could be any escape from this
course; for, granting that in certain districts of the
South there might be a considerable element of
population favourable to the Union, it is impossible

to doubt that in the main the people would be
thoroughly disaffected ; and how are popular institutions to be worked through the agency of a disaffected people ?   A·recourse to despotic expedients
would, therefore, so far as we can judge, be forced
upon the North.   Now, it is evident that such a
step involves considerations of the greatest gravity
—considerations before which the citizens of the
Union may well pause and ponder.   If, indeed, the
consequences of this policy could be certainly confined within the designed limits, there would, perhaps, be little need for hesitation.   At the worst, it
would be no more than the substitution of one form
of arbitrary power for another—of a civilized for a
barbarous despotism—and if the new government
were only equal to its task of reconstructing Southern society, its advent would be wholly a blessing.
But despotic principles once introduced into the
system of the Federal government, is it conceivable
that their influence would end in the attainment of
the object for the accomplishment of which they
were at the first invoked ?   Is it likely that the same
men, who should be exercising arbitrary authority
over the whole of the Southern States, would be
content, in governing the Northern, to confine themselves within constitutional bounds ?   Would there
not be the danger that habits acquired in ruling one
division of the republic would affect modes of action

in the other, and that, as soon as popular institutions became troublesome in the working, they would be superseded in favour of the more direct and obvious expedients of despotism ?   Besides it must be remembered that something more would be required to govern a disaffected South than a staff of officials.   The bureaucracy would need to be supported by an army, and the army would of necessity be at the disposal of the central government.   It would be easy, of course, to prescribe constitutional rules, to define with precision the limits of administrative authority ; but when the temper of arbitrary sway had been formed, when the example of an arbitrary system was constantly present to the eye and familiar to the thoughts, when the means of giving effect to arbitrary tastes were at hand, it is difficult to believe that the barrier of forms and definitions would be long respected, and that sooner or later the attempt would not be made to give to the principles of arbitrary government a more extended application.   The task of holding the South in subjection would thus, as it seems to me, inevitably imperil the cause of popular institutions in North America.   Now, the loss of popular government would be a heavy price to pay for the subjugation of the South, even though that subjugation involved the overthrow of the Slave Power.

It is satisfactory to find that there are politicians

in America who are alive to the momentous interests which this aspect of the question involves. In a remarkable speech lately delivered in New York, the danger to which I have adverted was very fairly and with much courage exposed. The speaker, however, contended that, by boldly following out a policy of emancipation—by striking at the root of disaffection through its cause—the danger in question might be evaded. The views expressed are so important, and, looking at the recent course of events, give so much promise of becoming fruitful, that I think it right to state them in the eloquent words of their author.

" Is this government, in struggling against rebellion, in re-establishing its authority, reduced to a policy which would nearly obliterate the line separating democracy from absolutism ? Is it really unable to stand this test of its character ? For this is the true test of the experiment. If our democratic institutions pass this crisis unimpaired, they will be stronger than ever; if not, the decline will be rapid and irremediable. But can they pass it unimpaired ? Yes. This republic has her destiny in her hands. She may transform her greatest danger and distress into the greatest triumph of her principles. There would have been no rebellion, had there not been a despotic interest incompatible with the spirit of her democratic institutions; and she has the glorious and inestimable privilege of suppressing this rebellion, by enlarging liberty instead of restraining it, by granting rights instead of violating them. . . . How can you rely upon the Southern people unless they are sincerely loyal, and how can they be sincerely loyal as long as their circumstances are such as to make disloyalty the natural condition of their desires and aspirations? They cannot be faithful unless their desires and aspirations change. And how can you change them? By opening before them new prospects and a new future. Look at the other side of the picture. Imagine slavery were destroyed in consequence of this rebellion. Slavery, once destroyed, can never be restored. . . . Southern society being, with all its habits and interests, no longer identified with slavery, that element of the population will rise to prominent influence which most easily identifies itself with free labour—I mean the non-slaveholding people of the South. They have been held in a sort of moral subjection by the great slave-lords. Not for themselves but for them they were disloyal. The destruction of slavery will wipe out the prestige of their former rulers; it will lift the yoke from their necks; they will soon think for themselves, and thinking freely they will not fail to understand their true interests. They will find in free labour society their natural element; and free labour

society is naturally loyal to the Union.   Let the
old political leaders fret as they please, it is the
free labour majority that will give to society its
character and tone.   This is what I mean by so
reforming Southern society as to make loyalty to
the Union its natural temper and disposition.   This
done, the necessity of a military occupation, the
rule of force, will cease ; our political life will soon
return to the beaten track of self-government, and
the restored Union may safely trust itself to the
good faith of a reformed people.   The antagonistic
element which continually struggled against the
vital principles of our system of government once
removed, we shall be a truly united people, with
common principles, common interests, common
hopes, and a common future."*

Such is the spirit in which the question of reconstructing the Union is now approached by some of
the leading minds of the North, and such are the
views which are now rapidly gaining ground through
the country.   While, however, readily acknowledging the proof which these speculations afford at once
of a full appreciation of the real difficulties to be
encountered and of philosophic boldness in meeting
them, I am unable to see that the remedy suggested
would obviate the danger which, it is admitted,

---

* Speech of the Hon. Carl Schurz, delivered in the Cooper
Institute, New York, 6th March, 1862.

would exist. In the reasoning which I have quoted
no account appears to be taken of the element of
time, so all-important to a realization of the results
anticipated. The abolition of slavery, it is truly
said, would strike directly at the authority of the
slave-lords. The stigma at present affixed to industry being removed, the industrial classes would
quickly rise in social importance, and a free labouring population would doubtless in the end predomi-
nate in the South. But these results could not
be accomplished in a moment. A disloyal people
would not be rendered loyal by a single stroke of
the manumitter's wand—

> "rerum imperiis hominumque
> Tot tantisque minor, quem ter vindicta quaterque
> Imposita haud unquam miserâ formidine privet."

The habits of obedience are not easily broken
through, traditional feelings are powerful, and the
influence of the slave-lords would probably long
outlive the institution from which it derives its
strength. A considerable period would, therefore,
of necessity, elapse before that pervading sentiment
of loyalty could be established, under the guidance
of which alone, as all admit, the rule of the Union
could be safely entrusted to popular institutions.

But there is another result which might follow
from the conquest of the South and the overthrow of
slavery, the probable effects of which on the settle-

ment of Southern society it may be worth while for a moment to consider. Is it not probable that, in the case we now contemplate, there would be an extensive immigration into the Southern States of free settlers from the North ? And what would be the effect of this new ingredient on the society of the South? I imagine it would in the main be a wholesome one. The new settlers would carry with them the ideas, the enterprise, the progressive spirit of free society, and would act as a leaven of loyalty on the disaffection of the South ; but I think it is equally plain they would introduce into Southern society, at all events for some time, a new element of disturbance. They would appear there as intruders, as the missionaries of a new social and political faith—a faith hateful to the old dominion, as living monuments of the humiliation of the Southern people. Is it not inevitable that between them and the old aristocracy a bitter feud would spring up—a feud which would soon be exasperated by mutual injuries, and might not impossibly be transmitted, as a heritage of hatred to future generations ? Now such a condition of society would be little favourable to the sudden conversion of the South to sentiments of loyalty; and, pending this happy consummation, how is the South to be governed? We are thus forced back upon our original difficulty—the difficulty of governing a disaffected South, from which, it seems to me, the path of despotism offers the only escape.

For these reasons, I cannot think that the North is well advised in its attempt to reconstruct the Union in its original proportions.*   At the same time I am far from thinking that the time for peace has yet arrived.   What, it seems to me, the occasion demands, and what, I think, the moral feeling of

---

* A writer in the *Semi-Weekly Times* (New York) complains that, in coming to this conclusion, I have not made " proper allowance for the part which the non-slaveholders, whose real interests are antagonistic to the owners of slaves, and identified with what will henceforth be the free-labour policy of the Federal government, may, by judicious management, be made to play in the reconstruction of the Union"; and that I do not " sufficiently weigh the influence which the extensive colonization of the South by free settlers from the North must have upon the political and social system of the South."   But if my friendly critic will turn to the preceding pages, he will find that I have not overlooked these important considerations.   It was indeed with a special view to present this aspect of the case in the strongest light that I quoted the passage from Mr. Schurz's speech, which, however, for the reasons I have assigned, appears to me to fail in its attempt to deal with the difficulties it so fairly states.   At the same time I am quite alive to what has been so well urged by this writer —the difficulty—he says " the impossibility"—" of a civilized nation's living side by side with such a monster as the Confederacy."   The character and aims of the Confederacy establish, in my opinion, the necessity of its being thoroughly humbled, as the indispensable preliminary to a permanent peace.   But this point once gained, I do not see why it might not for the future be kept within proper bounds by the presence of a negro army—the true and only solution, as it seems to me, of the grand problem.

Europe should support the North in striving for, is a degree of success which shall compel the South to accept terms of separation, such as the progress of civilization in America and the advancement of human interests throughout the world imperatively require. To determine the exact amount of concession on the part of the South which would satisfy these conditions is no part of my purpose. The attempt would be futile. It will suffice that I indicate as distinctly as I can that settlement of the controversy which would, in my judgment, adequately secure the ends proposed, and which on the whole is most to be desired.

Any scheme for the readjustment of political society in North America ought, it seems to me, to embrace two leading objects :— 1st, the greatest practical curtailment of the domain of the Slave Power; and 2nd, the reabsorption into the sphere of free society of as much of the present population of the Slave States as can be reabsorbed without detriment to the interests of freedom. On the assumption which I have made of the ability of the Northern people to subdue the South, these two conditions resolve themselves into one. This being assumed, the only obstacle to a complete reconstruction of the Union lies in the difficulty of combining in the same political system forms of society so different as those presented by the Northern and

Southern States. We may then, for the purpose of our discussion, confine our attention to the latter of the two conditions which have been laid down.

It will be remembered that, in considering, in a former chapter, the consequences of confining the Southern Confederacy within the area already settled under slavery, it was pointed out that slavery, thus restricted, would be at once arrested in its development, and that the check given to the system would be first felt in the older or breeding states. In these states the profits from slavery being derived chiefly from the sale, not from the employment, of slaves, so soon as the creation of new markets for the human stock was precluded, the reasons for maintaining the institution would cease. The slave-holders, obliged henceforward to look to the soil as the sole source of their profits, would be forced upon improved methods of cultivation ; and before the necessity for improved methods slavery would per-force disappear. Now, this being the position of slavery in the breeding states, it is evident that, so soon as the progress of the Northern armies shall have made it clear that the Slave Power must fail in its original design—still more when the South is menaced with positive curtailment of its dominions —the slaveholders of these states will understand that, so far as their interests are concerned, the institution is doomed. But this conviction will be brought home to them by still more cogent reasons than those which reflection on their economic condition would furnish. The breeding states are also the Border states, and they are therefore the states on which the evils of invasion must in the first instance fall. Already* nearly the whole of Virginia, Kentucky, Tennessee, and Missouri, is in possession of the Northern armies. Observe, then, the light in which, in the present aspect of affairs, the question of secession must present itself to a border slaveholder. He sees that for him the extinction of slavery is rendered certain in an early future. His slaves are flying to the Federal armies. His country is suffering all the evils of invasion. The tie which bound him to the Slave Power is hopelessly severed. In this position of affairs is it not probable that, were the opportunity of re-establishing social order upon a new basis presented to him, he would seize it, and, the old system of society having irrevocably passed away, that he would in good faith cast in his lot with a new order of things?

Such an opportunity has been created for the Border states by the adoption by Congress of Mr. Lincoln's recent message, recommending a co-operation on the part of the Federal government with such states as are willing to accept a policy of emancipation The scheme, indeed, has been pro-

* April, 1862.

nounced in this country to be chimerical—framed less with a view to the actual exigencies of the case than to catch the applause of Europe. I venture to say that never was criticism less appropriate, or censure more unjust. Practicality and unaffected earnestness of purpose are written in every line of the message. In the full knowledge evinced of the actual circumstances of the Border states, combined with the adroitness with which advantage is taken of their peculiar position as affected by passing events, there is displayed a rare political sagacity, which is not more creditable to its author than is the genuine sincerity which shines through his simple and weighty words. Had the scheme indeed been propounded at the outset of the contest (as so many well-meaning empirics among us were forward to advise)—while the Slave Power was yet unbroken, and the prospects of a future more prosperous than it had yet known seemed to be opening before it, there would have been some point in the strictures which have been indulged in, some ground for invidious comment ; but, proposed at the present time, it is, as I venture to think, a suggestion than which few more wise or more important have ever been submitted to a legislative body.*

* The condition on which the success of the President's scheme depended—the success of the Federal arms—has for the present failed of being realized ; yet the results already achieved are suffi-

Returning to our argument, it has been seen that in the event of the tide of war being decisively turned against the South, the position, alike industrial and geographical, of the Border states would greatly favour a reconstruction of society in them upon principles of freedom. Now, this result would

cient to show how complete that success would have been had the military position, even such as it was when the proposal was first brought forward, been maintained. As it was, even after the reverses sustained before Richmond, and the overcasting of the Federal horizon which followed, a strong minority of the representatives of the Border slave states, when addressed on the subject by the President on the rising of Congress, gave in their adhesion to. the scheme ; and at the recent elections Missouri and Delaware have pronounced unequivocally in its favour.

I have great satisfaction in quoting the following from the *Annuaire des Deux Mondes*, from which it will be seen that, in the view which I have from the first taken of the President's emancipation policy, I am supported by the high authority of M. Cucheval-Clarigny :—" Au milieu de ces discussions stériles éclata tout à coup un message du président. . . . Une émancipation graduelle semblait au président le mode le plus favorable à tous les intérêts, et M. Lincoln ne cachait pas que son but était d'élever une barrière infranchissable entre les états du centre et les états insurgés. Le principal mobile qui encourageait les rebelles à poursuivre la lutte contre l'Union était la conviction que, le jour où leur indépendence serait reconnue et la rupture de l'Union consommée, tous les états à esclaves demanderaient à être rattachés à la confédération du sud. Si les rebelles perdaient tout espoir d'accessions nouvelles, s'ils acquéraient la conviction que le territoire dévolu à l'esclavage ne pouvait plus s'accroître, la guerre devenait sans objet pour eux. . . . . La question de l'émancipation sortait tout à coup du domaine de la speculation pour entrer dans celui de la pratique. Les radicaux, qui s'en faisaient une

be powerfully helped forward by another circumstance in respect to which they differ from the
more southern states of the Confederacy—the presence in their population of a large element of free
cultivators. This interest, already in some of the
Border states* almost balancing that of slavery,

arme étaient réduits à confesser ouvertement qu'ils poursuivaient
un bouleversement social, ou, s'ils appuyaient le président, ils s'obli-
geaient à demeurer dans le cercle de la constitution. Les conserva-
teurs trouvaient dans le message l'assurance que le gouvernement
était déterminé à ne laisser porter aucune atteinte aux droits consti-
tutionnels des états. Quelque désagréable que la perspective, même
lointaine, de l'émancipation pût être pour les possesseurs d'esclaves,
la certitude que cette émancipation ne serait pas décrétée contre
leur volonté, et la garantie d'une indemnité préalable, que M.
Lincoln présentait comme le préliminaire indispensable de toute
mesure d'affranchissement, étaient deux considérations de nature à
rassurer plutôt qu'à alarmer les états du centre. Si l'émotion pro-
duite par le message de M. Lincoln fut des plus vives, l'impression
définitive ne fut pas défavorable : sénateurs et représentans se
trouvèrent tout à coup d'accord et se fondèrent sur l'importance
même de la proposition qui leur était faite pour en ajourner la
discussion jusqu'à ce qu'ils pussent connaître les sentimens de leur
commettants.   Par suite, les discussions sur l'esclavage furent
transférées de l'enceinte du congrès, où elles ne pouvaient aboutir,
dans l'intérieur des états à esclaves, où elles pouvaient seulement
recevoir une solution pratique."—*Annuaire des Deux Mondes,* 1861,
pp. 660–61.

* For example in Missouri. The position of slavery in that
state in 1856 is thus described by Mr. Weston :—" In large portions of Missouri slavery has never existed to any important
extent. The counties adjoining Iowa, ten in number, contained in
1856 57,255 whites, and only 871 slaves. Of the one hundred

would, it is evident, in the altered condition of affairs, rise rapidly into importance. Occupying that place in the social arrangements towards which the whole community was obviously tending, constantly increasing in numbers as the progress of emancipation brought new recruits to its ranks—a nucleus

and seven counties ninety-five, occupying four-fifths of the area of the state, contained in 1856 669,921 whites, and only 57,471 slaves, or nearly twelve to one. In twenty-five of these counties there was an absolute decrease of the number of slaves from 1850 to 1856. In the whole ninety-five counties the increase of slaves in that period was only 2,264. Slavery is not strong, and has never been so, except in twelve counties in the centre of the state, embracing about one-fifth of its area, and lying principally upon the Missouri river."—*Progress of Slavery*, p. 14. To which I add the following from the correspondent of the *Daily News* :—" By the force of circumstances beyond the control of politicians the edict of emancipation has been declared. Since 1860 the State has already lost one-half of her slaves. When the war began, Missouri had 104,000, but now it has only one-half that number. In some counties the average valuation of slaves has been diminished forty per cent. Many thousands have either become or made themselves contrabands, others have been carried by their masters to the South, and hosts have fled into Kansas." "In reference to Kentucky," says the Richmond correspondent of the *Times*, (Nov. 5, 1862) " it is idle to deny that there has been more disappointment here [Richmond] at her disloyalty to the South than at the apathy of Maryland. The condition of Kentucky, if the war lasts next year, will be appalling. On the other hand, if she had heartily thrown in her lot this autumn with the South, it is doubtful whether any attempt to carry the war further would have been made by the North. But in Kentucky and Maryland material considerations, wealth and comfort, have outweighed all other influences."

of loyalty around which all the best elements of
society might gather—this section of the population
would easily take the lead in the politics of their
several states, would give tone to the whole community, and determine its march.

It would thus seem that, the. might of the Slave
Power once effectually broken, the incorporation
of the Border states into a social system based on
industrial freedom would not present any insuperable difficulties. It would be only necessary to give
support to tendencies which the actual state of
things would call at once into operation. Now,
what might be done in the Border states, where a
slave society actually exists, might, it is evident, be
accomplished with much greater facility in those
districts of the South which, though enrolled as
slave states, have in reality yet to be colonized—
for example, in Texas and Arkansas. In Texas
population is represented by considerably less than
one person to the square mile ; in Arkansas, by
four ; and of this sprinkling of people three-fourths
in both states are composed of free persons.* To the
recovery of these states to the dominion of freedom
there would at least be no social or political obstacles which might not be easily overcome. Arkansas
and Texas recovered, Louisiana alone of the states
on the west of the Mississippi would remain to the

* See ante, p. 267, note.

Slave Power ; and is it not possible that Louisiana also might be recovered to freedom ? Doubtless its pro-slavery tendencies are intensely strong ; its slave population almost equals the free ; but the state is a small one, and the prize would be worth an extraordinary effort. Louisiana conquered, Arkansas and Texas recovered to freedom, the whole course of the Mississippi would be opened to the Western States ; and the Slave Power—shut up within its narrowed domain, bounded on one side by the Gulf of Mexico and the ocean, on the other by the line of the Alleghanies and the Mississippi,—might with some confidence be left to that process of natural decay which slave institutions, arrested in their expansion, inevitably entail.

I have hitherto discussed this question with reference to the interests of the Northern people on the one hand, and to those of civilization, as identified with the overthrow of the Slave Power, on the other. But there is another interest involved in the settlement of the American quarrel which may not seem at once to be identical with either of these—the interest of the present race of negro slaves. The mode of terminating the struggle which I have indicated as that which seems to me on the whole most desirable, though, if realized, it would probably bring freedom to a million of slaves, would yet, it is

not to be denied, leave some three millions still in
bondage ; and there are those who will probably
think that this after all would be but a sorry result
from the great opportunities of the present conjuncture, and from the great sacrifices which it has
already cost.   Far wiser, it will be said, as well as
more generous would it be, now that the hand
has been put to the plough, not to look back till the
work has been effectually accomplished, and the
great wrong once for all rased out.   With the
aspirations of those who hold this language I trust
I can sympathize ; but it seems to me that they fail
to appreciate the magnitude of the problem which
the policy they recommend involves.   No solution of
that problem would be complete, or would be worthy
of the enlightened views of the present time, which
did not include, besides the mere manumission of the
negro population, their protection against the efforts
of their former masters to recover their lost power,
and, no less, the provision for them of a career in the
future.   Now, let us suppose the first of these ends
to be accomplished—emancipation to be decreed—
and overlooking the objection to what would be the
necessary condition of an attempt to give effect to
the second—the establishment in the South of a despotic rule wielded by the central government—how,
let us ask, is it proposed to provide a career for four
millions of emancipated slaves ?   It will be said, the

land still remains to be cultivated ; and the labour of the negroes will be as necessary for its cultivation after they have been emancipated as before. The career for the emancipated negro would, therefore, be plain : he would, as a free labourer, hire his services to those who now take them by force. In a word, a population of four million slaves might be converted into a population of four million free labourers. This is, in truth, the only mode of solving the question that deserves serious attention ; for I do not think that the plans, of which we have lately heard something, of a wholesale removal of negroes from the American continent— even where they are not advanced for the purpose simply of discrediting the cause of emancipation— can be so regarded. But, taking the policy of immediate and universal emancipation in its best form, and judging it in a spirit of candour, is it a reasonable expectation that, looking at all the conditions of the case, the result which is contemplated would be realized,—that the negro, on the one hand, and the planter, on the other, would lend themselves to the scheme ? I am certainly not going to oppose to the proposal the exploded calumny of the incorrigible indolence of the negro. I am quite ready to admit, what nothing but the pernicious influence of slavery on the negro would ever have given a pretext for denying, and what our

West Indian experiment has now conclusively established,* that the negro in freedom is amenable to the same influences as the white man—that he can appreciate as keenly independence, comfort, and affluence, and that, like him, he will work and save and speculate to obtain these blessings ; neverthe-

* A very important contribution to our knowledge on the working of emancipation in the West Indies has just appeared from the pen of Mr. Edward Bean Underhill, from whose work, " *The West Indies, their Social and Religious Condition,*" I extract the following testimony of Captain Darling, the present governor of Jamaica, to the capacity of the negro for freedom :—" The proportion of those who are settling themselves industriously on their holdings, and rapidly rising in the social scale, while commanding the respect of all classes of the community, and some of whom are, to a limited extent, themselves the employers of hired labour, paid for either in money or in kind, is, I am happy to think, not only steadily increasing, but at the present moment is far more extensive than was anticipated by those who are cognizant of all that took place in this colony in the earlier days of negro freedom. There can be no doubt, in fact, that an independent, respectable, and, I believe, trustworthy middle class is rapidly forming. If the real object of emancipation was to place the freed man in such a position that he might work out his own advancement in the social scale, and prove his capacity for the full and rational enjoyment of personal independence secured by constitutional liberty, Jamaica will afford more instances, even in proportion to its large population, of such gratifying results, than any other land in which African slavery once existed. Jamaica at this moment presents, as I believe, at once the strongest proof of the complete success of the great measure of emancipation as relates to the capacity of the emancipated race for freedom, and the most unfortunate instance of a descent in the scale of agricultural and commercial importance as a colonial community."—pp. 45, 459.

less, while conceding all this, I confess I am unable
to see my way to the result that is here expected.

The grand difficulty to be encountered in any
scheme of emancipation which proposes to convert
suddenly a *régime* of forced into one of hired labour,
is the state of feeling which slavery leaves behind it
in the minds of those who have taken part in its
working. With the master there is a feeling of ex-
asperation which leads him to thwart the operation
of a system which has been forced upon him and
which is odious to him, combined with a desire to
re-establish under some new form his old tyranny ;
while the emancipated bondman naturally desires to
break for ever with a mode of life which is associated
with his degradation. These principles of disturbance were brought fully into play in the West
Indian experiment ;* but they were in that case

---

* "The House of Assembly at the time of emancipation possessed
the fullest powers to remedy any defect in that great measure. But
it abused its powers. Instead of enacting laws calculated to elevate
and benefit the people, it pursued the contrary course. By an
Ejectment Act it gave to the planters the right to turn out the enfranchised peasantry, without regard to sex or age, at a week's
notice, from the homes in which they had been born and bred ; to
root up their provision grounds, and to cut down their fruit trees
which gave them both shelter and food ; in order that, through
dread of the consequences of refusal, the negroes might be driven to
work on the planters' own terms. . . . Driven from his cabin on
the estate by the harsh or unjust treatment of his former master, the
free labourer had to build a cottage for himself. Immediately the
customs on shingles for the roof to shelter his family from the sea-

largely controlled by the condition of things in the West Indian islands. The strong arm of the British Government put an effectual restraint on the tyrannical temper of the masters ;* while in some of the islands the preoccupation of the land closed against the slave the one refuge from a hated lot. This, for example, was the case in Barbadoes, and in this island, accordingly, a system of hired industry was easily introduced. But the case of Barbadoes was exceptional, and, in the main, emancipation in the West Indies has issued, not in the conversion of a population of slaves into a population of labourers working for hire, but in the creation of a numerous

sons were more than doubled; while the duty on the staves and hoops for sugar hogsheads, the planters' property, was greatly reduced. And when the houses were built, they were assessed at a rate which, in some parishes, bore so heavily on the occupants, as to lead to the abandonment of their dwellings for shanties of mud and boughs."— *The West Indies*, &c., pp. 216-218.

" Some proprietors at emancipation drove their labourers from the estates, and one was mentioned who was living at the time on the north side of the island. He swore that he would not allow a ' nigger' to live within three miles of his house ; of course the man was speedily ruined."—*Ibid.* pp. 268, 269.

* " If the House of Assembly has had any policy at all in its treatment of the labouring classes, it has been a 'policy of alienation.' Only the perpetual interposition of the British government has prevented the enfrachised negro from being reduced to the condition of a serf by the selfish partisan legislation of the Jamaica planters. . . . As slaves the people were never instructed in husbandry, or in the general cultivation of the soil ; as free men, the legislature has utterly neglected them, and they have had to learn as they

class of small negro proprietors, each cultivating in independence his own patch of ground. It may thus be stated generally that, wherever the waste land was abundant, the West Indian experiment, so far as the point at present under consideration is concerned, broke down. The plantations were extensively deserted, and the negroes, instead of becoming hired labourers, became peasant farmers on the vacant land. Those principles of disturbance which slavery leaves after it, though largely controlled, were yet sufficiently powerful to prevent the general establishment of a system of hired labour.*

Now what would be the chance of replacing

could the commonest processes of agriculture. No attempt has been made to provide a fitting education for them ; for the paltry grant of some £2,500 a year cannot in any sense be said to be a provision for their instruction. . . . Speaking of this feature of Jamaica legislation, Earl Grey, writing in 1853, says:—'The Statute Book of the island for the last six years presents nearly a blank, as regards laws calculated to improve the condition of the population and to raise them in the scale of civilization.' . . . Happily the present governor, following in the steps of many of his predecessors, deals impartially with every class, strives to prevent as far as possible the mischievous effects of the selfish policy that has been pursued, and exerts himself to rescue the government from the grasp of personal interest and ambition."—*Ibid.* pp. 222, 223.

* The following is Mr. Underhill's conclusion as to the general results of the experiment in Jamaica :—" Emancipation did not, indeed, bring wealth to the planter ; it did not restore fortunes, already trembling in the grasp of mortgagees and usurers ; it did not bring back the palmy days of foreign commerce to Kingston, nor assist in the maintenance of protective privileges in the markets

negro slavery with hired labour in the Southern States? If we look to the condition of society there, we find that the usual disturbing causes exist in exaggerated force, while there is little to counteract them in the other conditions of the case. Nowhere else has pro-slavery fanaticism been so strong; the belief in the moral soundness of the

of Great Britain; it did not give wisdom to planters, nor skill to agriculturists and manufacturers; but it has brought an amount of happiness, of improvement, of material wealth and prospective elevation to the enfranchised slave in which every lover of man must rejoice. Social order everywhere prevails. Breaches of the peace are rare. Crimes, especially in their darker and more sanguinary forms, are few. Persons and property are perfectly safe. The planter sleeps in security, dreads no insurrection, fears not the torch of the incendiary, travels day or night in the loneliest solitudes without anxiety or care. The people are not drunkards, even if they be impure; and this sad feature in the moral life of the people is meeting its check in the growing respect for the marriage tie, and the improved life of the white community in their midst. . . . The general prospects of the island are improving. Estates are now but rarely abandoned, while in many places portions of old estates are being brought again under cultivation. It is admitted by all parties that sugar cultivation is profitable. At the same time, it is very doubtful whether any large proportion of the emancipated population will ever be induced to return to the estates, or, at least, in sufficient numbers to secure the enlargement of the area of cultivation to the extent of former days. Higher wages will do somewhat to obtain labourers, and they can be afforded, and the return of confidence will bring capital; but the taste and habit of independence will continue to operate, and induce the agricultural classes to cling to the little holdings which they so industriously occupy."—*The West Indies*, &c. pp. 455, 457.

institution has been nowhere so implicit ; nowhere, therefore, would the introduction of a system of free industry. have to encounter on the part of the masters such violent prejudices.   Again, the desire of the emancipated negro to break with his former mode of life could scarce fail to be here extremely strong ; for, although the treatment of the slaves was perhaps harsher in the West Indies than it has for the most part been in the Confederate States, the degradation of the race had neither there nor elsewhere reached so low a point; and, as a principle of repulsion, the feeling of shame would probably be not less powerful than that of hatred.   On the other hand, who can suppose,—bearing in mind the unworthy antipathy to the negro which still animates the great majority of the American people, and which perhaps emancipation would do little to remove ; bearing in mind the effects of a long complicity with slavery on the traditions of the Federal government —who, I say, impressed with these facts, can suppose that the negro of the Southern States would in that people and government find efficient protectors ? Would there be no fear that the protector might have less sympathy with the victim than even the tyrant against whom protection was claimed ?   But even on the assumption that the spirit of the Federal government and of the Northern people was excellent, would the task of protecting the negro be feasible in the South? Throughout the whole slave domain, but especially in the more southern of the Slave States, there are, as we know, vast regions of wilderness. Over these wanders a miserable white population, idle, lawless, and cherishing for the negro a contempt, which, on his being raised to their level by emancipation, would be quickly converted into hatred. Now, remembering what has happened in those West Indian islands which offer the nearest analogy to the present case—remembering what has occurred, for example, in Trinidad*—is it not almost

* "Three years after emancipation, in 1841, the condition of the island [Trinidad] was most deplorable: the labourers had for the most part abandoned the estates, and taken possession of plots of vacant land, especially in the vicinity of the towns, without purchase or lawful right. Vagrancy had become an alarming habit of great numbers; every attempt to take a census of the population was baffled by the frequent migrations which took place. Criminals easily evaded justice by absconding to places where they were unknown, or by hiding themselves in the dense forests which in all parts edged so closely on the cleared lands. Drunkenness increased to an enormous degree, assisted by planters who freely supplied rum to the labourers to induce them to remain as cultivators on their estates. High wages were obtained only to be squandered in amusement, revelry and dissipation; at the same time, these high wages induced a diminished cultivation of food, and a corresponding increase in price and in the importation of provisions from the neighbouring islands and continent. The labourers steadily refused to enter into any contracts which would oblige them to remain in the service of a master: this would too much have resembled the state of slavery from which they had but just emerged."—*The West Indies, &c.*, pp. 68–69.

certain that, so soon as emancipation was decreed the negroes would betake themselves to these wilds? and, dispersed over this vast region, what would be their fate? How could they be protected? How could they be trained to a higher mode of life? They would there encounter the white man in a condition as wretched as their own. His example could not fail to influence them. They would acquire his vagabond tastes, and emulate his idleness. They would be wholly at his mercy. Efficient protection would be impossible over a region so vast. The growth of regular industry would be hopeless ; and the too probable result would be that the whole South would be abandoned to the dominion of nature, and negro and white man go to ruin together.*

* It is proper here to add that the course of events since the publication of the first edition of this work has tended in some degree to diminish the force of the considerations set forth in the above passage. According to reliable accounts the negroes in Louisiana, in Western Florida, and on the coasts of the Carolinas—in short wherever the experiment has been tried—have shown themselves quite ready to engage with their former masters at reasonable wages ; and, as a matter of fact, considerable bodies of negroes are now employed upon the footing of free labourers in all these localities. Still it should be remembered that up to the present time the experiment has been conducted on a limited scale, which of course renders it proportionally more manageable ; and, secondly, that, as now tried, the most serious obstacle to its success —the temptation to squat on the waste lands—is effectually counteracted by the condition of the country, which obliges the negro to have recourse for safety to the Federal lines.

On the other hand, looking at the problem of emancipation, as it would present itself under that settlement of the American question which I have ventured to indicate as desirable, I am unable to see that it would involve any difficulty which a government, really bent on accomplishing its object, might not be fairly expected to overcome. In the first place, it would, as thus presented, at once assume more manageable proportions. The evil might be dealt with in detail, and the experience acquired in the earlier efforts might be made available at the further stages of the process. The attack would in the first instance be directed against the weakest part of the system—the institution in the Border states. In those states, not only is slavery less strongly established than in the states further south, it is also milder in its character. The relation subsisting between master and slave being less embittered, the obstacles to a re-establishment of their connexion upon a new footing would be less formidable. The wilderness, indeed,—the greatest difficulty of the case—would not be wholly absent even in the Border states ; but its dimensions would here be less vast, and these, as the abolition of slavery drew a fresh immigration from the adjoining states of the North, would in all probability be rapidly reduced. Even should the negroes repair to the wilds in considerable numbers, the case would not be so hopeless.

They would meet here in many districts, not the " mean whites," but a population of free cultivators, whose example, it is not to be doubted, would exercise on their character and pursuits an influence as wholesome as that of the others would be baneful. In these peasant cultivators the free negro would behold industry in its most respectable and most prosperous form ; and, with their example before him, he would probably settle down into the same condition of life with them.

But while in the reannexed states a career would be provided for the emancipated negro, his brother, still left in bondage in the South, would ere long find that for him also a new era was opening. Cut off from the rich virgin soils of the south-west the older states of the Confederacy would quickly reach the condition of Virginia and Maryland, The inevitable goal would soon come in sight, and the foreseen necessity of a change would gradually reconcile the minds of the planters to a policy of emancipation. The spirit in which the task would be undertaken when prescribed to them as it were by Nature herself, would, it may fairly be expected, be far different from that with which it would be encountered, if enforced at the bayonet's point by hostile and hated Northerns. Self-interest, no longer overborne by passion or pride, would teach the necessity of calmly considering a position of which the urgency could no longer be concealed or evaded ; and the full knowledge and large experience of the planters might be expected to conduct them to that solution which would be most in accordance with the welfare of the negro and their own. Meanwhile, the policy of emancipation once commenced, its effects would not be confined to the states which adopted it.   The working states, deprived of their supply of labour from the North, would be compelled to adopt new maxims of management. The life of the slave would become for his master an object of increased consideration; his comfort would be more attended to, and his condition would rapidly improve.   With the progress of time the destiny of the older states would overtake these also, and thus, by a gradual but sure process, the greatest blot on modern civilization would be expunged from American soil.

APPENDICES.

APPENDICES.

APPENDIX A.*

SOUTHERN TACTICS IN EUROPE.

THE *Richmond Inquirer* of December 20th, 1861, contained a document which throws a curious light on some of the causes which have been acting on public opinion in England during the past year. The writer had just returned to the South from a mission to London, in which he had been associated with Messrs. Yancey and Mann, and describes the state in which he found English opinion on American subjects on his arrival here in July, 1861, and the influences brought to bear by himself and his associates upon the members of the London Press, with a view to advancing the Southern cause with the English public. After stating the general expectation which prevailed in the South when he left it in June last, " that the manufacturing necessities of England and France would force them to a speedy recognition and interference with the Federal blockade ;" and " the equally confident impression that the commercial enterprise of England would spring at once to the enjoyment of the high prices the blockade established, by sending forward cargoes of arms, ammunition, medicines, and other stores most needed in the Confederacy ;" and after describing the causes in the public opinion of England which prevented these hopes being realized, the writer proceeds as follows :—" I have thus endeavoured, in this most hurried and imperfect manner, to sketch some of the difficulties which met our commissioners on the very threshold of their mission. That they have addressed themselves

* See page 22.

to these difficulties with zeal and efficiency will not be doubted by the millions in the South to whom their abilities and character are as familiar as household words. During my stay in London I was frequently at the rooms of Colonel M——, and can thus bear personal testimony to his zeal and efficiency. He seemed to appreciate the necessity of educating the English mind to the proper view of the various difficulties in the way of his progress; and, with but limited means of effecting his objects, he worked with untiring industry for their accomplishment; and, as I have also written, a distinguished member of Congress is, I believe, doing all that talent, energy, and a peculiar fitness for his position can accomplish. Without any other aid than his intimate knowledge of English character, and that careful style of procedure which his thorough training as a diplomatist has given him, he has managed to make the acquaintance of most of the distinguished representatives of the London Press, whose powerful batteries thus influenced are brought to bear upon the American question. This of course involves an immense labour, which he stands up to unflinchingly. So much for his zeal. His efficiency, with that of his colleague, is manifested in the recognition of our rights as a belligerent, and in the wonderful revolution in the tone of the English Press. . . . The influence of this lever upon public opinion was manifest during my stay in Paris. When I first went there, there was not a single paper to speak out in our behalf. In a few days, however, three brochures were issued which seemed to take the Parisian Press by storm. One of them was the able and important letter of the Hon. T. Butler King to the Minister; another, 'The American Revolution Unveiled,' by Judge Pequet, formerly of New Orleans—whose charming and accomplished lady, by the way, is a native of Richmond; and a third, 'The American Question,' by Ernest Bellot des Minières, the agent of the French purchasers of the Virginia canals. These works each in turn created a great deal of attention, and their united effect upon the French mind shows the effective character of this appliance. Messrs. Bellot and Pequet deserve well of the Confederacy for their powerful and voluntary advocacy. I can, and with great pleasure do, bear testimony to the valuable and persevering efforts

of Mr. King both in Paris and London. Among the first acquaint-
ances I had the pleasure of making while in London was Mr.
Gregory, M.P., to whom I carried letters of introduction from a
Virginia gentleman long resident in Paris, who very kindly either
introduced or pointed out to me the distinguished members of
parliament. He had been, I found, a traveller in Virginia, and
inquired after several persons, among whom was Mr. John B.
Rutherford, of Goochland. During an hour's walk upon the pro-
menade between the new parliament houses and the Thames, he
plied me with questions as to the 'situation' in the Confederacy,
and seemed greatly encouraged by my replies; more so, he said,
than at any time since the revolution commenced."

APPENDIX B.*

SLAVE LABOUR.

" I AM here shewn tools," says Mr. Olmsted, " that no man in
his senses, with us, would allow a labourer, to whom he was paying
wages, to be encumbered with; and the excessive weight and clum-
siness of which, I would judge, would make work at least ten per
cent. greater than with those ordinarily used with us. And I am
assured that, in the careless and clumsy way they must be used by
the slaves, anything lighter or less rude could not be furnished
them with good economy, and that such tools as we constantly give
our labourers, and find our profit in giving them, would not last out
a day in a Virginia cornfield—much lighter and more free from
stones though it be than ours.

" So, too, when I ask why mules are so universally substituted
for horses on the farm, the first reason given, and confessedly the
most conclusive one, is that horses cannot bear the treatment that
they always *must* get from negroes; horses are always soon foun-

* See page 53.

dered or crippled by them, while mules will bear cudgelling, and lose a meal or two now and then, and not be materially injured, and they do not take cold or get sick, if neglected or overworked. But I do not need to go further than to the window of the room in which I am writing, to see at almost any time, treatment of cattle that would insure the immediate discharge of the driver by almost any farmer owning them in the North." In another State, a Southern farmer describes to him " as a novelty, a plough ' with a sort of wing, like,' on one side, that pushed off and turned over a slice of the ground; from which it appeared that he had, until recently, never seen a mould-board; the common ploughs of this country being constructed on the same principle as those of the Chinese, and only rooting the ground like a hog or a mole—not cleaving and turning."—*Seaboard Slave States*, pp. 46, 47, 402.

APPENDIX C.*

FAILURE OF THE SOUTH IN MANUFACTURES.

It is not, of course, intended to be maintained that no mechanical or manufacturing industry of any sort is carried on in the Slave States—no society could exist on such terms, though how closely the Southern States approximate to this condition may be seen from the fact, that even for so simple a production as shoes Virginia has been dependent almost exclusively on the North (De Bow's *Industrial Resources*, vol. ii. p. 130). What I mean to assert is, that the amount of industry of this kind carried on in the South is so small, that in the computation of the national resources it may for practical purposes be disregarded; and this, notwithstanding the existence of a few factories in some of the Southern towns, Mr. De Bow admits as fully as I have stated it. Indeed, no inconsiderable portion of the four volumes of his *Industrial Resources* is taken up with lamentations over this very circumstance—the exclusive

* See page 70.

devotion of the industry of the country to an exhaustive system of agriculture, to the almost entire neglect of manufactures, followed by exhortations to the introduction of the latter. Take, for example, the following passage. Replying to the question, what has become of the industrial profits of the South, the writer says :— " Much of it has been paid to the neighbouring states for provisions, mules, horses, and implements of husbandry ; much has been paid for clothing and other articles of manufacture, all induced by the system of applying all, or nearly all the labour of the country, to the production of one staple only, and by neglecting the encouragement of manufactures. . . . She is yearly wearing out her soil in the production of one great staple, which has become ruinously low in price by reason of its great supply. She parts with this staple at prime cost, and purchases almost all her necessary appliances of comfort from abroad, not at prime cost, but burdened with the profits of merchants, the costs of transportation, duties, commissions, exchange, and numerous other charges, all of which go to support and enrich others at her expense. This is the true reason that she is growing poorer while the rest of the world is growing rich, for it is easy for the world to enrich itself from such a customer on such terms. If she were wise, she would cease to carry on a traffic in which she always has been and always must be a loser ; she will set up for herself, and instead of parting with the products of all her labour to support the balance of the world, she will manufacture her own clothing, and, not stopping at this, proceed to manufacture the whole of her crop, and thereby draw upon the world for a portion of her former losses." Passages of this kind (and the economic literature of the South abounds with them) throw a curious light on the pretensions of the Southern States to enlightened views in political economy, and show upon what quicksands those persons are building who support the Confederacy in the expectation of its adopting a free commercial policy.

APPENDIX D.*

THE ' MEAN WHITES.'

A WRITER in the *Saturday Review* has denied the existence of any class in the South which answers to the description given in this passage. He denies that even the names, " mean white," " white trash," have any place—out of the negroes' quarters—in the Southern vocabulary; and he treats the impression which prevails in this country of the existence of such people as an example—to be classed with " the world-famous wife market in Smithfield"—of the delusions to which nations are liable respecting the social condition of other countries. This position the Reviewer seeks to establish, for the most part by strong assertion, but in some degree by an appeal to statistics. His argument from statistics I will examine : his assertions I will give the reader an opportunity of comparing with those of English and American visitors to the Southern States, as well as with the testimony of Southern men of position and character, addressing Southern audiences, and speaking in the presence of the facts which they describe.

And, first, as to the statistical argument—the Saturday Reviewer writes as follows :—" We know from the census that there were in 1850, 1,114,000 free families in the Southern States, and 563,000 farms ; so that more than half the white population is employed in agriculture alone. And agriculture, in its statistical acceptance, does not by any means include all who derive their subsistence directly from the produce of the soil. We see, therefore, that there were of planters and farmers, strictly so-called, 563,000 families, each settled on land of its own, and possessing from fifty to five thousand acres of cleared and uncleared ground."

I must take leave to say that the Reviewer does not know these statements from the census. No such return as the second of those which he quotes is to be found in the census; but such a return is to be found in a partisan work, lately published by the Hon. James Williams, late American minister in Turkey—" *The South Vindi-*

* See page 83.

cated;" and it is grossly incorrect. The number of farms in the Southern States in 1850, as given in Colton's Atlas, was not 563,000 but 373,106—that is to say, the Reviewer represents the number of farms in the South as more than one-half greater than it actually is. Assuming, as I suppose I am justified in doing, that the Reviewer's statistics are borrowed from the pages of Mr. Williams, it will be instructive to note the following facts. In the table from which the Reviewer quoted, the number of farms in Maryland is set down at 211,860, while the number in Virginia is set down at 77,013, that in Kentucky at 74,777, and that in Tennessee at 72,735. Now no one, who had the most superficial knowledge of the industrial condition, or even of the geography, of the South, could have looked at these figures, and not have seen that they contained an enormous error. The three chief farming states of the South are Virginia, Kentucky and Tennessee; the smallest of them is three times as large as Maryland; and yet Maryland is represented as containing nearly as many farms as all these states combined. But, had there been any doubt upon this point, a comparison of this table with one immediately preceding it must have removed it. In a table given in the preceding page the agricultural population of Maryland is set down at 28,588; the number of farms, we have seen, is given at 211,860; whence it would follow, combining these numbers, that every member of the agricultural population of Maryland is on an average master of seven farms and a half ! Such is the avidity with which any statements are swallowed by those who reason to support a foregone conclusion; and such is the notable conclusion, which this writer, who affects profound disdain for " those who derive their notions of the South from *Uncle Tom's Cabin* and Mr. Olmsted's *Journeys,"* blindly accepts ! No less unquestionable an authority than the Hon. James Williams in the *South Vindicated* will satisfy the severe requirements of the *Saturday Review.*

And now let us observe how this gigantic blunder affects the Reviewer's argument. The purpose of that argument is to dispose of the charge of idleness brought against the bulk of the Southern population by producing proof of the existence of industry in the

South sufficient in quantity to provide them with occupation.
Thus from his imaginary premises of 563,000 farms, the Reviewer
concludes that "there were of planters and farmers, strictly so
called, 563,000 families, each settled on land of its own, and
possessing from fifty to five thousand acres of cleared and uncleared
land." We have seen, however, that the number of farms, instead
of 563,000, was only 373,000 ; and this reduction at once throws
on the Reviewer's hands 190,000 families, comprising according to
the census proportion 1,092,000 individuals, for whom he has not
even attempted to suggest any honest means of livelihood. But the
case is in reality much stronger than this. The returns of farms include plantations, and we all know that it is common for a single
planter to own several plantations. Nor does the census save us from
this source of error ; since Professor De Bow, the superintendent of
the census of 1850, expressly informs us that " where the party owns
several plantations in different counties or in different states, he will
be entered more than once." It follows, then, that the 373,000 farms
by no means represent 373,000 families. What the proportion of
families to farms may be it is not possible to say with exactness,
but we may arrive at it approximately as follows :—The Reviewer
assumes (and the assumption is perhaps a fair one) that the owner
of five slaves and upwards may be taken to represent the planting,
as distinguished from the farming, interest. Adopting this view,
and applying it to the census returns of slaveholders, we arrive at
173,022 as the number of planters in the South in 1850. It
would probably be not more than a fair allowance for the case of
pluralists to say that these 173,022 planters absorbed 200,00c
plantations. Deducting these from the aggregate of farms and
plantations we obtain 173,000 farms disposable for the remaining
population ; and what was its number ? We arrive at this by
deducting the number of planters' families from the aggregate number of families in the South.

Total of white and free coloured families in 1850   .   1,114,687
Deduct planters' families   173,022
                                                    ———————
Remaining population, number of families   .   .   941,665

We have thus 173,000 farms, properly so called, disposable among a population of 941,665 families. The point to be determined is the number of families to which these may be supposed to have given employment. Of this the census affords us no direct evidence; but we know that the farming population in the Southern, as in the Northern, States, consists for the most part of peasant proprietors; the land held by such, as a general rule, not exceeding what a single family is competent to cultivate; and, secondly that, where the farms exceed this limit, slave labour is obtainable and is much preferred by Southern farmers to such free labour as the country can provide. Under these circumstances it is evident that the class of free farm labourers, who are not members of the farmer's family, must be exceedingly small. It will probably be a liberal estimate if we suppose that each farm, in addition to the farmer's family, gives employment on an average to one-fourth of a family of free labourers. This would bring the whole number of families absorbed by the 173,000 farms to 216,000. And this, I apprehend, represents approximately the position in which in 1850 the case actually stood. These 216,000 families, comprising, according to the census proportion, 1,242,000 individuals, are principally distributed over the Northern portion of the Border states, more especially through western Virginia, Kentucky, and eastern Tennessee; and this portion of the Southern population, as I have intimated in more than one passage in this volume, forms a substantially foreign element in the society of the South, having no affinities with the system in contact with which it finds itself, and being a source of weakness instead of strength to the Slave Power.

Taking now the farming and planting population together, as it stood in 1850, it might, according to the above calculation, be distributed as follows :—

Families engaged in farming 216,000
Planters' families 173,022

Total of farming and planting families . . 389,022
But the total number of families in the South at this time was 1,114,687. Deducting the former from the latter, there remained

725,665 families, which, according to the census proportion, would comprise 4,172,574 individuals. Here was a vast population existing in the Southern States over and above what the planting and farming industry, on the most liberal computation of its resources, gave employment to. The question is how did this vast population find the means of support ? The Reviewer replies as follows :—" There is a very numerous class employed, at enormous wages, in the internal carrying trade of the South. There is the working population of the cities, also numerous and exceedingly well-paid. There are the traders of every sort—those of the cities and small villages, and those who establish their ' stores' at cross-roads, and supply the farming population of large districts with everything which they consume that cannot be grown on their own farms. None of these classes are poor or degraded ; and these altogether embrace no inconsiderable proportion of the non-agricultural population. Besides or below these, and the class of farmers, comes a numerous body which is not reckoned among the agriculturists. The collection of rosin or turpentine affords employment to thousands ; and the class of backwoodsmen is also large."

The answer of the Reviewer, stated generally, amounts to this, that the white population, who are neither planters nor farmers, nor engaged in farming operations, find employment in distributing the produce which the planters and farmers raise. Now I maintain that this is a palpable absurdity. The whole productive population in the Southern States in 1850, including under this head all the plantation slaves, the white farming population with such slaves as they employ, and the small number of whites and blacks engaged in productive operations in the towns, could scarcely have exceeded in all four million persons ; but, assuming them to have numbered five millions, we are asked to believe that the mere business of distributing the products raised by this population would give employment to a population nearly as large. In no considerable country in the world does the population engaged in distributing wealth nearly equal the population engaged in producing it. In Ireland the proportion borne by the former to the latter department of the population was in 1850 about one to three; but probably nowhere does the distributive population stand in so small a ratio to the productive as in the Southern States ; and this for obvious reasons. In the first place the largest class of consumers in the South is that of negro slaves—a stationary population, without surplus expenditure, whose wants are restricted to a few invariable commodities which are supplied with routine regularity.   Again, the magnificent river system of the South affords unparalleled facilities for internal transport, reducing in a proportional degree the quantity of industry required for carrying it on ;* and, lastly, a considerable portion of the expenditure of the Southern wealthy class has always taken place in Northern towns.   These causes, tending at once to simplify and facilitate the work of distribution, concur to render the proportion which this department of industry bears to that engaged in production greatly smaller in the South than elsewhere ; and I shall therefore probably overstate the case, if I take this proportion as one to four.   But assuming this to be the proportion, and assuming that five millions in the South are engaged in production —also I am convinced an exaggeration—a million and a quarter of persons would suffice for the whole business of distribution.   But the population available for this purpose was, in 1850, not a million and a quarter, but upwards of four millions.   How did the vast remaining population of nearly three millions find employment?

The truth is, the distributive industry of the South, which has been suggested by the Reviewer as furnishing the means of regular employment to the mass of the white population, and which, as we have just seen, would be altogether insufficient for this purpose, is in reality performed in a very slight degree by the native white people, but mainly by negroes and foreign immigrants, many of the latter being occasional residents, who would not find their place in the census at all.   I shall now proceed to adduce some evidence bearing upon this point ; and I shall take the several occupations in the order in which they occur in the passage of the *Saturday Review* which I have quoted.

* " Minnesota is 1500 miles above New Orleans, but the wheat of Minnesota can be brought down the whole distance without change of the vessel in which it is first deposited."—Trollope's *North America*, vol. ii., p. 127.

And, first, as to the allegation that "there is a very numerous class employed at enormous wages in the internal carrying trade of the South"—the following passage from Mr. Stirling's *Letters from the Slave States* throws some light upon this as well as upon some others of the Reviewer's suggestions. "On the Georgian railway Irish labourers were lately employed ; now they have slaves. The American railway officials prefer the latter, but only, I suspect, because Irishmen refuse to be driven. On the Mississippi and Alabama rivers Irish and negroes are employed indiscriminately. On the St. John's only slaves are employed ; few or no Irish go so far South. The captain of the Charleston steamer told me he paid eighteen dollars per month for slaves, and sixteen and seventeen for Irish ; but he prefers the former, ' for,' said he, naively, ' if an Irishman misbehaves, I can only send him ashore.' The alternative in the case of the nigger was ' understood.' Then, as to waiters,—at the St. Charles Hotel, New Orleans, they were all Irish ; at the Pulaski House, Savannah, they are all slaves ; at the Charleston Hotel, Charleston, they are partly Irish and partly slaves."* And to precisely the same effect is the testimony of Mr. Russell of Kilwhiss:—" I got on board a steamer at Natchez for New Orleans, this afternoon, and found it full of passengers, and the accommodation as good as in the one in which I had ascended the river. Calls at different plantations were frequently made to take in cotton and sugar. As many as forty labourers, one half Irishmen, the other half negroes, are kept on board to save time in taking in the produce of the plantations." We have here no mention of white natives : the only workmen spoken of are Irish and negroes. It is quite possible indeed that the ' mean white' may do an occasional job in this way ; and Mr. Olmsted tells us that this is the case in some parts of Virginia, in one district of which he says " they mostly follow boating—hiring as hands on the bateaus that navigate the small streams and canals, but never for a longer term at once than a single trip of a boat, whether that might be long or short. At the end of the trip they were paid by the day,"† Are these the

---

* pp. 229–30.　　　　　† *Seaboard Slave States,* p. 82.

people that the planters and their agents would be likely to trust to as the main resource for conducting the internal carrying trade of the South?

Again, we are told "there is the working population of the cities also numerous and exceedingly well-paid. There are traders of every sort," &c. Now, in the first place, the white city population of the South, if we exclude a few towns such as Baltimore and St. Louis, which are on the borders of the Free States, and owe their prosperity far more to Northern than to Southern influences, is by no means large; and secondly that portion of the city population to which the South is indebted for such urban industry and enterprise as it possesses is principally of foreign origin. "Of those Southern towns which I have named," says Mr. Trollope [New Orleans, Charleston, Savannah, Mobile, Richmond and Memphis] the commercial wealth is of Northern creation. The success of New Orleans as a city can be no more attributed to the Louisianians than can that of the Havana to the men of Cuba, or of Calcutta to the natives of India."* But the following account from a Southern journal, the New Orleans *Commercial Bulletin,* respecting the founding of a Southern town, will perhaps convey a better idea than any general statements how little the prosperity, such as it is, of Southern towns owes to the industry or enterprise of the inhabitants of the South. The description refers to the laying out of the new town of Brashear on Berwick Bay, on the route between New Orleans and Galveston. "No more favourable site," says the *Bulletin,* "could have been selected for a town, which in a few years may become a flourishing city. . . . . . Nearly the whole of this property has been sold to mechanics, artizans, and store-keepers. . . . . . A feature or two in this sale is worthy of notice. *The purchasers, with a few exceptions, not exceeding five or six, are naturalized citizens, principally Germans, with some Spaniards and Frenchmen, and a few Irish.*"† On which Mr. Weston, from whom I have borrowed the quotation, remarks—" These 'mechanics,

* And see Stirling's *Letters from the Slave States,* pp. 320, 321.
† *Progress of Slavery,* pp. 48, 49.

artizans, and storekeepers,' who 'appreciated' the advantages of Brashear, and who had the means wherewithal to buy and pay for lots in it, were, it seems, scarcely any of them native white citizens of Louisiana. At that point, so remote from the free States, it is not easy to see of what materials the new town could have been constituted, *but for the fortunate presence of Europeans,* 'principally Germans,' who stood ready, with well-filled pockets and skilful hands, to lay the foundations of a 'flourishing city.'"*

But, lastly, " the collection of rosin and turpentine affords employment to thousands." It may be true that a small number of the white people find in a few localities a desultory occupation in this way; but it is certain that the bulk of the industry in the pine forests is carried on by negroes. In a detailed account, extending over ten pages, given by Mr. Olmsted of the process of collecting turpentine and rosin in North Carolina,† the only workmen spoken of are negroes. Of the poor whites he gives the following description :—" The negroes are decidedly superior in every moral and intellectual respect to the great mass of the white people inhabiting the turpentine forest. Among the latter there is a large number, I should think a majority, of entirely uneducated, poverty-stricken vagabonds. I mean by vagabonds, simply, people without habitual, definite occupation or reliable means of livelihood. They are poor, having almost no property but their own bodies; and the use of these, that is, their labour, they are not accustomed to hire out statedly and regularly, so as to obtain capital by wages, but only occasionally by the day or job, when driven to it by necessity. A family of these people will commonly hire, or 'squat' and build, a little log cabin, so made that it is only a shelter from rain, the sides not being chinked, and having no more furniture or pretension to comfort than is commonly provided for a criminal in the cell of a prison. They will cultivate a little corn, and possibly a few roods of potatoes, cow-peas and coleworts. They will own a few swine, that find their living in the forest; and pretty certainly, also, a rifle

* *Progress of Slavery,* pp. 49–50.
† *Seaboard Slave States,* pp. 338–348.

and dogs; and the men, ostensibly, occupy most of their time in hunting."*

But lastly, "the class of backwoodsmen is large." And "here at least" the Reviewer admits that an untravelled visitor "might be excused for supposing that he had found that 'mean white' species which is supposed to be a growth of slave soil peculiar to the South;" but here again he would be mistaken. Backwoodsmen, we are reminded, are to be found also in the North. There is, however, the Reviewer admits, a difference between the two cases, "owing," as he tells us, "to the different character of Northern and Southern cultivation, and the different laws of their progress. In the North, civilization advances evenly, like the wave of a tide slowly but continually gaining on the western shore. In the South it has overflowed the land like an inundation, taking possession of those soils which suited it, and leaving an island of wilderness here and there in the midst of a settled and busy people. And the wilderness forms a great part of the country, abounding even in the oldest and richest states. Alabama is the only state in which the acreage of 'unimproved' farm land is not at least double that of 'improved;' and improved and unimproved together amount to only a little more than one-fifth of the whole area of the Southern States.† Everywhere there may be found forests abounding in game, and presenting all the facilities and temptations of savage life. Within twenty miles of Mobile, you may meet with herds of deer; and so generally is this the case, that in most parts of the South venison is cheaper than beef. Nowhere is it an unheard of thing for a villager to shoot a wild turkey in his own barnyard. Everywhere—in the midst of cultivation, and in the neighbourhood of cities—may be found the backwoods and the backwoodsman."

I think it must be admitted that the field provided by the Re-

---

* *Seaboard Slave States*, pp. 348, 349.

† This statement does not give a favourable idea of the state of agriculture in the South, yet in truth the impression it leaves falls immensely short of the reality. Of the four million acres of "improved land" in South Carolina, Mr. Russell tells us that but a million and a half are in cultivation.—See *North America*, &c. p. 294.

viewer for his backwoodsmen is a sufficiently spacious one ; and that it is therefore not without reason he has told us that "the class of backwoodsmen is large." He speaks indeed of " civilization over-flowing" the South like an " inundation," " leaving an island of wilderness here and there in the midst of a busy and settled people ;" but from his subsequent description, it seems plain that his metaphor has by some accident been inverted, and that it is the wilderness which should represent the " inundation," and civilization the occasional " island ;" for he tells us that of what is in the census called " land in farms " in the South not one-third is "improved," while " improved and unimproved together amount to only one-fifth of the area of the Southern States." There can therefore be no doubt that the backwoodsmen of the South are furnished with an ample range. Now, no one has ever ventured to say that there is anything corresponding to this in the Northern States. It is only, according to the Reviewer's own account, on the extreme margin of the advancing tide of civilization that there is any place for the species, which is, consequently, in the Northern States numerically insignificant. But there is another difference between the Northern and Southern backwoodsmen, which the Reviewer has failed to point out, but which is nevertheless pertinent to our inquiry. The backwoodsman of the Northern States performs for the society to which he belongs a really useful, nay an indispensable office. He is the pioneer of progress. Without his assistance the expanding wave of civilization would be arrested. Will the Reviewer inform us what social ends are served by the Southern backwoodsman ?

We see, then, that in the functions which they perform, no less than in number, the Northern and the Southern species stand upon a different footing. The backwoodsman of the North represents an insignificant fraction of the whole population existing on the outskirts of civilization, where he discharges a task indispensable to Northern society : the backwoodsman of the South exists over the whole area of the Southern States, discharges no useful office, but preys upon the wealth which surrounds him. Is it true, as the Reviewer asserts, that these two men "represent precisely the same variety of the human race"? The following descriptions of the two classes, proceed, I think it will not be denied, from competent hands :—

" Florida is the Paradise of an idle man. Shooting and fishing will easily supply him with food ; and, if he wishes to be very luxurious, by scratching the ground he may have a few sweet potatoes, or a little Indian corn. Land has been bought in Florida at a cent per acre ; but for that matter our ' cracker' need not buy land at all—he may squat, and take his chance of being turned out. It is not every one who would wish to dispossess a ' cracker' so long as the ' cracker' had his rifle and an ounce of lead. Having thus established himself on land of his own, or a patch of Uncle Sam's, he may also, if he pleases, become a grazier at small expense of labour or money. Having bought, borrowed, or stolen a few head of cattle, he simply marks them, and turns them out into the woods. In the spring he collects the calves, and puts his brand upon them ; and this, absolutely, is all the care or trouble he takes, except catching them when a purchaser appears. In this way some of these Florida squatters accumulate vast herds of cattle, without any exertion on their part. Nay, so lazy and careless of comfort are they, that I am assured there are men in these forests, owning 5,000 or 6,000 head of cattle, who have not even milk to their coffee ; ' and that,' said Captain B——, ' I call pretty damned shiftless.'

" This easy, lazy, good-for-nothing kind of life is very common among all the ' poor whites' of the seaboard slave states, but it seems to have reached its climax in Florida. Here the plentiness of game and cheapness of land attract many idlers from the neighbouring states ; and many a man squats in Florida who has made other states too hot to hold him. Florida is the Alsatia of the Union."*

So much for the Southern backwoodsman : now for his analogue in the North :—

"The primary settler, therefore, who, however, will not usually have been the primary owner,—goes to work upon his land amidst

* Stirling's *Letters from the Slave States*, pp. 224, 225.

all the wildness of nature. He levels and burns the first trees, and raises his first crop of corn amidst stumps still standing four or five feet above the soil; but he does not do so till some mode of conveyance has been found for him. So much I have said hoping to explain the mode in which the frontier speculator paves the way for the frontier agriculturist. But the permanent farmer generally comes on the land as the third owner. The first settler is a rough fellow, and seems to be so wedded to his rough life, that he leaves his land after his first wild work is done, and goes again further off to some untouched allotment. He finds that he can sell his improvements at a profitable rate, and takes the price. He is a preparer of farms rather than a farmer. He has no love for the soil which his hand has first turned. He regards it merely as an investment; and when things about him are beginning to wear an aspect of comfort,—when his property has become valuable, he sells it, packs up his wife and his little ones, and goes again into the woods. The western American has no love for his own soil, or his own house. The matter with him is simply one of dollars. To keep a farm which he could sell at an advantage from any feeling of affection,—from what we should call an association of ideas,—would be to him as ridiculous as the keeping of a family pig would be in an English farmer's establishment. The pig is a part of the farmer's stock in trade, and must go the way of all pigs. And so it is with house and land in the life of the frontier man in the western states.

"But yet this man has his romance, his high poetic feeling, and above all his manly dignity. Visit him, and you will find him without coat or waistcoat, unshorn, in ragged blue trousers and old flannel shirt, too often bearing on his lantern jaws the signs of ague and sickness; but he will stand upright before you and speak to you with all the ease of a lettered gentleman in his own library. All the odious incivility of the republican servant has been banished. He is his own master, standing on his own threshold, and finds no need to assert his equality by rudeness. He is delighted to see you, and bids you sit down on his battered bench without dreaming of any such apology as an English cottier offers to a Lady

Bountiful when she calls. He has worked out his independence, and shows it in every easy movement of his body. He tells you of it unconsciously in every tone of his voice. You will always find in his cabin some newspaper, some book, some token of advance in education. When he questions you about the old country he astonishes you by the extent of his knowledge. I defy you not to feel that he is superior to the race from which he has sprung in England or in Ireland. To me I confess that the manliness of such a man is very charming. He is dirty and perhaps squalid. His children are sick, and he is without comforts. His wife is pale, and you think you see shortness of life written in the faces of all the family. But over and above it all there is an independence which sits gracefully on their shoulders, and teaches you at the first glance that the man has a right to assume himself to be your equal." *

The reader may look on this picture and on that. If these two men " represent precisely the same variety of the human race," it must be allowed that the limits within which a variety may vary without losing its identity are tolerably extensive.

I have now examined in turn the several modes of industry which have been suggested as possible means of employment for the five millions and a half of population in the South, whose pursuits are un-ascertained, and I submit that the assumptions of the Reviewer are utterly overthrown by the evidence which has been adduced. The whole distributive industry of the South would not suffice to absorb more than one-fourth of the available population; and we find that, in point of fact, the white natives of the South take little part in it. The internal carrying trade is conducted principally by negroes and Irish immigrants; three-fourths of the commerce of the country are in the hands of foreigners; in their hands also are most of the mechanical and other trades of the cities; and the work of the pine forests is performed, at all events principally, by negroes. On the other hand, it is admitted that four-fifths of the whole Southern country are little better than wilderness, and offer strong attractions to those whose tastes lead them towards a wild life. These facts alone, even in the absence of all positive evidence as to the character

* *North America*, by Anthony Trollope, vol. i. pp. 197-199.

and pursuits of the bulk of the Southern people, would go far, I think, to justify the popular impression which the Reviewer treats with such scorn ; but, in truth, the case does not rest upon presumptive grounds. We have the most distinct and unequivocal testimony, both from Southerns themselves, and from impartial English writers, as to the point in question ; and this testimony, of which I shall now adduce some specimens, is, I submit, fully adequate to sustain the description of the Southern population which I have given in the text.

In a paper read before the South Carolina Institute in 1851 by Mr. William Gregg, the following passages occur :—

" From the best estimates which I have been able to make I put down the white people, who ought to work, and who do not, or who are so employed as to be wholly unproductive to the state, at one hundred and twenty-five thousand. . . . The appropriation annually made by our legislature for our school fund every one must be aware, so far as the country is concerned, has been little better than a waste of money. . . . While we are aware that the Northern and Eastern states find no difficulty in educating their poor, we are ready to despair of success in this matter, for even penal laws against the neglect of education would fail to bring many of our country people to send their children to school. . . . Any man who is an observer of things could hardly pass our country without being struck with the fact that all the capital, enterprise, and intelligence is employed in directing slave labour ; and the consequence is that a large proportion of our poor white people are wholly neglected, and are suffered to while away an existence in a state but one step in advance of the Indian of the forest. It is an evil of vast magnitude." The whole population of South Carolina, by the census of 1850, numbered 274,563 persons; and of these Mr. Gregg tells us that there are 125,000 " who ought to work and do not," whose condition is " but one step in advance of the Indian of the forest." Now 125,000 persons are not far from half of the whole population of the State : they would probably be three-fourths of the population who are capable of working.

Again, in a paper advocating the introduction of " domestic manufactures in the South and West," published by Mr. Tarver of

Missouri, I find the following :—" The free population of the South may be divided into two classes—the slaveholder and the non-slaveholder. I am not aware that the relative numbers of these two classes have ever been ascertained in any of the states, but I am satisfied that the non-slaveholders far outnumber the slaveholders—perhaps by three to one. In the more southern portion of this region, the non-slaveholders possess, generally, but very small means, and the land which they possess is almost universally poor, and so sterile that a scanty subsistence is all that can be derived from its cultivation ; and the more fertile soil, being in the possession of the slaveholder, must ever remain out of the power of those who have none. This state of things is a great drawback, and bears heavily upon and depresses the moral energies of the poorer classes. . . . The acquisition of a respectable position in the scale of wealth appears so difficult, that they decline the hopeless pursuit, and many of them settle down into habits of idleness, and become the almost passive subjects of all its consequences. And I lament to say that I have observed of late years that an evident deterioration is taking place in this part of the population, the younger portion of it being less educated, less industrious, and in every point of view less respectable than their ancestors. . . . To the slaveholding class of the population of the south-west, the introduction of manufactures is not less interesting than to the non-slaveholding class. The former possess almost all the wealth of the country." In a paper written with the same view by the Hon. J. H. Lumpkin of Georgia, we find the following description of the whites of that State :—" It is objected that these manufacturing establishments will become the hot-beds of crime. . . . But I am by no means ready to concede that our poor, degraded, half-fed, half-clothed, and ignorant population—without Sabbath schools or any other kind of instruction, mental or moral—will be injured by giving them employment, which will bring them under the oversight of employers, who will inspire them with self-respect by taking an interest in their welfare."

I shall conclude these quotations by the following from an English writer of unimpeachable authority :—" The white inhabitants of Florida, as of all the Slave States more or less, constitute but two classes—the planters or rich class, and the poor class, variously

denominated 'crackers,' 'white trash,' 'poor whites,' 'mean whites.'
. . . This social characteristic I consider the most remarkable and
important feature of Southern civilization. It is only by keeping
this clearly and constantly in mind, that we can at all understand
the social and political organization of the South; and only thus
can we duly appreciate the amazing difference between Northern
and Southern development. The essence of Northern, as of English
civilization, is the *progressiveness* of the labouring class, and the
consequent rapid rise of an easy, affluent, well-educated, and law-
abiding class, recruited from day to day, and from hour to hour,
from the ranks of the lower class; the individuals raised being,
from the nature of things, those most remarkable for energy, foresight, and self-reliance. Where men of industry, integrity, and
intelligence can easily rise to a condition of independence, a nation
is in a good condition, even though the improvident and sinful
find their deserved portion of misery. On the contrary, where the
labouring class forms a stereotyped, unprogressive caste, stagnation
is the necessary characteristic of the community. The richer class
may accumulate wealth, but there can be no dissemination of com-
fortable existence, no healthy growth of an independent, self-made,
self-reliant class. Society is divided into a wealthy dominant class,
and a wretched, ignorant class, at once insubordinate and servile.
Such is essentially the social condition of the Slave States of this
Union; and the cause obviously is the discouragement thrown over
free labour by the institution of slavery. The white poor man
disdains to 'work like a nigger;' he tries, instead, to live by his
rifle or his fishing-rod. If these fail, he plants a few sweet potatoes,
or loafs about the town, doing odd jobs which have not the restraint
of regular labour. He hates a trade; he will not be a smith or a
carpenter, to compete with his rich neighbour's slaves, and probably
be beaten by them. How, then, can such a man rise? How can
he ever escape from his dependent and degraded position? How
shall a man become a capitalist who will not first be a labourer?
This is the secret of the 'white trash' of the Southern States.
Hence the political rowdyism of slave communities, where an ignorant and idle mob, accustomed to the use of deadly weapons, is

constantly prowling about the country, and congregating in the cities. Hence, too, the want of material progress : there is neither efficient labour nor abundant capital. The very elements of civilization are wanting."*

It would be easy to multiply these quotations, but the reader will probably consider what I have given to be sufficient. I must, however, make one short quotation more. The Saturday Reviewer, not content with questioning my general description, affects to sneer at my language. He quotes as absurd my statement that the " 'mean white' ekes out a wretched subsistence by hunting, by fishing, by hiring himself out for occasional jobs, by plunder." The Reviewer, in his entire ignorance of Southern literature, is not aware that these words are not mine, but those of Southern as well as Northern writers, and that it is owing to their triteness alone that they have not been placed in quotation marks. For example, Governor Hammond of South Carolina thus describes the same class :—" They obtain a precarious subsistence by occasional jobs, by hunting, by fishing, by plundering fields or folds, and too often by what is in its effects far worse—trading with slaves, and seducing them to plunder for their benefit."† The reader can now judge if my picture has been overcharged.

But what is the probable number of this "mean white" population of the Southern States ? It is from the nature of the case impossible to ascertain this with any degree of precision. In the first edition of this work I set it down at five millions. I think it possible that this may be an over-statement. The proportion of these people to the whole population has been stated by several trustworthy writers as about seven-tenths ; and, after a careful examination of the subject, I am inclined to think that this is about the true proportion; but, in applying it, we must confine the aggregate with which we compare the "white trash" to slave society strictly so called. In writing the passage as it stood in the first edition, I did not sufficiently attend to—what, however, I had

* Stirling's *Letters from the Slave States,* pp. 221–3 : and see to the same effect Russell's *North America,* pp. 156, 296, 301, 302.

† De Bow's *Industrial Resources,* vol. iii. p. 35.

distinctly pointed out in other passages—the considerable foreign element of free society existing in the Southern States. Deducting this element, and taking the "white trash" as constituting seven-tenths of the remainder, we should arrive at somewhat over four millions as the probable number of these people at the present time.[*] I have therefore in the present edition set down the number at this sum. I need scarcely say that the change does not in the least degree affect the general argument of my work. Four millions of people, such as we know the "mean whites" to be, existing in a community of which the aggregate (excluding, as I have just ex-plained, that portion which is properly foreign) does not exceed six millions, must form a sufficiently formidable element of mischief.

APPENDIX E.[†]

THE SLAVE ARISTOCRACY IN BRAZIL.

A PRECISELY similar phenomenon—such, to borrow the words of M. Elisée Reclus, is the " étroite solidarité du mal"—is presented by Brazil :—" Au milieu de tous ses satellites, le propriétaire féodal, qui du reste a le plus souvent titre de comte ou de baron et possède toute l'autorité politique et judiciaire, est en réalité roi dans son domaine ; il a ses vassaux et ne reconnaît pour suzerains que l'em-pereur et le congrès de Rio-Janeiro, composé pour la plus grande part de planteurs comme lui. La non-existence du majorat et la constitution si libérale du Brésil ne peuvent rien contre cette féoda-

---

* It will be remembered that between 1850—the period to which the reason-ing in the early portion of this note applies—and 1860, the date of the last United States census, the total white population in the Southern States had increased from 6,184,000 to 8,039,000. Of these 8,039,000 rather more than 2,000,000 would probably represent the foreign element of free society in the South: there would thus remain of whites, identified industrially and morally with the institution, about 6,000,000. It is to this number, and not to the aggregate white population of the South, that the proportion indicated above should be applied in order to obtain the probable number of the ' mean white' population.

† See page 96.

lité territoriale que la nature même des choses a fait naître, ·et qui devient chaque jour plus puissante, car, dans tous les pays où il existe, l'esclavage est le fait primordial et crée une société qui lui ressemble.   C'est ainsi qu'aux Etats-Unis des institutions bien plus démocratiques encore que celles de l'empire brésilien n'ont pas empêché la formation d'une oligarchie de planteurs qui a fini par mener la république aux abîmes."

APPENDIX F.*

INDUSTRIAL REVOLUTION IN VIRGINIA.

THE progress of this movement is thus described by the *Southern Planter* :—" Every farm was greatly impoverished—almost every estate was seriously impaired—and some were involved in debt to nearly their value.   Most of the proprietors had died, leaving families in reduced circumstances, and in some cases in great straits.   No farm whether of a rich or a poor proprietor had escaped great exhaustion, and no property great dilapidation, unless because the proprietor had at first been too poor to join in the former expensive habits of his wealthier neighbours.   There was nothing left to waste, but time and labour ; and these continued to be wasted in the now fruitless efforts to cultivate to profit, or to replace the fertility of soil which had been destroyed.   Luxury and expense had been greatly lessened, But on that account the universal prostration was even the more apparent.   Many mansions were falling into decay.   Few received any but trivial and indispensable repairs.   No new mansion was erected, and rarely any other farm-building of value.   There was still generally prevailing idleness among proprietors ; and also an abandonment of hope, which made every one desirous to sell his land and move to the fertile and far West, and a general emigration and dispersion was only prevented by the impossibility of finding purchasers for the lands, even at half the then low estimate of

* See page 125.

market prices." The consequences are further described by Mr. Olmsted :—" Notwithstanding a constant emigration of the decayed families, and of the more enterprising of the poor, the population steadily augmented. . . . If the apparent wealth of the country was not increasing, the foundation of a greater material prosperity was being laid in the increase of the number of small but intelligent proprietors, and in the constantly growing necessity to abandon tobacco, and substitute grains, or varied crops, as the staple productions of the country. The very circumstance that reduced the old pseudo-wealthy proprietors was favourable to this change, and to the application of intelligence to a more profitable disposal of the remaining elements of wealth in the land. While multitudes abandoned their ancestral acres in despair, or were driven from them by the recoil of their fathers' inconsiderate expenditures they were taken possession of by ' new men,' endowed with more hopefulness and energy if not more intelligence than the old."— *Seaboard Slave States,* pp. 274–276.

APPENDIX G.*

COMPETITION OF FREE AND SLAVE LABOUR IN THE SOUTH.

A WRITER in the *Saturday Review* (Nov. 2, 1861), in noticing a work of Mr. Olmsted's, reasons as follows :—" It would be hasty to infer, as a great many philanthropists have done, that free labour would answer better than slave labour in the South. The Southern planters are keen enough speculators to have discovered the fact if it were true. In reality the experiment has been tried and resulted in favour of *slave* labour." The experiment no doubt has been tried, and with the result alleged ; but how far the experiment, as it has been conducted, is conclusive, the reader will be enabled to judge when he reads the following passage from Mr. Olmsted, in a review of one of whose works the above argument occurred :—"The

* See page 146.

labourer, who in New York gave a certain amount of labour for his wages in a day, soon finds in Virginia that the ordinary measure of labour is smaller than in New York : a 'day's work' or a month's does not mean the same that it did in New York. He naturally adapts his wares to the market. . . . The labourer, finding that the capitalists of Virginia are accustomed to pay for a poor article at a high price, prefers to furnish them with the poor article at their usual price, rather than a better article, unless at a more than correspondingly better price. . . . Now let the white labourer come here from the North or from Europe—his nature demands a social life—shall he associate with the poor, slavish, degraded negro, with whom labour and punishment are almost synonymous ? or shall he be the friend and companion of the white man ? . . . Associating with either or both, is it not inevitable that he will be rapidly demoralized—that he will soon learn to hate labour, give as little of it for his hire as he can, become base, cowardly, faithless,—'worse than a nigger' ?" The case is simple. The moral atmosphere generated by slavery in the South corrupts the free labourer, whether native or imported : thus corrupted, he fails in competition with the slave; but does it follow from this that, if slavery no longer existed, free labour would be less efficient in the South than slave labour is at present ? For that is the point.

APPENDIX H.*

POPULAR EDUCATION IN VIRGINIA.

THE following extract is from a review of Howison's History of Virginia, published in De Bow's *Industrial Resources*, &c., vol. iii. p. 460 :—" Before drawing our article to a conclusion, we will give a few extracts from the work of Mr. Howison, which we have had under review. He writes with good sense and much candour, which we admire; but we must beg leave to differ with him in the matter

* See page 153.

of *slavery*—to which he seems mainly to attribute the decline, and perhaps the extinction of his native state. We coincide with him entirely in the importance of a more thorough system of education. He says:—' It is with pain we are compelled to speak of the horrible cloud of ignorance that rests upon Virginia. In the eastern section there are 29,863, and in the western, 28,924—making a total of 58,787 white persons, over 20 years of age, who cannot read or write. This, however, is not all. It is computed that there are in the state 166,000 children, between 7 and 16 years of age, and therefore fit for school. Of these, about 28,000 poor children attend the Free and Lancasterian schools an average of twelve weeks in the year for each child. 12,000 more children are sent to colleges, academies, and classical schools. The remaining 126,000 attend no school at all, except what can be imparted by poor and ignorant parents!

" 'This deplorable condition has been long felt and deplored by Virginia's most virtuous sons. Efforts have been made to ameliorate it. Education conventions have assembled, and many animated debates have taken place. The legislature has moved from time to time, and during the session of 1845-6 its movement was decided and beneficial. Nevertheless, the evil remains almost untouched. We pretend not to suggest any remedy. But it will be pertinent to the subject to add, that in the whole State of Massachusetts— containing, in 1840, 737,699 persons, there were but 4,448 white persons, over 20 years of age, who could neither read nor write.' "

APPENDIX I.*

MR. STIRLING'S ARGUMENT FOR THE EXTINCTION OF SLAVERY THROUGH ECONOMIC CAUSES.

MR. STIRLING relies upon the following considerations as containing the solution of the problem. " Within the last ten or fifteen

* See page 158.

years the value of slaves has risen fifty per cent. at least. During
the same time the price of bacon has risen 100 to 200 per cent.
Let this process only be continued for ten years longer, and where
will be the profits of the cotton-planter? And here we may perhaps find the long-looked-for solution of the nigger question. When
slave labour becomes unprofitable, the slave will be emancipated.
South Carolina herself will turn abolitionist when slavery ceases to
pay. When she finds that a brutalized race cannot and will not
give as much efficient labour for the money as a hired class of superior workers, it is possible that she may lay aside the cowhide, and
offer wages to her niggers."—*Letters from Slave States*, pp. 182, 183.
The argument is palpably fallacious. It is the same as if one were
to argue that the high rent of land must ultimately destroy agriculture. In each case the high price of the natural agent—land or slaves
—results from the comparative profitableness of capital invested in
the employment of one or the other. When the high price of land
leads landlords to throw up their estates, an analogous course of
conduct may be expected from slaveholders from an analogous
inducement. The high price of the slave's food is scarcely to the
point, since this must tell also against the free labourer ; at all
events, so long as the slave fetches any price, it is a proof that he
is considered to be worth at least more than his keep.

APPENDIX J.*

ECONOMIC STRENGTH OF SLAVERY.

" So long," says Mr. Merivale, " as there is new soil to break up
so long the continuance of slavery is secured ; because workmen
must be had at all hazards, and it is more profitable to cultivate a
fresh soil by the dear labour of slaves, than an exhausted one by
the cheap labour of freemen. It is secured, I mean, so far as the
immediate interests of the masters can prevail in maintaining it.

* See page 162.

. . . It seems but too evident [assuming that there is ' new soil to break up'] that no economical cause can be assigned on which we may rely for the extinction of slavery, and that those who have persuaded themselves that nations will gradually attain a conviction that its maintenance is unfavourable to their interests are under a delusion."—*Colonization and the Colonies*, pp. 307–309. New edition.

"Until the institution of slavery," says one of the most accurate observers of the economical phenomena of North America, " be weakened, as it was in Europe, by the redundancy of the predial population, I have as little hope of slavery relaxing its grasp in the United States for many years to come as of people denying themselves the luxuries of cotton, sugar, and tobacco. I have failed to discover a single element in active operation which points to a different conclusion."—Russell's *North America*, p. 293.

Nor does M. Elisée Reclus, judging the question from the experience of Brazil, regard the case as more hopeful. " Certains optimistes ont encore la naïveté de croire que la servitude involontaire finira par s'éteindre d'elle-même au Brésil. Le mal ne meurt pas ainsi : sa nature est d'empirer sans cesse, de gagner de proche en proche, de corrompre tout ce qui l'entoure, et de disparaître seulement à la suite d'une crise violente où toutes les forces vitales se réunissent pour l'expulser."

APPENDIX K *

SPIRIT OF THE SLAVE LAWS.

IT is true that, "the wilful, malicious, and premeditated" killing of a slave is now by law a capital offence in all the Slave States; but, putting aside the difficulty, which often amounts to an impossibility, of establishing the facts, owing to the exclusion of the evidence of coloured persons, what is a " wilful, malicious, and premeditated

* See page 172.

killing ?" We may infer at least what it is *not* from the provisos added to most of the statutes which legislate for the crime. Thus the statute of Tennessee subjoins the proviso :—" provided this act shall not be extended to any person killing any slave in the act of resistance to his lawful owner or master, or any slave *dying under moderate correction" ;* and that of Georgia, the following :—" *unless such death should happen by accident in giving such slave moderate correction.*" If the reader would appreciate the spirit which pervades the Black Code of the South, let him reflect on the contrast afforded by the following laws of South Carolina. By an act of 1754, it is made a capital felony, without benefit of clergy, " to inveigle, steal, and carry away, or to hire, aid or counsel any person or persons to inveigle, steal or carry away any slave or slaves, or *to aid any slave in running away,* or departing from his master's or employer's service." " This law," says the Hon. J. O'Neil, " has remained ever since unchanged, and has been sternly enforced as a most valuable safeguard to property." On the other hand, by the 37th section of the act of 1740—also still in force—it is provided that " if any person shall wilfully cut out the tongue, put out the eye, castrate, or cruelly scald, burn, or deprive any slave of any limb or member, or shall inflict any other cruel punishment, *other than by whipping, or beating with a horse-whip, cow-skin, switch or small stick, or by putting irons on or confining or imprisoning such slave,* every such person shall for every such offence forfeit the sum of £100 current money, equal to 61 dollars, 23 cents," or £14 13s. 4d. sterling. Thus, while for performing a simple act of humanity— the rendering of assistance to an unfortunate creature seeking to escape from his tormentors—the law awards the punishment of death, it gives, on the other hand, its direct sanction to the act of beating without limit a fellow creature with a horse-whip or cow-skin, and the infliction of any torture which the ingenuity or malignity of man may invent, in the application of irons to the human body, or, if the master wills it, the perpetual incarceration of the slave ; and, in case this does not satisfy the master's propensity for cruelty, it provides that he may indulge it still further to almost any conceivable extent at the low cost of £14 13s. 4d.; this sum to

be enforced in the rare case in which the act would be performed in
the presence of a white man who is willing to give evidence against
the criminal, otherwise the act to receive absolute impunity.

I subjoin the celebrated judgment of Judge Ruffin of North
Carolina, which sets the legal position of slavery in the South in a
clearer light than any other statement I have met with.

"The defendant was indicted for an assault and battery upon
Lydia, the slave of one *Elizabeth Jones.* On the trial it appeared,
that the defendant had hired the slave for a year; that during the
term the slave had committed some small offence, for which the
defendant undertook to chastise her; that while in the act of so
doing, the slave ran off; whereupon the defendant called upon her
to stop, which being refused, he shot at and wounded her. The
judge in the court below charged the jury, that if they believed the
punishment inflicted by the defendant was cruel and unwarrantable,
and disproportionate to the offence committed by the slave, that in
law the defendant was guilty, as he had only a special property in
the slave. A verdict was returned for the slave, and the defendant
appealed.

Ruffin, J. A judge cannot but lament, when such cases as the
present are brought into judgment. It is impossible that the
reasons on which they go can be appreciated but where institutions similar to our own exist, and are thoroughly understood.
The struggle, too, in the judge's own breast between the feelings of
the man and the duty of the magistrate is a severe one, presenting
strong temptation to put aside such questions, if it be possible. It
is useless, however, to complain of things inherent in our political
state. And it is criminal in a court to avoid any responsibility
which the laws impose. With whatever reluctance, therefore, it is
done, the court is compelled to express an opinion upon the extent
of the dominion of the master over the slave in North Carolina. . .
The question before the court has indeed been assimilated at the
bar to the other domestic relations; and arguments drawn from the
well-established principles which confer and restrain the authority
of the parent over the child, the tutor over the pupil, the master
over the apprentice, have been pressed on us. The court does not

recognise their application. There is no likeness between the cases. They are in opposition to each other, and there is an impassable gulf between them. The difference is, that which exists between freedom and slavery—and a greater cannot be imagined. In the one, the end in view is the happiness of the youth, born to equal rights with that governor, on whom the duty devolves of training the young to usefulness in a station which he is afterwards to assume among freemen. To such an end, and with such a subject, moral and intellectual instruction seem the natural means ; and for the most part they are found to suffice. Moderate force is superadded, only to make the others effectual. If that fail, it is better to leave the party to his own headstrong passions, and the ultimate correction of the law, than to allow it to be immoderately inflicted by a private person. With slavery it is far otherwise. The end is the profit of the master, his security, and the public safety ; the subject, one doomed in his own person and his posterity to live without knowledge, and without the capacity to make any thing his own, and to toil that another may reap the fruits. What moral considerations shall be addressed to such a being, to convince him what it is impossible but that the most stupid must feel and know can never be true,—that he is thus to labour upon a principle of natural duty, or for the sake of his own personal happiness ; such services can only be expected from one who has no will of his own, who surrenders his will in implicit obedience to that of another. Such obedience is the consequence only of uncontrolled authority over the body. There is nothing else which can operate to produce the effect. The power of the master must be absolute, to render the submission of the slave perfect. I must freely confess my sense of the harshness of this proposition. I feel it as deeply as any man can. And as a principle of moral right, every person in his retirement must repudiate it. But in the actual condition of things it must be so. There is no remedy. This discipline belongs to the state of slavery. They cannot be disunited, without abrogating at once the rights of the master, and absolving the slave from his subjection. It constitutes the curse of slavery to both the bond and the free portions of our population. But it is inherent in the relation of master and slave.

That there may be particular instances of cruelty and deliberate barbarity, where in conscience the law might properly interfere, is most probable. The difficulty is to determine, where *a court* may properly begin. Merely in the abstract it may well be asked, which power of the master accords with right. The answer will probably sweep away all of them. But we cannot look at the matter in that light. The truth is, that we are forbidden to enter upon a train of general reasoning on the subject. We cannot allow the right of the master to be brought into discussion in the courts of justice. The slave, to remain a slave, must be made sensible that there is no appeal from his master; that his person is in no instance usurped, but is conferred by the laws of man at least, if not by the law of God. . .

"Judgment below reversed; and judgment entered for the defendant."—Wheeler's *Practical Treatise on the Law of Slavery,* pp. 244-8.

APPENDIX L.*

RECENT IMPORTATION OF AFRICAN SLAVES INTO THE SOUTH.

In the *Saturday Review* (Oct. 18, 1862, p. 471) it is asserted that " not one hundred Africans have, since 1808, been landed on the Southern coast." The following evidence, which I extract from the *Reports of the American Anti-Slavery Society,* will enable the reader to form an opinion on the accuracy of this statement :—

"About the first of December last, the yacht Wanderer, (which, after a temporary detention in New York, last June, on suspicion of being destined for the Slave Trade, was released, for want of proof satisfactory to the cautious authorities), came in from the African coast, and landed several hundred Slaves, near Brunswick, Georgia ; whence they were speedily distributed in that and other States. The Augusta *Chronicle,* of December 16th (opposed to the

* See page 245.

traffic), says that 'about 270 of the cargo are now on a plantation
in South Carolina, two or three miles below this city, on the
Savannah river, and we suppose will soon be offered for sale. . . . .
The success of this enterprise by the owners of the Wanderer
establishes the fact that if the Southern people intend to suppress
this traffic they must rely upon themselves. The coast of the
Slaveholding States is so extensive that the entire navy of the
United States cannot maintain the law inviolable.' The Augusta
Despatch says, 'we learn on good authority, that the cargo consisted
of 420. . . . Citizens of our city are probably interested in the
enterprise. It is hinted that this is the third cargo landed by the
same company, during the last six months. . . . One of our citizens
has bought from the lot a stout boy, about fourteen years old, for
250 dollars.' To show 'what practical good can result from the
agitation of the revival of the slave-trade, we point to this cargo
of sturdy labourers, delivered from the darkness and barbarism of
Africa, to be elevated and Christianized on our soil ;' and 'to the
price paid for this son of the jungles, compared with the exorbitant
prices paid for less valuable negroes here ; and we claim that these
results are the beginning of the blessings to flow in upon the
South' from that agitation. 'This trade may be called piracy, by
a false construction of a foolish law, but the day will come when
the South will make it the right arm of her legitimate commerce.'
A writer in the Edgefield (South Carolina) *Advertiser* makes 'an
authorized announcement that the slaves brought by the Wanderer
have been landed in Edgefield District, and most of them are now
within its confines. This act has been done by a combination of
many of the first families in Georgia and South Carolina, from
purely patriotic motives.' A correspondent of the New York *Times*
writes from Montgomery (Alabama), on December 24th, that he has
'just seen the negroes brought from Africa by Captain Corrie,' of
the Wanderer. 'They are real Congo negroes. They came here
from Macon, Georgia. . . . So far as a successful landing of a cargo
of native Africans on our Southern coast can effect that result, the
African slave-trade has actually been re-opened.' The Atlanta
(Georgia) *Intelligencer* states that 'forty negroes said to be direct

from Africa,' and believed to be part of the Wanderer's cargo, passed through Atlanta by railroad, going west, on the 23rd of December. A little later, a despatch from Savannah says that 'scores have been transported by railroads and steamers throughout the South.' The Vicksburg (Mississippi) *Sun* speaks of two of them as 'smuggled into Mississippi,' and living 'on a plantation bordering on the Mississippi central railroad, between Canton and Durant.' Other papers, in different parts of the South, mention parties of them as having been in their respective neighbourhoods. With all this publicity as to where they were, we hear of no earnest effort of the government to get possession of the captives, and restore them to freedom and home. One of them was 'arrested' on the coast, a few days after the landing, but was soon after 'abducted' at night from the place where he had been put for safe keeping; no pains having been taken to guard him securely, though the marshal had been warned of a probable attempt at abduction. Two others were taken in Macon, and sent to Savannah, where they were kept several weeks in jail, and then given up by a justice of the peace to C. A. L. Lamar (the openly avowed owner of the Wanderer), who claimed them as his property, supporting his claim by proof that they had been seen in his possession. This, it seems is, by Georgia law, presumptive proof of good title to black men. The United States attorney and the marshal had notice of the proceedings, but declined to interfere, the latter expressly disclaiming any right to detain the Africans. A deputy-marshal, in Telfair County, arrested thirty-six on their way to Alabama in charge of one or two men, put them in the county jail, and reported to the marshal at Savannah what he had done. The marshal replied that he 'had telegraphed and written to the authorities at Washington, and had received no answer respecting the Africans known to be in the country, and his advice was to turn them loose and let them go on their way.' The deputy did so; the persons from whom they had been taken resumed the charge of them, and pursued their journey. A few weeks after this, some persons from Worth County, who had assisted in the arrest, having visited Savannah, Lamar made oath, before a justice of the peace, that they had stolen from him certain negroes of the value of at least 2,000 dollars; whereupon they were arrested and bound over for trial at the October term of the Worth superior court, on a charge of larceny.

" We do not hear of even an attempt to secure any of the remaining hundreds of the imported Africans, and the whole cargo seems now to have sunk into the mass of the slave population and disappeared.

" On the first public knowledge of the Wanderer's arrival, three of her crew were arrested, and, after examination, bound over to answer at the next term of the United States District Court, in Savannah.   Six weeks later, the captain surrendered himself to the United States marshal, in Charleston (South Carolina), and was held to bail in 5,000 dollars.   Indictments were found against him in Savannah, but warrants for his arrest were refused by the judge of the South Carolina District, on the ground that, having been bound over to appear in that District, it was there he ought to be indicted.   As yet we have heard of no further proceedings in these cases.

" The vessel was condemned as a slaver, and sold at auction, on the 12th of March, but to Lamar himself, and, it is said, for less than a quarter of its value.   He claimed it as his property, unjustly taken from him; and appealed to the crowd not to bid against him. Very few did so ; only one, it seems, to any considerable amount; and him he knocked down, amid general applause.   It is affirmed that 'the marshal seemed to favour Lamar, not dwelling an instant after his last bid.   Thus, instead of promptly taking measures to hold him to account for the piracy in which his own repeated public avowals prove him to have been the real principal, the government restored to him, with a legal title, and at a price little more than nominal, the forfeited instrument of its perpetration; very probably to be used in repeating the crime.   He has since, however, been indicted for aiding and abetting in the slave-trade, and for having in his possession, and for claiming, Africans recently imported ; but, as a Savannah jury will try him, he is in little danger of conviction.

" Two parties of the newly-imported Africans having been brought to Mobile, Judge Campbell, of the United States Circuit Court for the Southern District of Alabama, took occasion from that fact, in charging the grand jury, at Mobile, on the 12th of April, to expound very distinctly the law concerning the slave-trade; denouncing in emphatic terms the 'piratical efforts lately made to make slaves of Africans, *in despite of the treaties and laws* of the United States;' and 'invoking the active and diligent efforts of the grand jury to bring the malefactors to justice.' We do not yet hear of any remarkable 'diligent efforts' to that end. But the news may not have had time to reach us."—Annual Report for the year ending May 1, 1859, pp. 45–48.

"The St. Augustine (Florida) *Examiner*, of July 21, gives an account of a case in Florida, in which the Federal authorities had notice of a slaver's being off the coast, but, upon going to the region indicated, were told that the vessel (schooner Experiment), had landed her cargo near Jupiter's Inlet, six weeks before, and of course the 'birds had flown.' 'We understand more are expected shortly,' adds the *Examiner*, coolly taking it for granted that caution is needless, and censure uncalled for, in speaking of the business. The Pensacola (Florida) *Observer* confirms, on the authority of Colonel Blackburn, United States Marshal, a statement sent from Jacksonville, on the 16th of last July, that 'a cargo of six hundred Africans has been landed on the Florida coast, near Smyrna;' and says, that 'as soon as the landing was effected, the vessel was set on fire and abandoned to the elements.'"—Annual Report for the year 1861, p. 22.

APPENDIX M.

THE PHILOSOPHY OF SECESSION.

By the Hon. L. W. SPRATT.

BEING A PROTEST AGAINST A DECISION OF THE SOUTHERN CONGRESS.

From the *Charleston Mercury*, 13th February, 1861.

To the Hon. John Perkins, Delegate from Louisiana :

From the abstract of the Constitution for the Provisional Government, published in the papers of this morning, it appears that the slave trade, except with the Slave States of North America, shall be prohibited. The Congress, therefore, not content with the laws of the late United States against it, which, it is to be presumed, were re-adopted, have unalterably fixed the subject by a provision of the Constitution. That provision, for reasons equally conclusive, will doubtless pass into the Constitution of the permanent government. The prohibition, therefore, will no longer be a question of policy, but will be a cardinal principle of the Southern Confederacy. It will not be a question for the several States, in view of any peculiarity in their circumstances and condition, but will be fixed by a paramount power, which nothing but another revolution can overturn. If Texas shall want labour she must elect whether it shall be hireling labour or slave labour; and if she shall elect slave labour she must be content with that only which comes from other States on this continent, and at such prices as the States on this continent shall see proper to exact. If Virginia shall not join the Confederacy of the South, she is at least assured of a market for her slaves at undiminished prices ; and if there shall be, as there unquestionably is, a vast demand for labour at the South; and if there shall be, as there unquestionably will be, a vast supply of pauper labour from the North and Europe, and the States of the South shall be in danger of being overrun and abolitionized, as the States of the North have been overrun and abolitionized, there must be no power in any State to counteract the evil. Democracy is right, for it has the approval of the world; slavery wrong, and only to be tolerated in consideration of the property involved ; and while the one is to be encouraged, therefore the other is to be presented in such attitude as to be as little offensive as it may be to the better sentiment of an enlightened world.

Such I take to be a fair statement of the principles announced in the earliest utterance of the Southern Republic; and I need scarcely say that I deprecate them greatly. I fear their effects upon the present harmony of feeling ; I fear their effects upon the fortunes of the Republic; and I will take the liberty of intervening and of presenting reasons why I think we should not take such action at the present time. I may seem presumptuous, but I have a stake too great to scruple at the measures necessary to preserve it. I take a liberty, without permission, in making you the object of this letter; but our personal relations will assure you that I have but the simple purpose, if possible, to be of service to my country ; and if, in representing a measure so offensive, I may seem wanting in respect for the " spirit of the age," I have but to say that I have been connected with the slave trade measure from the start. I have incurred whatever of odium could come from its initiation ; I have been trusted by its friends with a leading part in its advancement; and so situated, at a time when prejudice or a mistaken policy would seem to shape our action to a course inconsistent with our dignity and interests, I have no personal considerations to restrain me, and feel that it is within my province to interpose and offer what I can of reasons to arrest it.

Nor will I be justly chargeable with an unreasonable agitation of this question. We were truly solicitous to postpone it to another time; we were willing to acquiesce in whatever policy the States themselves might see proper to adopt. But when it is proposed to take advantage of our silence, to enter judgment by default, to tie the hands of States, and so propitiate a foreign sentiment by a concession inconsiderate and gratuitous, it is our privilege to intervene; and I am in error if your clear conception of the questions at issue, and your devotion to the paramount cause of the South, will not induce you to admit that the odium is not on us of introducing a distracting issue.

The South is now in the formation of a Slave Republic. This, perhaps, is not admitted generally. There are many contented to believe that the South as a geographical section is in mere assertion of its independence ; that it is instinct with no especial truth— pregnant of no distinct social nature; that for some unaccountable reason the two sections have become opposed to each other; that for reasons equally insufficient there is disagreement between the peoples that direct them ; and that from no overruling necessity, no impossibility of coexistence, but as mere matter of policy, it has been considered best for the South to strike out for herself and establish an independence of her own. This, I fear, is an inadequate conception of the controversy.

The contest is not between the North and South as geographical sections, for between such sections merely there can be no contest; nor between the people of the North and the people of the South, for our relations have been pleasant, and on neutral grounds there is still nothing to estrange us. We eat together, trade together, and practise yet, in intercourse, with great respect, the courtesies of common life. But the real contest is between the two forms of society which have become established, the one at the North, and the other at the South. Society is essentially different from government—as different as is the nut from the bur, or the nervous body of the shell-fish from the bony structure which surrounds it; and within this government two societies had become developed as variant in structure and distinct in form as any two beings in animated nature. The one is a society composed of one race, the other of two races. The one is bound together but by the two great social relations of husband and wife and parent and child; the other by the three relations of husband and wife, and parent and child, and master and slave. The one embodies in its political structure the principle that equality is the right of man; the other that it is the right of equals only. The one embodying the principle that equality is the right of man, expands upon the horizontal plane of pure democracy; the other embodying the principle that it is not the right of man, but of equals only, has taken to itself the rounded form of a social aristocracy. In the one there is hireling labour, in the other slave labour; in the one, therefore, in theory at least, labour is voluntary, in the other involuntary; in the labour of the one there is the elective franchise, in the other there is not; and, as labour is always in excess of direction, in the one the power of government is only with the lower classes; in the other the upper. In the one therefore, the reins of government come from the heels, in the other from the head of the society; in the one it is guided by the worst, in the other by the best, intelligence; in the one it is from those who have the least, in the other from those who have the greatest, stake in the continuance of existing order. In the one the pauper labourer has the power to rise and appropriate by law the goods protected by the State—when pressure comes, as come it must, there will be the motive to exert it—and thus the ship of State turns bottom upwards. In the other there is no pauper labour with power of rising; the ship of State has the ballast of a disfranchised class: there is no possibility of political upheaval, therefore, and it is reasonably certain that, so steadied, it will sail erect and onward to an indefinitely distant period.

Such are some of the more obvious differences in form and constitution between these two societies which had come into contact within the limits of the recent Union. And perhaps it is not the least remarkable, in this connection, that while the one, a shapeless, organless, mere mass of social elements in no definite relation to each other, is loved and eulogized, and stands the ideal of the age; the other comely, and proportioned with labour and direction, mind and matter in just relation to each other, presenting analogy to the very highest developments in animated nature, is condemned and reprobated. Even we ourselves have hardly ventured to affirm it—while the cock crows, in fact, are ready to deny it; and if it shall not perish on the cross of human judgment, it must be for the reason that the Great Eternal has not purposed that still another agent of his will shall come to such excess of human ignominy.

Such are the two forms of society which had come to contest within the structure of the recent Union. And the contest for existence was inevitable. Neither could concur in the requisitions of the other; neither could expand within the forms of a single government without encroachment on the other. Like twin lobsters in a single shell, if such a thing were possible, the natural expansion of the one must be inconsistent with the existence of the other; or, like an eagle and a fish, joined by an indissoluble bond, which for no reason of its propriety could act together, where the eagle could not share the fluid suited to the fish and live, where the fish could not share the fluid suited to the bird and live, and where one must perish that the other may survive, unless the unnatural Union shall be severed—so these societies could not, if they would, concur.

The principle that races are unequal, and that among unequals inequality is right, would have been destructive to the form of pure democracy at the North. The principle that all men are equal and equally right, would have been destructive of slavery at the South. Each required the element suited to its social nature. Each must strive to make the government expressive of its social nature. The natural expansion of the one must become encroachment on the other, and so the contest was inevitable. Seward and Lincoln, in theory at least, whatever be their aim, are right. I realized the fact and so declared the conflict irrepressible years before either ventured to advance that proposition. Upon that declaration I have always acted, and the recent experience of my country has not induced me to question the correctness of that first conception.

Nor is indignation at such leaders becoming the statesmen of the South. The tendency of social action was against us. The speaker, to be heard, must speak against slavery ; the preacher, to retain his charge, must preach against slavery ; the author, to be read, must write against slavery ; the candidate, to attain office, must pledge himself against slavery ; the office-holder, to continue, must redeem the pledges of the candidate. They did not originate the policy, but they pandered to it ; they did not start the current, but they floated on it ; and were as powerless as drift-wood to control its course. The great tendency to social conflict pre-existed ; it was in the heart of the North—it was in the very structure of Northern society. It was not a matter of choice but of necessity that such society should disaffirm a society in contradiction of it. It was not a matter of choice but of necessity that it should approve of acts against it. In possession of power, it flowed to political action on the South, as fluids flow to lower levels. The acts of individuals were unimportant. If I had possessed the power to change the mind of every Republican in Congress, I would not have been at the pains to do so. They would have fallen before an indignant constituency, and men would have been sent to their places whose minds could never change. Nor, in fact, have they been without their use. As the conflict was irrepressible, as they were urged on by an inexorable power, it was important we should know it. Our own political leaders refused to realize the fact. The zealots of the North alone could force the recognition ; and I am bound to own that Giddings, and Greeley, and Seward, and Lincoln, parasites as they are, panderers to popular taste as they are, the instruments, and the mere instruments, of aggression, have done more to rouse us to the vindication of our rights than the bravest and best among us.

Such, then, was the nature of this contest. It was inevitable. It was inaugurated with the government. It began at the beginning, and almost at the start the chances of the game were turned against us. If the foreign slave trade had never been suppressed, slave society must have triumphed. It would have extended to the limits of New England.

Pari passu with emigrants from Europe came slaves from Africa. Step by step the two in union marched upon the West, and it is reasonably certain had the means to further union been admitted, that so they would have continued to march upon the West, that slave labour would have been cheaper than hireling labour, that, transcending agriculture, it would have expanded to the arts ; and that thus one homogeneous form of labor and one homogeneous form of society, unquestioned by one single dreamer, and cherished at home and honoured abroad, would have overspread the entire available surface of the late United States. But the slave-trade suppressed, democratic society has triumphed. The States of New York, New Jersey, Pennsylvania, and Deleware found an attractive market for their slaves. They found a cheaper pauper labour to replace it ; that pauper labour poured in from Europe ; while it replaced the slave, it increased the political power of the Northern States. More than five millions from abroad have been added to their number ; that addition has enabled them to grasp and hold the government. That government, from the very necessities of their nature they are forced to use against us. Slavery was within its grasp, and forced to the option of extinction in the Union, or of independence out, it dares to strike, and it asserts its claim to nationality and its right to recognition among the leading social systems of the world.

Such, then, being the nature of the contest, *this Union has been disrupted in the effort of slave society to emancipate itself ;* and the momentuous question now to be determined is, shall that effort be successful ? That the Republic of the South shall sustain her independence, there is little question. The form of our society is too pregnant of intellectual resources and military strength to be subdued, if, in its products, it did not hold the bonds of amity and peace upon all the leading nations of the world. But in the independence of the South is there surely the emancipation of domestic slavery ? That is greatly to be doubted. Our property in slaves will be established. If it has stood in a government more than half of which has been pledged to its destruction, it will surely stand in a government every member of which will be pledged in its defence. But will it be established as a normal institution of society, and stand the sole exclusive social system of the South ? That is the impending question, and the fact is yet to be recorded. That it will so stand somewhere at the South I do not entertain the slightest question. It may be overlooked or disregarded now. *It has been the vital agent of this great controversy.* It has energized the arm of every man who acts a part in this great drama. We may shrink from recognition of the fact ; we may decline to admit the source of our authority ; refuse to slavery an invitation to the table which she herself has so bountifully spread ; but not for that will it remain powerless or unhonoured. It may be abandoned by Virginia, Maryland, Missouri ; South Carolina herself may refuse to espouse it. The hireling labourer from the North and Europe may drive it from our seaboard. As the South shall become the centre of her own trade, the metropolis of her own commerce, the pauper population of the world will pour upon us. It may replace our slaves upon the seaboard, as it has replaced them in the Northern States ; but concentrated in the States upon the Gulf it will make its stand, condensed to the point at which the labour of the slave transcends the want of agriculture, it will flow to other objects ; it will lay its giant grasp upon still other departments of industry ; its every step will be exclusive ; it will be unquestioned lord of each domain on which it enters. With that perfect economy of resources, that just application of power, that concentration of forces, that security of order which results to slavery from the permanent direction of its best intelligence, there is no other form of human labour that can stand against it, and it will build itself a home and erect for itself, at some point within the present limits of the Southern States, a structure of imperial power and grandeur—a glorious Confederacy of States that will stand aloft and serene for ages amid the anarchy of democracies that will reel around it.

But it may be that to this end another revolution may be necessary. It is to be apprehended that this contest between democracy and slavery is not yet over. It is certain that both forms of society exist within the limits of the Southern States; both are distinctly developed within the limits of Virginia; and there, whether we perceive the fact or not, the war already rages. In that State there are about 500,000 slaves to about 1,000,000 whites; and as at least as many slaves as masters are necessary to the constitution of slave society, about 500,000 of the white population are in legitimate relation to the slaves, and the rest are in excess. Like an excess of alkali or acid in chemical experiments, they are unfixen in social compound. Without legitimate connection with the slave, they are in competition with him. They constitute not a part of slave society, but a democratic society. In so far as there is this connection, the State is slave; in so far as there is not, it is democratic; and as States speak only from their social condition, as interests, not intellect, determine their political action, it is thus that Virginia has been undecided—that she does not truly know whether she is of the North or South in this great movement. Her people are individually noble, brave, and patriotic, and they will strike for the South in resistance to physical aggression; but her political action is, at present, paralyzed by this unnatural contest, and as causes of disintegration may continue—must continue, if the slave trade be not re-opened—as there will still be a market at the South for her slaves—as there will still be pauper labour from abroad to supply their places, and more abundant from industrial dissolutions at the North, and the one race must increase as the other is diminished—it is to be feared that there the slave must ultimately fail, and that this great state must lose the institution, and bend her proud spirit to the yoke of another democratic triumph. In Maryland, Missouri, Kentucky, and even Tennessee and North Carolina, the same facts exist, with chances of the like result.

And even in this State [South Carolina] the ultimate result is not determined. The slave condition here would seem to be established. There is here an excess of 120,000 slaves, and here is fairly exhibited the normal nature of the institution. The officers of the State are slave-owners and the representatives of slave-owners. In their public acts they exhibit the consciousness of a superior position. Without unusual individual ability, they exhibit the elevation of tone and composure of public sentiment proper to a master class. There is no appeal to the mass, for there is no mass to appeal to ; there are no demagogues, for there is no populace to breed them ; judges are not forced upon the stump; governors are not dragged before the people; and when there is cause to act upon the fortunes of our social institution, there is perhaps an unusual readiness to meet it. The large majority of our people are in legitimate connection with the institution—in legitimate dependence on the slave; and it were to be supposed that here at least the system of slave society would be permanent and pure. But even here the process of disintegration has commenced. In our larger towns it just begins to be apparent. Within ten years past as many as 10,000 slaves have been drawn away from Charleston by the attractive prices of the West, and labourers from abroad have come to take their places. These labourers have every disposition to work above the slave, and if there were opportunity would be glad to do so; but without such opportunity they come to competition with him; they are necessarily resistive to the contact. Already there is the disposition to exclude him; from the trades, from public works, from drays, and the tables of hotels, he is even now excluded to a great extent. And when enterprises at the North are broken up; when more labourers are thrown from employment; when they shall come in greater numbers to the South they will still more increase the tendency to exclusion; they will question the right of masters to employ their slaves in any works that they may wish for ; they will invoke the aid of legislation ; they will use the elective franchise to that end ; they may acquire the power to determine municipal elections ; they will inexorably use it; and thus this town of Charleston, at the very heart of slavery, may become a fortress of democratic power against it. As it is in Charleston, so also is it to a less extent in the interior towns.

Nor is it only in the towns the tendency appears. The slaves, from lighter lands within the State, have been drawn away for years for higher prices in the West. They are now being drawn away from rice culture. Thousands are sold from rice fields every year. None are brought to them. They have already been drawn from the culture of indigo and all manufacturing employments. They are yet retained by cotton and the culture incident to cotton; but as almost every negro offered in our markets is bid for by the West the drain is likely to continue. It is probable that more abundant pauper labor may pour in, and it is to be feared that even in this State, the purest in its slave condition, democracy may gain a foothold, and that here also the contest for existence may be waged between them.

It thus appears that the contest is not ended with a dissolution of the Union, and that the agents of that contest still exist within the limits of the Southern States. The causes that have contributed to the defeat of slavery still occur; our slaves are still drawn off by higher prices to the West. There is still foreign pauper labor ready to supply their place. Maryland, Virginia, Kentucky, Missouri, possibly Tennessee and North Carolina, may lose their slaves, as New York, Pennsylvania, and New Jersey have done. In that condition they must recommence the contest. There is no avoiding that necessity. The systems cannot mix; and thus it is that slavery, like the Thracian horse returning from the field of victory, still bears a master on his back; and, having achieved one revolution to escape democracy at the North, it must still achieve another to escape it at the South. That it will ultimately triumph none can doubt. It will become redeemed and vindicated, and the only question now to be determined is, shall there be another revolution to that end? It is not necessary. Slavery within the seceding States at least is now emancipated if men put forward as its agents have intrepidity to realize the fact and act upon it. It is free to choose its constitution and its policy, and you and others are now elected to the high office of that determination. If you shall elect slavery, avow it and affirm it not as an existing fact, but as a living principle of social order, and assert its right, not to toleration only, but to extension and political recognition among the nations of the earth. If, in short, you shall own slavery as the source of your authority, and act for it, and erect as your are commissioned to erect, not only a Southern, but a Slave Republic, the work will be accomplished. Those States intending to espouse and perpetuate the institution will enter your Confederacy; those that do not, will not. Your Republic will not require the pruning process of another revolution; but, poised upon its institution, will move on to a career of greatness and of glory unapproached by any other nation in the world.

But if you shall not; if you shall commence by ignoring slavery, or shall be content to edge it on by indirection; if you shall exhibit care but for a Republic, respect but for a democracy; if you shall stipulate for the toleration of slavery as an existing evil by admitting assumptions to its prejudice and restrictions to its power and progress, re-inaugurate the blunder of 1789; you will combine States, whether true or not, to slavery ; you will have no tests of faith; some will find it to their interest to abandon it; slave labor will be fettered ; hireling labor will be free ; your Confederacy is again divided into antagonist societies ; the irrepressible conflict is again commenced ; and as slavery can sustain the structure of a stable government, and will sustain such structure, and as it will sustain no structure but its own, another revolution comes—but whether in the order and propriety of this, is gravely to be doubted.

Is it, then, in the just performance of your office, that you would impose a constitutional restriction against the foreign slave trade ? Will you affirm slavery by reprobating the means of its formation ? Will you extend slavery by introducing the means to its extinction ? Will you declare to Virginia if she shall join, that under no circumstances shall she be at liberty to restore the integrity of her slave condition ? that her five hundred thousand masters without slaves

shall continue ? that the few slaves she has shall still be subject to
the requisitions of the South and West ? that she shall still be
subject to the incursions of white laborers, without the slaves to
neutralize their social tendencies? and thus, therefore, that she must
certainly submit to be abolitionized, and when so abolitionized that
she must surely be thrown off, to take her fortunes with the Abolition States ? Will you say the same to Maryland, Kentucky, Missouri, North Carolina, and Tennessee? Will you declare to the State
of South Carolina that, if the canker of democracy eats into her
towns and cities ; if her lighter lands are exposed, her forms of
culture are abandoned, she must still submit to it ? To Texas, that
to her imperial domain no other slaves shall come than those she
may extort from older States; and that she must submit to be the
waste she is, or else accept the kind of labor that must demoralize
the social nature of the State ? Will you do this, and yet say that
you erect slavery and affirm it, and, in your ministrations at its
altar, own it as the true and only source of your authority ?
Individually, I am sure you will not. I am too well assured of
your intelligent perception of the questions at issue, and of your
devotion to the great cause you have espoused, to entertain a doubt
upon that subject ; but others may, and that I may meet suggestions likely to arise, I will task your indulgence further.

Then why adopt this measure ? Is it that Virginia and the
other Border States require it ? They may require it now, but is it
certain they will continue to require it ? Virginia and the rest have
never yet regarded slavery as a normal institution of society. They
have regarded the slave as property, but not slavery as a relation.
They have treated it as a prostitution, but have never yet espoused
it. Their men of intellect have exhibited enlightened views upon
this subject, but their politicians who have held the public ear have
ever presented it as a thing of dollars, and to be fought for, if need
be, but not to be cherished and perpetuated. And is it certain that
when better opinions shall prevail; that when they join, if they
shall join, a Slave Republic, a Republic to perpetuate the institution,
when there shall be less inducement to sell their slaves, and the

assurance that when they shall sell them they will fall under the rule of a democracy which must unfit them for association in a slave confederacy—the people of these States may not solicit an increase of slaves? And is it policy to preclude the possibility of such an increase? But admit the change may never come, yet against all the evils to result from the slave trade these States are competent to protect themselves. The failure of the general government to preclude that trade by constitutional provision by no means precludes them from such a prohibition. If they may never want them, they may keep them out, without the application of a Procrustean policy to all the other States of the Confederacy. It may be said that without such general restriction the value of their slaves will be diminished in the markets of the West. They have no right to ask that their slaves, or any other products, shall be protected to unnatural value in the markets of the West. If they persist in regarding the negro but as a thing of trade—a thing which they are too good to use, but only can produce for others' uses—and join the Confederacy, as Pennsylvania or Massachusetts might do, not to support the structure, but to profit by it, it were as well they should not join, and we can find no interest in such association.

Is it that the Cotton States themselves require it? If so, each for itself may adopt the prohibition. But they do not. The political leaders of the country are not ready for the proposition, as they were not ready for the measure of secession. Many leaders of the South, many men who meet you in Convention, have been forced to that position by a popular movement they had never the political courage to direct; and so, perhaps, in any case the whole machinery of society must start before the political hands upon the dial-plate can indicate its progress; and so, therefore, as this question is not moved—as the members of this Congress are charged to perfect the dissolution of the old government, but have not been instructed as to this permanent requisition of the new—they may be mistaken, as they would have been mistaken, if by chance they had met six months ago and spoken upon the question of secession. And they are mistaken, if, from any reference to popular feeling, they inaugurate the action now proposed. The people of the Cotton States want labour; they know that whites and slaves cannot work together. They have no thought of abandoning their slaves that they may get white labour; and they want slaves, therefore, and they will have them—from the Seaboard States, if the slave trade be not opened, and they cannot heartily embrace a policy which, while it will tend to degrade the Seaboard States to the condition of a democracy, will compel them to pay double and treble prices for their labour.

It may be said in this connection that, though the Cotton States might tolerate the slave trade, it would overstock the country and induce a kind of social suffocation. It is one of the most grievous evils of the time that men have persisted in legislating on domestic slavery with what would seem to be an industrious misapprehension of its requisities. It is assumed that it is ready to explode, while it is in an ordinary state of martial law, *(sic)* as perfect as that which, in times of popular outbreak, is the last and surest provision for security and order. It is assumed that the negro is unfit for mechanical employments, when he exhibits an imitative power of manipulation unsurpassed by any other creature in the world; and when, as a matter of fact, we see him daily in the successful prosecution of the trades, and are forced to know that he is not more generally employed for reason of the higher prices offered for him by our fields of cotton. It is assumed that he cannot endure the cold of Northern States, when he dies not more readily in Canada than Domingo, and when the finest specimens of negro character and negro form to be met with in the world are on the northern borders of Maryland and Missouri. It is assumed that whenever he comes in contact with free society we must quail before it, when it is evident that the question which shall prevail is dependent on the question which can work the cheapest; and when it is evident that with slaves at starvation prices—slaves at prices to which they will be reduced by the question whether we shall give them up or feed them—at prices to which they will be reduced when the question comes whether they shall starve the hireling or the hireling the slave, the system of domestic slavery, guided always by its best intelligence, directed always by the strictest economy, with few invalids and few inefficients, can under-work the world.   And it is assumed that, hemmed in as we will be, but a slight addition to our slaves will induce disastrous consequences. But it is demonstrable that negroes are more easily held to slavery than white men; and that more in proportion, therefore, can be held in subjection by the same masters; and yet in the Republic of Athens of white slaves there were four to one; and in portions of the Roman Empire the proportion was greater still; and upon this ratio the slaves might be increased to forty millions, without a corresponding increase among the whites, and yet occur no disaster; but on our rice lands, isolated to a great extent where negroes are employed in thousands, there is often not one white man to one hundred slaves.   Nor is there greater danger of an overcrowded population.   Slaves may be held to greater density than freemen; order will be greater, and the economy of resources will be greater. Athens had seven hundred to the square mile, while Belgium, the most densely populated state of modern Europe, has but about three hundred and eighty-eight to the square mile; and with a population only as dense as Belgium, South Carolina could hold the population of the Southern States, and Texas three times the present popula-tion of the Union.

Is it that foreign nations will require it?   As a matter of taste they might perhaps.   There is a mode upon the subject of human rights at present, and England, France, and other states that are leaders of the mode, might be pleased to see the South comply with the standard of requirement, and, provided only no serious incon-venience or injury resulted, would be pleased to see the South sup-press not only the slave trade, but slavery itself.   But will our failure to do so make any greater difference in our relations with those states?   Men may assume it if they will, but it argues a pitiable want of intelligence and independence, an abject want of political spirit to suppose it.   France and England trade in coolies, and neither will have the hardihood to affirm that between that and the slave trade, there is an essential difference, and practising the one they cannot war with us for practising the others. Nor, in fact, do they wage war upon the slave trade. Spain permits the trade in Cuba, though she acknowledges the mode by professing to prohibit it. Portugal and Turkey do not even so much. Even England lends her ships to keep the slave trade open in the Black Sea; and almost every slave bought in Africa is paid for in English fabrics, to the profit of the English merchant, and with the knowledge of the British government. In view of these facts, it were simple to suppose that European states will practise sentiment, at the expense of interest. And have they interest in the suppression of the slave trade? Three years ago in my report to the Commercial Convention at Montgomery, I said that European states are hostile to the Union. Perhaps "they see in it a threatening rival in every branch of art, and they see that rival armed with one of the most potent productive institutions the world has ever seen : they would crush India and Algeria to make an equal supply of cotton with the North; and, failing in this, they would crush slavery to bring the North to a footing with them, but to slavery without the North they have no repugnance; on the contrary, if it were to stand out for itself, free from the control of any other power, and were to offer to European states, upon fair terms, a full supply of its commodities, it would not only not be warred upon, but the South would be singularly favoured—crowns would bend before her; kingdoms and empires would break a lance to win the smile of her approval ; and, quitting her free estate, it would be in her option to become the bride of the world, rather than, as now, the miserable mistress of the North."

This opinion seemed then almost absurd, but recent indications have rendered it the common opinion of the country ; and as, therefore, they have no repugnance to slavery in accordance with their interests, so also can they have none to the extension of it. They will submit to any terms of intercourse with the Slave Republic in consideration of its markets and its products. An increase of slaves will increase the market and supply. They will pocket their philanthropy and the profits together. And so solicitude as to the feeling of foreign States upon this subject is gratuitous : and so it is that our suppression of the slave trade is warranted by no necessity to respect the sentiment of foreign States. We may abnegate ourselves if we will, defer to others if we will, but every such act is a confession of a weakness, the less excusable that it does not exist, and we but industriously provoke the contempt of States we are desirous to propitiate. Is it that we debase our great movement by letting it down to the end of getting slaves ? We do not propose to reopen the slave trade ; we merely propose to take no action on the subject. I truly think we want more slaves. We want them to the proper cultivation of our soil, to the just development of our resources, and to the proper constitution of society. Even in this State I think we want them ; of eighteen million acres of land, less than four million are in cultivation. We have no seamen for our commerce, if we had it, and no operatives for the arts ; but it is not for that I now oppose restrictions on the slave trade. I oppose them from the wish to emancipate our institution. *I regard the slave trade as the test of its integrity. If that be right, then slavery is right, but not without* ; and I have been too clear in my perceptions of the claims of that great institution—too assured of the failure of antagonist democracy, too convinced the one presents the conditions of social order, too convinced the other does not, and too convinced, therefore, that the one must stand while the other falls, to abate my efforts or pretermit the means by which it may be brought to recognition and establishment.

Believing, then, that this is a test of slavery, and that the institution cannot be right if the trade be not, I regard the constitutional prohibition as a great calamity. If the trade be only wrong in policy it would be enough to leave its exclusion to the several States that would feel the evils of that policy; but it is only upon the supposition that it is wrong in principle, wrong radically, and therefore never to be rendered proper by any change of circumstances which may make it to our interest, that it is becoming in the general government to take organic action to

arrest. The action of the confederacy is, then, a declaration of
that fact, and it were vain to sustain the institution in the face of
such admissions to its prejudice.

It will be said that at the outset of our career it were wise to
exhibit deference to the moral sentiment of the world; the obligation is as perfect to respect the moral sentiment of the world
against the institution. The world is just as instant to assert that
slavery itself is wrong, and if we forego the slave trade in consideration of the moral feeling of the world, then why not slavery also?
It were madness now to blink the question. We are entering at
last upon a daring innovation upon the social constitutions of the
world. We are erecting a nationality upon a union of races, where
other nations have but one. We cannot dodge the issue ; we cannot disguise the issue; we cannot safely change our front in the
face of a vigilant adversary. Every attempt to do so, every refusal
to assist ourselves, every intellectual or political evasion, is a point
against us. We may postpone the crisis by disguises, but the slave
republic must forego its nature and its destiny, or it must meet the
issue, and our assertion of ourselves will not be easier for admissions
made against us. And is it not in fact from a sense of weakness
that there is such admission? Is there a man who votes for this
measure but from misgivings as to slavery, and as to the propriety
of its extension? Therefore is there not the feeling that the finger
of scorn will be pointed at him without ; and is he who doubts the
institution, or he who has no higher standard of the right than
what the world may say about it, the proper man to build the
structure of a slave republic? The members of that Convention
are elected to important posts in the grand drama of human history.
Such opportunity but seldom comes of moulding the destiny of men
and nations. If they shall rise to the occasion, they shall realize
their work and do it, they will leave a record that will never be
effaced; but if they shall not—if they shall shrink from truth, for
reason that it is unhonored; if they shall cling to error, for reason
that it is approved, and so let down their character, and act some
other part than that before them, they will leave a record which

their successors will be anxious to efface—names which posterity will be delighted to honor.

Opinions, when merely true, move slowly; but when approved, acquire proclivity. Those as to the right of slavery have been true, merely so far, but they came rapidly to culmination. *I was the single advocate of the slave trade in* 1853 ; *it is now the question of the time.* Many of us remember when we heard slavery first declared to be of the normal constitution of society ; few now will dare to disaffirm it. Those opinions now roll on ; they are now not only true but are coming to be trusted ; they have moved the structure of the State, and men who will not take the impulse and advance must perish in the track of their advancement. The members of your Convention may misdirect the movement—they may impede the movement—they may so divert it that another revolution may be necessary ; but if necessarily that other revolution comes, slavery will stand serene, erect, aloft, unquestioned as to its rights or its integrity at some points within the present limits of the Southern States, and it is only for present actors to determine whether they will contribute or be crushed to that result.

I hope you will pardon this communication ; it is too long, but I have not had time to make it shorter. I hope also you will find it consistent with your views to urge the policy I have endeavoured to advance. If the clause be carried into the permanent government, our whole movement is defeated. It will abolitionize the Border Slave States—it will brand our institution. Slavery cannot share a government with democracy—it cannot bear a brand upon it ; thence another revolution. It may be painful, but we must make it. The Constitution cannot be changed without. The Border States, discharged of slavery, will oppose it. They are to be included by the concession ; they will be sufficient to defeat it. It is doubtful if another movement will be so peaceful; but no matter, no power but the Convention can avert the necessity. The clause need not necessarily be carried into the permanent government, but I fear it will be. The belief that it is agreeable to popular feeling will continue. The popular mind cannot now be worked up to the task of dispelling the belief; the same men who have prepared the provisional will prepare the permanent constitution ; the same influence will affect them. It will be difficult to reverse their judgment in the conventions of the several States. The effort will at least distract us, and so it is to be feared this fatal action may be consummated ; but that it may not is the most earnest wish I now can entertain.

Respectfully, your obedient servant,

L. W. SPRATT.

THE END